TERI DEGLER

THE DIVINE
FEMININE
FIRE

TERI DEGLER

THE DIVINE FEMININE FIRE

CREATIVITY AND YOUR YEARNING

TO EXPRESS YOUR SELF

Dreamriver Press

Dreamriver Press LLC
www.dreamriverpress.com
or contact at:
12 Franklin Avenue
Flourtown, PA 19031-2006
U.S.A.

First Dreamriver Press edition, 2009

ISBN-13: 978-0-9797908-4-3
ISBN-10: 0-9797908-4-0

Library of Congress Control Number: 2009928589

1. OCC036050   BODY, MIND & SPIRIT / Spirituality /
                Divine Mother, The Goddess, Quan Yin
2. SEL009000   SELF-HELP / Creativity

Designed by George D. Matthiopoulos

This book is printed on 100% recycled paper.

Preserving our environment
Dreamriver Press chose Legacy Hi-Bulk
Natural 100% post-consumer recycled paper for
the pages of this book printed by Webcom Inc.

© **Mixed Sources**
Product group from well-managed
forests, controlled sources and
recycled wood or fiber
www.fsc.org Cert no. SW-COC-002358
© 1996 Forest Stewardship Council

FSC

Printed and bound in Canada

For Anya, Britta, Christine, Kavita, and Wendi
—who so bravely and generously shared
their personal stories for this book—
and all the other wonderful women who,
filled with the divine feminine fire,
are moving forward on their
creative-spiritual journeys.

Permission Credits
The author and publisher would like to thank the following
for granting their permission to use material in this book.

Penguin Group U.K. for translations of Mahadeviakka's poetry
in *Speaking of Shiva*, © A.K. Ramanujan, 1973.

University of California Press for material
from Barbara Newman's *Sister of Wisdom: St. Hildegard's Theology
of the Feminine* and *Voice of the Living Light: Hildegard of Bingen
and her World*, © The Regents of the University of California,
1987 and 1998, respectively.

Paulist Press for excerpts from *Mechthild of Magdeburg:
The Flowing Light of the Godhead*, translated and introduced
by Frank Tobin, Copyright © Frank Tobin. Paulist Press, Inc.
New York/Mahwah, N.J. Reprinted by permission of Paulist Press, Inc.
www.paulistpress.com.

Kavita for permission to reprint poetry from *Love Songs
of the Undivided*. All India Press, © Kavita, 1994.

Every effort was made to contact copyright holders of copyrighted
material contained herein that exceeds generally accepted "fair use".
In case of inadvertent omission the author and publisher express
gratitude for the use of excerpted material.
See also the Bibliography and Suggested Reading section.

About the Cover Art
The artwork used for the cover is a detail from a painting
by Sandy Brand entitled *Vulnerable*. The contrast between our usual
associations with vulnerability and the extraordinary power expressed
in the painting underscore the idea that it is often in opening ourselves
and becoming vulnerable that we are able to truly experience the power
of the divine feminine fire that exists within each and every one of us.
The painting in its entirety and other examples of Sandy's brilliant
artwork can be seen at www.sandybrand.com.

CONTENTS

Acknowledgements

In writing this book I received a tremendous amount of help, support, and encouragement. Although it would be impossible to list every person I'm indebted to, I want to acknowledge as many as I can. First of all, I want to thank Sandy Brand for the use of her extraordinary painting for the cover art. I also want to express great gratitude to Dale Pond who put in countless hours checking for errors and offering helpful suggestions—and to Paul Pond and Eileen Holland who read the manuscript in its early stages and offered invaluable insight.

My heartfelt appreciation goes out to Oriah Mountain Dreamer, Edward Lawrence, Dorothy Walters, and Marion Woodman for taking time out of their extremely busy schedules to read and comment on the manuscript.

Gene Kieffer from the Kundalini Research Foundation in the U.S. and everyone associated with the Institute for Consciousness Research in Canada were, as always, wonderfully supportive in a variety of ways. They include Mike Bradford, Sabine Brüstle, Muriel Ford, Tom Howe, Beverley Viljakainen, Alf Walker, and Ted Wood—and I can't forget to bless Sabine's mom, Gaby, for all the marvelous *Pfirsich Kuchen* she brought to meetings!

Laura Arsie's wonderful photography and David McMaster's technical support—along with his priceless assistance with my website and newsletter—have been enormously appreciated, as has been the support of singer-songwriter Pam Gerrand and the inspiration and perceptive advice Evelyn Wolff has so unselfishly given.

Jean Kowalewski from the S. Walter Stewart Library was a great help. Rabbi Jerry Steinberg has provided invaluable information and insight on Judaism and Kabbalah over the years. Other friends and associates who have been extremely supportive include Phyllis Brown, Glenn Copeland, Evy Cugelman, Wendi Gramantik, Christine Kobielski, Carol Mark, Nancy Volk, and Peggy Voth. Superb artists Janine Kinch and Shelley Yampolsky gave advice on a number of the creativity exercises. Jeannine Keenan, Renate Karner, and Jørgen Pedersen were also very helpful.

Academics who were extremely generous with their time and knowledge include Rick Rogers from Eastern Michigan University, Adele Reinhartz of the University of Ottawa, Monica Sandor and

Jacalyn Duffin of Queen's University, Johanna Stuckey of the Centre for Feminist Research at York University, and David Gordon White of the University of California at Santa Barbara. Any errors I made in their various areas of expertise are mine alone.

Last but certainly not least, my deep gratitude goes out to my superb agent, Natasha Kern, my outstanding editor, Alexandra Pel, and my wonderful husband, Kaz Kobielski—both for doing the drawings for the book and for being so unfailingly supportive.

INTRODUCTION

One day when I first came up with the idea for this book I was discussing it with my friend Beverley, who is a yoga teacher, Sanskrit scholar, and long-time student of the Vedas. Bursting with enthusiasm, I told her I wanted to write a book about the divine feminine—one that compared Shakti from yoga and Hinduism, Sophia from Christianity, and Shekinah from Judaism and showed how they were all related to not just our yearning to be creative but to the personal transformation so many of us are undergoing as individuals and that the world itself is experiencing. Just as enthused as I was, she grabbed me and enveloped me in a huge hug. "Oh, Teri," she said "that is wonderful! I am so thrilled that you are willing to take on such an important and massive project!"

"Massive project?" I thought. "What the heck is she talking about? I'll have this peanut cracked in a year!" *That* was eight years ago. Beverley was right: researching this book was an enormous undertaking. Part of the reason for this is that there is a good deal of controversy among scholars regarding the divine feminine in general and goddess traditions in particular. According to the scholars, some of the popular writings on these topics contain less-than-careful research and a hazardous tendency to assume theories or hypotheses are fact.

Because I feel the topic of the divine feminine is so critically important, so essential to our understanding of where we are and what is happening to us, I wanted to avoid this. I wanted to be absolutely sure every word I wrote about this cosmic creative force was as accurate as it could possibly be: checking and double-checking and tracing everything I read back as far as my limited ancient language skills would allow me to go. And then, because I wanted this to be an approachable, highly readable book, the hard part came: recognizing that I had to toss many of the specifics of the research and *all* of the academic language out the window! Only scholars—and the occasional slightly obsessed person like me—would, I realized, be interested in the degree of detail I dug up in all those years of research.

Doing away with all this excess material left what I believe is the essential core of information you need for understanding this divine energy—how she manifests, how she exists within you, how she is propelling your spiritual journey, how she is the power that is making you yearn for what is right and good and true. In order to share this information with you, I take you back to sacred texts from Christianity, Judaism, yoga and Tantra and explore them. This, then, is not the kind of "1-2-3 Steps to Enlightenment and Eternal Happiness" type of book that is so popular today! But I think I can safely say it won't be difficult to read either. To make sure the book would be as interesting—and, especially, as relevant to your daily life—as possible, the "informative" bits are interwoven with the daring tales of highly creative women mystics from long ago and the stories of ordinary, everyday women— just like you and me—who have turned their contemporary spiritual journeys into fascinating adventures.

The book is organized in two parts. After a chapter that provides a little background and a bit of my own story (I think the reader has a right to know the person behind the words they're reading!), Part I continues with the intriguing tale of Mahadevi Akka, a twelfth-century Hindu saint. Part II begins with the equally amazing story of Mechthild of Magdeburg, a thirteenth-century Christian mystic. These two women—from such vastly different cultures and belief systems—stand like two pillars East and West. The extraordinary similarity of their experiences—from the intense passion and blatant sexual overtones in their writings to their detailed descriptions of how they experienced the Divine—does more to reveal the way the divine feminine works in our lives than almost anything I could have imagined. This is particularly true because these mystics' experiences are not only astonishingly alike, they are similar in ways we might have never imagined to spiritual experiences that people like you and me are having today.

Both Parts I and II contain women's stories—as well as myths, sagas, and legends. Part I lays more of the groundwork, while Part II focuses more on how to apply this knowledge to enrich your creative expression and your daily life. Each chapter (except the last) ends with a creativity exercise designed to move this process along and help you tune into the divine feminine as the source of creative inspiration. Some of these exercises involve writing and others use simple art materials. They each feature creative visualization— which is explained in case you've never tried it before—and they are activities you can benefit from whether you are a professional in the arts or someone who is just beginning to explore your yearning to be creative.

So often we put this yearning on the back burner; we think we'll allow ourselves time to be truly creative when all our "important" work is done. This is often true even if you work in the arts. For, if you are like me, you sometimes get so caught up in how your creative work can earn you a living, you lose touch with your true creative spirit and your sense of what a sacred act creative expression really is. However, as you'll see in the following pages—whether you are a professional or a beginner—the yearning to express yourself is as essential as your desire to become a better person, to help end suffering, or to save Mother Earth. The yearning for all these things is, in fact, all *one* yearning— and it comes to us from the divine feminine. That this should be so shouldn't be as startling as it is. After all, the divine feminine, in her myriad forms, has been seen throughout history as the creative force, the "mother", of the universe. It should come as no surprise then that she is also the creative force within us or that she is the fount of the creative inspiration we all long for.

All this emphasis on the feminine might lead one to believe this is a book for women only, but I did not intend that to be the case. Although the book is certainly about the cosmic feminine and full of the stories of women, contributions of many men—from Pierre Teilhard de Chardin to Gopi Krishna—are included. Far more importantly, of course, both the divine feminine and the divine masculine exist, and should be balanced, within each one of us, and the key to not only increasing the creative inspiration in our lives but also to understanding the transformation we are experiencing lies in understanding how the divine feminine is working in our lives—and this is true for men and women alike.

Before going on to explore these ideas in depth in the following chapters, a few issues need to be addressed. One is the way terms from yoga and Hinduism are spelled. If you are familiar with these terms, you might notice some inconsistencies. In general, I've used proper Sanskrit diacritical marks on terms unless they have become fairly common in English without them. Thus the yogic term for "life energy" is written simply as *prana* and not *prāna*. Regarding dates, you'll also notice that, in order to be more inclusive, BCE (Before the Common Era) and CE (the Common Era) have been used rather than BC and AD.

The "Notes" section for each chapter includes bits of academic information I just couldn't bear to leave out, as well as some general interest material that was too detailed to include in the text. You will find them at the back of the book along with a fairly extensive "Bibliography and Suggested Reading" section. Although I didn't list every book I used in doing the research, I've included the important ones and broken them into categories so that if you decide you want to read more about Mechthild of Magdeburg, for instance, you can easily find the books.

Those "house-keeping" issues out of the way, I invite you to dive into *The Divine Feminine Fire* and wish you the same joyful journey of discovery and creativity that I had in researching it and weaving it all together.

PART I

CHAPTER ONE

The Call of the Creative Spirit

If you have picked up this book and begun to read, chances are you have experienced the power of the creative spirit. This power is not a figment of your imagination; it is not an abstract concept. It is real. It is a force that manifests itself, not just mentally and spiritually, but physically. If you don't believe this, the next time you feel the urge to create, sit with the feeling. Go to a place of stillness, become completely in touch with your body, bring your consciousness to bear on this urge, and you will feel it *in* your body: a sensation, perhaps almost imperceptible, that begins in the nest of your pelvis, then rises up, reaches your heart and throat, and bursts into an aching, a longing, a profound need.

Ideally, when this feeling is upon us we are able to let it out, to allow it to flow into the creation of beautiful words, stirring melodies, graceful movements, or vibrant colors on a canvas. But all too often we use all our might to try to push it back down and dam it up so that it can't escape.

Whether you are a professional in the arts or a person who is just beginning to express yourself creatively, you probably already know that we do all of this out of fear. We are afraid we aren't good enough, talented enough, or skilled enough to create. Or we are bullied by guilt, by the belief that creativity is frivolous and that we have no right to take time from our *real* jobs of breadwinning and nurturing to allow ourselves the "luxury" of creative expression.

You are probably already aware that you *can* overcome all the fear and guilt that block your creativity. This book is here to affirm this awareness and to acknowledge the work you may have already done on overcoming your fears. More importantly, however, it is here to say that not only can you allow yourself to be creative, but that you *must*.

The reason for this is simple. *When you feel you are being moved by the creative spirit, you are in fact being moved by the divine feminine.* The haunting call we feel to be creative is a cry that comes not just from the feminine side of our being but, at its most profound level, from a cosmic feminine force. Now, I admit this is a sweeping statement. And although it is one I have believed for years, it is also one I wouldn't have had the courage to make quite so blatantly if I hadn't learned what I did in the five years I spent researching this book. The reason for this will become clear as you read the stories that follow of the extraordinarily creative women mystics and the ordinary women who have been profoundly touched by the creative spirit. These stories will help you understand how this force is working in your life, how opening up to its power will help you move forward both creatively and spiritually, and why trying to suppress this force is a little like trying to cork a volcano with a coconut.

This awesome feminine force is the single most important factor in our personal creative and spiritual unfoldment, and yet it would be a mistake to ignore, as some contemporary spiritual movements have done, the divine masculine principle. For it too exists and, as will be discussed in some detail later, has an essential role in creative expression. Still, the divine feminine will be emphasized far more heavily than the masculine in the following pages. The most obvious reason for this is, as we all know, the Divine has been "masculinized" for centuries while the divine feminine has been ignored, denigrated, and suppressed.

But there are other reasons, too. One is simply that it is time. The idea that we are at a critical point in history is a widespread one in the contemporary spiritual movement, and some of our greatest thinkers believe it is a particularly crucial time in terms of the divine feminine. Marion Woodman, one of the most widely respected Jungian analysts of our day, concluded her wonderful book *Dancing in the Flames: The Dark Goddess in the Transformation of Consciousness* with an eloquent plea for us to realize that our most crucial job right now is to learn to *embody* the divine feminine. Writers from the East echo this idea. Right up to his death in 1984, the yogi and philosopher Gopi Krishna wrote and spoke tirelessly on the idea that absolutely nothing is more important at this time in history than understanding how this divine feminine force is awakening in the lives of individuals around the planet and what this means for the human race.

Implicit in these and many other great thinkers' perspectives is the notion that the divine feminine is in some way related to evolution. In other words, the cosmic feminine not only creates the universe, as she is seen to do in so many traditions, but also keeps propelling it along; moving both the cosmos as a whole and all the individual forms of consciousness within it towards some specific goal.

Allusions to this idea can be found in many goddess traditions and in the three manifestations of the divine feminine that will be examined most closely in this book: Shakti, the all-powerful cosmic feminine principle in Hinduism; Sophia, the powerful creative force known as Wisdom in the Old Testament; and Shekinah, the feminine face of God in the Jewish mystical tradition.

It is this force I'm referring to when I talk about the *feminine fire*. This feminine fire is a primordial, elemental force that is powerful beyond our wildest imaginings. *It is, in fact, power itself.* Ironically, I didn't discover anything about how this concept is viewed in the Judeo-Christian tradition as Sophia and the Jewish mystical tradition as Shekinah until years after I had begun learning about it in the rich sacred tradition known as Tantra and the philosophical teachings that form the basis of hatha yoga. There, this feminine, generative force is known as Shakti.

The first time I came across the concept of Shakti was many years ago when I traveled to Kashmir with a group of friends to meet Gopi Krishna. While we were there we walked up into the foothills of the Himalayas to his home near the little village of Nishat and listened to him speak for several days about this mighty force. During one of the talks someone in the audience asked if it was possible to control this power. Gopi Krishna just shook his head and laughed. If, he said, you could take a ball of fire no bigger than a baseball from the center of the sun and bring it within two hundred miles of the surface of the earth, the heat from that small ball would scorch the ground beneath it. Then, he suggested, try to imagine not just that small ball of burning energy, but the energy of the entire sun. Next, he said, try to imagine not just the energy of that sun but of all the billions of suns in the universe. And then imagine, not just the energy of all suns, but the force that moves all these suns and all the planets around the universe. That force, he said, is Shakti.

This image leaves little doubt about our inability to *control* this divine feminine energy, and yet the imagery also suggests that this is the energy of life, of creation itself, and that it must pulse through each of us and have a role to play in our daily lives. Indeed this is the case, for yogic tradition tells us there is not only a cosmic Shakti, but also a shakti that makes her home in each one of us as individuals.

The cosmic Shakti—a sort of "capital S" Shakti—is Divine. In the story of creation told in some Hindu traditions nothing existed in the beginning but the One, the Absolute. In other words, there was nothing anywhere but God Consciousness. The next stage of the universe to come into existence was divine masculine consciousness. Known as Shiva, this masculine principle is sometimes characterized as being Consciousness itself or Pure Thought—absolute, quiescent, static Thought. This is a very difficult concept for our Western minds to comprehend, because what we're talking about here is thought without thinking. Thinking implies mental movement, change, or activity—and with Shiva, in the beginning, there is only *stillness*.

Fortunately, we don't have to worry about "thought without thinking" for long, for once masculine consciousness comes into being it is instantaneously followed by the creation of divine feminine consciousness. This feminine principle is known as Shakti. The One has now become Two: Shiva, the static masculine principle, and Shakti, the dynamic feminine principle. Once Shakti springs into action, the cosmos begins to burst into existence. Her essence begins to divide and subdivide into the various attributes and properties that make up the universe until the process of creation begins to explode exponentially, and the myriad aspects of the universe as we know it are propelled into being.

Although there would be no universe at all without both Shakti and Shiva, it is Shakti who is the driving force behind creation. Without her, Shiva is powerless. This concept is portrayed graphically in the many Hindu paintings and statues that show Shiva lying on the ground with Shakti dancing joyously on his supine and lifeless form. Another example is found in the Hindu sacred texts known as the *Purānas*, where it says, "Just as the moon does not shine without moonlight, so also Shiva does not shine without Shakti."

Shakti is, thus, the creative force that has generated the entire cosmos into existence. But her role doesn't end there. Once the cosmos has been created, she continues to propel evolution throughout time. Her job is not just to create more creatures and more highly advanced creatures, but also to bring the myriad forms of existence closer and closer to God Consciousness until, ultimately, all creation is propelled in a vast circle that leads it back to the One. In this sense, Shakti is *the* evolutionary force. As this great cosmic power, Shakti is sometimes envisioned as a great goddess, indeed the greatest of all goddesses, who is known as Kundalini.

The shakti—with a small "s"—that manifests in the individual can also be seen as having an evolutionary role. The easiest way to understand this is to consider it in terms of yoga. The word yoga comes from the Sanskrit *yuj*, a word that forms the root of the English word yoke, which means, of course, to unite or join. In this same sense, the goal of yoga is Union. This is the ultimate Union —the union of the individual self with the Divine or, as it is said in some yoga traditions, the Realization that the individual self is, and always has been, already one with the Divine.

Shakti with a small "s" is often referred to as kundalini-shakti or just kundalini. In one sense, she can be thought of as the trigger that brings this sublime realization—often called enlightenment—about. In the pictures seen so often of the cross-legged yogi with the seven chakras (wheels or vortices often referred to simply as "energy centers")

drawn on his body, kundalini-shakti is depicted symbolically as a serpent coiled three-and-a-half times around the base of the yogi's spine. When this dormant serpent awakens, it is able to travel up the spine, through the chakras, to reach the seventh chakra. Known as the crown chakra, this center is sometimes called the seat of Shiva. Thus it is said that when shakti makes her way to the crown, she unites with Shiva and brings about God Consciousness—Oneness with the Divine—in the individual.

Although all this about Shakti as the evolutionary force might seem a bit abstract and immaterial to you, nothing could be further from the truth. For what it all means is, in short, that Shakti is propelling *your* evolution. She is moving you along and pushing you forward. Another way to look at this is to say she is transforming you and, in particular, transforming your consciousness. Although this transformation is occurring gradually over time in each and every human being, for many of us today this process is being accelerated. In Tantric and yogic traditions this accelerated transformation is related to the "awakening" of kundalini-shakti in the body. Although this process—and the surprising parallels that can be found in Western traditions—are described in more detail later, what is essential to understand now is that the deep yearning you have to create is inextricably linked to both this accelerated process and the way cosmic Shakti is expressing herself in the world today.

This realization didn't come to me all at once. It grew gradually over a number of years and developed out of an image that Gopi Krishna planted in my mind on that long-ago trip to India. At the time, he was describing the wave of interest in the spiritual that had first begun to sweep North America during the seventies—the curiosity about meditation, the exploration of alternative religions, the fascination with the paranormal, the attraction to Eastern traditions like Zen Buddhism—then he chuckled and said, "That, *that*—is kundalini!"

This statement triggered a vision in my mind's eye of a great force, like an oceanic wave, that was flowing through each and every one of us who was actively searching for something "spiritual" in our lives. I could see this powerful force sweeping us along. I could feel its power moving through me and I felt part of something unimaginably immense. At exactly that instant I understood that our vast, collective yearning—whether it was to know the Divine or to bring peace to the world or to end suffering—was kundalini-shakti. That deep yearning was Shakti's voice. And it was real; it was visceral; it was something I was holding in my body; it was something we were *all* holding in our bodies.

It took me much longer to associate Shakti—or in fact anything spiritual at all—with the great yearning I had always felt to express myself creatively. For most of my life, I'd seen my desire to draw, paint, and write as, at best, an indulgence and, at worst, a whim. Even after I had managed to become a professional writer, I always felt like I was cheating fate somehow and that I would eventually have to suffer for being allowed to work at something that was essentially so frivolous. These feelings were enforced, of course, by society's general attitude about the arts and, even more specifically, by my family—a good example of this is how, even after my sixth or seventh book was published, my mother would call and offer to send me back to school so that I could renew my long-elapsed teaching credentials and get a "real" job.

The casting aside of these negative feelings and coming to understand the true nature of creative longing began one morning when I was attending a conference on spirituality in Monterey, California. Just before dawn broke, I went out onto the beach to do Tai Chi. With the blue-green waves washing onto the shore and my bare feet digging into the cold, damp sand, I began to move slowly through the set of exercises. As I focused my eyes on the horizon and began the fluid move known as "Wave Hands Like Clouds", something in my perception shifted. The line separating sky and water began to dissolve. Sky and water became one, water became one with the sand, and slowly all boundaries, all lines of demarcation dissolved. Suddenly, I could see, actually physically see, that all edges were illusion. Everything that had once appeared to be separate to me was in fact One— one vast, limitless expanse of pulsating life energy. Intense sensations began to rush through my body, and my heart exploded with love for this Oneness and everything it contained.

The connection between this profoundly spiritual experience and creativity began to make itself known later that same day. As I was sitting in one of the talks at the conference, a lengthy poem poured out of me that would become the first in a series of the best I have ever written. This poetry, along with many other pieces of writing, came to me over the next several months in exact tandem with the rushes of energy I was experiencing. The pulsations would begin near the base of my spine, move upward and burst, usually near my heart but sometimes near my throat. Words would begin to flow into my mind in rhythmic cadences that kept time with the surges of energy moving through my body, and I would have to write them down. I could not *not* write. It was impossible to resist this compulsion.

Still, even though the spiritual experiences and the creative rushes were occurring at the same time, I might never have realized that their source was the same if it hadn't been for how intense this sensation was. It was so potent, so consuming, that I had no choice but to sit with it, to be with it—to look it, as it were, in the eye. At some point in the process of being flooded with this feeling, I suddenly *recognized* it: although it was vastly more emphatic, it was the same old yearning I'd felt for so many years; it was the longing to become a better person, to discover my true self, to learn to meditate, and to live by spiritual principles. It was the passion that had driven me to fight for social justice issues and to become an environmental activist. And I finally realized that it *felt* exactly the same as the yearning that had compelled me to spend hours drawing as a child, to paint and write poetry as a teenager, to begin university as an art major, and to eventually end up as a writer. It felt the same because it was the same. It was all Shakti, calling out with a Siren's call.

The moment I recognized this in myself for what it truly was, I began to see it working in others. And as I taught an increasing number of workshops on creativity, I began to realize just why recognizing this yearning as Shakti's voice was so important. One reason for this was that I discovered there were so many other women who had the same conflicted feelings about their longing to be creative that I had had. Even though most of them had never put it into words, they saw their spiritual yearning and their creative yearning as forces that pulled them in opposite directions: the spiritual towards the high and worthy; the creative towards the frivolous and self-indulgent. While they had been diligently honoring their spirituality, they had been ignoring, minimizing, or at worst, denigrating, the creative side of their natures.

If you are anything like me or the many women I have met in these workshops, you have been enduring this same disharmony in your life: your spirituality is something you work at; your creativity is something you play at. And you play at it only when you have time, when nothing else—your work, your family, your relationship, your dog, your goldfish—is deemed more important. Even if you are a professional in the arts, you have probably had to work long and hard to convince yourself (if you are indeed convinced!) that you are not cheating fate by being allowed to do something so wonderful with your life.

This dichotomy will vanish when you understand that the yearning you feel is the voice of Shakti. You can begin to see your longing for creative expression as an integral part of your spiritual path; not as a guilty pleasure to be enjoyed only when you have nothing "better" to do. If you are not already a professional in the arts, it might even mean that you would eventually commit yourself full-time to your creative pursuits. But this is not by any means always—or even often—necessary. What is vastly more important is learning how to listen to the voice of Shakti. Then and only then will you know that you are moving in the direction she is calling you to go. And this direction, though it may take you on many marvelous creative adventures during your lifetime, is ultimately about transformation.

In the ancient Tantric and yogic texts this transformation is described, at least in terms of its ultimate goal, as a process that can turn the ordinary spiritual seeker into an enlightened saint or sage. These texts almost always describe a monumental mystical experience that, classically, signals the onset of enlightenment. In these descriptions, the mystical experience itself is almost always portrayed as including a vision of blindingly brilliant, radiant light; sensations of bliss, joy, and love that defy description; and an unfathomable awareness of being one with the Divine or with all of creation.

Although not all instances of enlightenment begin with a mystical experience (some yogis are said to be born enlightened; others to attain this state through a gradual, almost imperceptible process), in the cases most often described in the yogic texts this type of experience marks the beginning of a transformation in which the yogi develops certain traits that either weren't present before or present only in a lesser degree. One of the most important of these traits is a compassion and concern for others that encompasses a passionate desire to end the suffering of humankind. Another is a kind of charisma; people are drawn to the rare yogis who have reached this state and delight in being in their presence. Yet another trait is the development of *siddhis*. Known as *iddhis* in Tibetan Buddhism, these are paranormal abilities and include such things as prophesying the future, accurately interpreting dreams, and, in extreme cases, the manipulation of the natural environment.

Probably the most significant trait of all, however, is the facility to receive divine inspiration. In the highest cases of enlightenment this takes the form of revelation: the great founders of spiritual traditions, for instance, brought new knowledge, new ways of seeing the world, new codes for conduct and behavior that revolutionized thinking in their time and place. But even the yogis who reached only lesser levels of enlightenment would receive some degree of inspiration. In fact, being able to receive inspiration was once used as a test to verify the authenticity of an awakening. When a yogi would come to his guru and claim to have reached the higher state of consciousness known as *samādhi*, the guru would present him with a passage from a sacred text like the *Upanishads* and tell him to meditate upon it and bring back a commentary. If the commentary the yogi returned with was a completely new interpretation of the passage and one that brought a new level of understanding to others, the yogi was deemed to have indeed reached a high level of samādhi. Another way this divine inspiration manifested was what we would now think of as inspired creativity. The Tantras and other yogic texts are replete with references to how poetry and other beautiful words would flow like ambrosia from the mouths of the enlightened ones.

Interestingly enough, the first time I came across a listing of the characteristics of higher consciousness, it was not in a Tantric text or even in anything written by a yogi; it was in a book called *Cosmic Consciousness*, published in 1901 by a medical doctor named Richard Maurice Bucke. Born in England and raised in Canada, Bucke worked in the field of psychiatry in its early days. Widely and highly well-respected in North America and Europe for his innovations in the care of the mentally ill, he became president of what were then known as the American Medico-Psychological Association and the Psychological Section of the British Medical Association.

Bucke was both a medical man and a mystic of sorts. Late one night, when he was visiting England and driving his buggy down a lonely road, he was, quite without warning, enveloped in flaming white light and filled with an inexpressibly moving sense of bliss and union. This experience altered both his scientific and his spiritual life. He soon developed a number of therapeutic techniques that made the treatment of the mentally ill under his care far more compassionate and humane.

At the same time he began a quest to understand exactly what had happened to him that night on the lonely road. A long-time admirer of Walt Whitman, Bucke sensed that Whitman must have had similar types of experiences. He sought Whitman out, and eventually the two became close friends. (The story of their friendship is told in the 1990 movie *Beautiful Dreamers*.) Around this time, Bucke also began to study the lives of the great spiritual masters. Being a scientist at heart, he methodically isolated the characteristics of both their mystical experiences and their personal traits. Eventually he developed the hypothesis that brief mystical experiences like the one he had had were fleeting tastes of a higher state of consciousness and that founders of the great religious traditions had not only reached this higher state but had lived in it. But Bucke didn't study just spiritual masters like Christ and Buddha, he also delved into the lives of the greatest creative geniuses like Dante and William Blake and found that many of them, too, had had some type of mystical experience and exhibited to some degree the personal characteristics he'd isolated in the lives of the great spiritual teachers. Although Bucke had no way of knowing it at the time—few if any Sanskrit texts would have been available to him in translation—his descriptions of both mystical experiences and the individual characteristics were virtually identical to those listed in Tantric and yogic texts.

Based on his findings, Bucke developed the theory that the individuals he had studied were all, to one degree or another, harbingers of a higher level of consciousness that all of humankind was evolving towards. Although *Cosmic Consciousness*, first published in 1901, contains some bits of information we now know to be incorrect, Bucke's basic premise has stood the test of time and has profound implications for those of us on the spiritual path today. One is that this experience is universal: both the mystical experience and the characteristics developed after this experience were similar regardless of the religion or spiritual practice the individual followed. Another, and one that is perhaps even more significant for those of us who are experiencing the call to creativity as part of our spiritual path, is that his descriptions of people who had reached lesser and greater degrees of cosmic consciousness open the way for us to see the whole process of awakening and transformation as one that exists on a continuum.

To continue with the metaphor of shakti awakening from her sleep and traveling upwards to reach Shiva, we could say that when the two actually meet, the manifestations are profound, cataclysmic, and beyond the limits of language to describe. They are also extremely rare. According to the yogic tradition, this level of awakening has been reached by only a handful of saints and mystics. It would lie at the far end of the continuum, with the experiences of the great spiritual teachers like Christ, Moses, Buddha, Mohammed and so on at the very furthest end. The experiences of the vast majority of us would lie at the other end. For most of us, the sleeping shakti is just beginning to awaken. Stirring in fits and starts, she sometimes moves a little way upwards, and sometimes returns to rest in the cradle of the pelvis—but all the while opening windows here and there, giving us provocative glimpses of what lies beyond, and transforming us by beginning to awaken, to one degree or another, the characteristics of cosmic consciousness within us.

When we look at mystical experience in terms of this continuum, at the far end of the spectrum we find, for example, Buddha reaching Nirvana, and fairly close to this we might find the Hindu saint Rama-krishna's experience of being utterly dissolved in God Consciousness. A little further along would be the twelfth-century Christian mystic Mech-thild of Magdeburg, who at times experienced being "one love and one fire and one breath and one light with God". Way at the other end of the spectrum would be an experience like the one I had on the beach; significant and life-altering as it was to me, it was the merest hint of what the true mystics have experienced.

As an example of paranormal abilities or siddhis—known as *charisms* in the Christian tradition and often mentioned in both the Old and New Testaments—we find, at the far end of the continuum, Jesus raising Lazarus from the dead; a little further along we might find the Old Testament Joseph, who was able to tell the Pharaoh exactly what was going to happen with the harvest for the next fourteen years; and at the other end we would find the vast majority of us, who find that we have a "psychic" experience now and then or that our intuition is far stronger than it once was.

This same continuum can be seen with inspired creativity. At one end of the spectrum we have the revealed teachings brought to us by the great religious masters, and a little further along we have the poetry of a Rumi and the music of a Hildegard of Bingen. Lying at various points closer to the other end of the spectrum we find the creative work of most of us who have found ourselves on the path that combines creativity and spirituality.

You probably aren't surprised to discover that your work lies at this end of the spectrum—you are aware that you haven't turned into a Rumi or a Hildegard *yet*. But this "yet" is really the crux of what this book is about. If the divine feminine is really propelling the evolution of consciousness and if inspired creativity is indeed one of the manifestations of this transformation of consciousness, it means that although the degree of inspiration we receive may be *quantitatively* different from that of a Rumi or a Hildegard, it is *qualitatively* the same. *The essence of the experience is the same.* What flowed through Rumi flows through us. And if we aren't able to contain it and express it with the same purity or clarity just yet, it doesn't mean we won't be able to—or to, at least, steadily increase the amount of inspired creativity that blesses our lives.

The stories in the following pages give evidence again and again that this is so. As you will see, the Hindu saint Mahadevi's experience of kundalini-shakti is virtually identical to the Christian mystic Mechthild of Magdeburg's experience of the Holy Spirit—and the way this experience manifested in extraordinary creativity is also the same. But even more importantly for everyday people like you and me, the experiences of the ordinary women whose stories are told in this book contain the very same elements.

Very early on in my research I was struck by how these women's experiences, although essentially spiritual in nature, contained such a powerful physical element. As you read on you'll see this particularly clearly in the stories of Mahadevi and Mechthild. These women felt the movement of kundalini and the Holy Spirit intensely in their bodies. In spite of the fact that they were both in celibate religious orders, they wrote frankly of the physical sensations they experienced and often used blatantly sexual terms to express this in their poetry. Although this aspect of sexuality in creativity and spirituality is an extremely important phenomenon (see Chapter Thirteen), what struck me early on was simply the sheer physicality of what they were describing.

An explanation for this can be found in the sacred symbolism of Tantra, where the most fundamental image is the concept of a macro-cosm and a microcosm. In this symbolic imagery, the human body is a microcosm that replicates the entire macrocosm. In this macrocosm, the dance between cosmic Shakti and Shiva described earlier is per-petually being played out: Shakti, in her yearning to return to Shiva and to Oneness, is continually propelling the universe through the stages of evolution that will lead everything in creation back to union with the Absolute. At the same time, this great cosmic dance is being played out and mimicked in the microcosm that is the human body, where kundalini-shakti lies at the base of the spine, yearning to be reunited with her Shiva. For his part, Shiva sits above the crown of the head longing for the return of his Beloved so that the individual can experience divine union, or the oneness of cosmic consciousness. In this dance of cosmic longing and love-play, kundalini is the *embodied* manifestation of the divine feminine.

This macrocosmic/microcosmic view of the universe made perfect sense to me; undoubtedly at least in part because it tallied with how intensely *in the body* even my own very minor mystical experiences had been, and I became very excited about it. But what thrilled me even more was discovering something I had never heard expounded anywhere before, and this was that both Sophia and Shekinah, exactly like Shakti, could be seen as the *embodiment* of the divine feminine. And, even more amazingly to me, I found that it was in this embodied state that they, exactly like kundalini-shakti, worked their transformative magic.

As mentioned earlier, Marion Woodman believes that learning to embody the divine feminine is one of, if not the most, important pursuits for those of us on the spiritual path today. In this, she is joined by many other thinkers who have brought our attention to the feminine aspect of the Divine in recent years. But just how little information is available on this—especially that focuses on the purely practical—was brought home to me just about the time I finished researching this book.

I had just taught a creative writing workshop in the Rocky Mountains and the organizer, Peggy, was driving me to the airport. As I gazed out the car window, I couldn't help thinking what a perfect setting it was for the discussion on the divine feminine that we were having. As we rolled along, Peggy began to talk about how deeply the concept of the divine feminine had moved her and how much it had meant to her. She told me how from the very first time she had come in contact with the idea of embodying the divine feminine she had longed to do it. She spoke about this in very abstract terms for a few moments and then said, bluntly, "But to tell you the truth," she said, "until today I really had no idea what 'embodying the divine feminine' really meant. And I had no idea how the heck to *do* it."

The moment she made this comment I felt like a boulder had rolled off one of the passing hills and hit me on the head. Immediately, I realized that if she had indeed gleaned any specific information on embodying the divine feminine from my workshop, it had been purely by accident: for it had never, ever occurred to me that someone in the audience might be asking the eminently practical question "How do I do this?" If it had, I would have shouted out what I had discovered: "You don't have to *do* anything! You *already* embody the divine feminine!"

Shakti, Shekinah, and Sophia can all be seen to represent the Divine with us, the Divine in our bodies. This means that the way to embody the divine feminine is to realize that you have embodied her all along. Of course, this is, like so much on the spiritual path, simple but not easy. It is much like the yogi master telling his students that the way to become one with God is to realize you have been one with God all along.

Still, what I have learned from the women whose stories are told in this book is that there are very specific steps you can take if you want to *realize* this—and by this I mean make it real in your life and, in so doing, discover how this embodied divine feminine can become an ever-expanding source of inspired creativity for you. The first step in this is simply to become increasingly able to recognize her in your life. To help you do this, you need to become more familiar with Shakti, Sophia, and Shekinah and how she has been portrayed in the sacred stories, myths, and legends that reveal the secrets of her inner workings. Doing this prepares you for the second, and in a way most essential step, which is learning to listen to her when she calls to you. Perfecting this ability to listen also involves the third step: learning to hold her great power in your body—learning to sit with her, to simply be with her. As you become increasingly comfortable with these three steps, it becomes easier and easier to accomplish the forth step. And this is to express her, to allow her to flow upwards and outwards from both the very depth—and the very heart of your being. For the more you are willing to express her, the more willing she is to flow back into your life and fill you with her sweet grace once again.

Inspiration—Only a Breath Away

There is no better place to see where the ideas expressed in this chapter come together than in the word "inspiration". It actually comes to us from the Latin that means "to bring spirit in", and in this way embodies both creativity and spirituality. It tells us that creative inspiration comes from drawing in the Divine. And because "inspiration" also refers to "breathing in", it creates an image of creative inspiration flowing into our lives as simply and surely as the air we breathe.

This relationship between creative inspiration and breathing can also be found in the yogic literature where the word prana refers both to breath and to the all-sustaining life force. If you've done much yoga, you probably know that breathing exercises are known as pranayama.

Before going on to explore this relationship between prana and creativity, the following exercise will help you create a sacred space where you can tune into this life force, recognize it as the source of inspiration within your own soul, and allow it to flow into your creative expression. Use this exercise whether you want to be creative or simply find a creative solution to an everyday problem. Just ask for an answer to your problem before you begin, or have your pen, paintbrush, musical instrument, etc. at hand.

Because it begins with the most basic of type of pranayama, it is a good introductory exercise for those of you who have never done any type of creative visualization or meditation. If you are already familiar with pranayama, just skip to point number four.

1. Begin by exhaling, gently emptying your lungs of all air, to a slow count of eight.
2. To a count of eight, breathe in deeply—gently filling up the bottom of your lungs first, then the middle, then the top.
3. To do this, allow your muscles to expand, beginning with the muscles around the stomach, then those around your chest and ribs. Allow the air to rise up until it almost feels like it is massaging the base of your throat. This is natural breathing; it is the way a baby breathes. Hold for a count of four.
4. Then exhale to a count of eight. Begin by emptying first the bottom, then the middle, then the top of your lungs by gently contracting the

muscles you expanded. Feel yourself becoming increasingly still, deeply relaxed, and in tune with your inner self.

5. *Allow yourself to become increasingly aware that you are breathing in prana—the radiant life force.*

6. *Concentrate on this radiance, see it glowing and sparkling within you until you are aware that you are filled with a luminous, resplendent white light. Stay for a while in this space allowing the radiance of the light to intensify.*

7. *Once you feel yourself filled with this shimmering light, visualize—or just imagine—it flowing upwards. See it moving to your heart, resting there for a moment and intensifying with each heartbeat. Then see it flowing to your shoulders, down your arms, out the hands, into the fingers that are resting on your paper and holding your pen—or into whatever creative tool you chose to have at hand.*

CHAPTER TWO

I Burn, Desiring What the Heart Desires

The first gentle nudges from the divine feminine are often experienced as yearning. Whether this yearning is felt as soft waves of longing or as an almost unbearable aching hunger, it is a call from some deep level of your being. Since you have been drawn to this book, you will almost certainly have experienced this yearning at one time or another as a deep-seated desire for creative expression. But it may have touched you in many other ways as well: as a simple desire to discover who you really are or to understand the reason for your existence; as a great passion to end suffering and right the wrongs in the world; as hunger to know God not with your mind but with your heart; as an awareness that any inner emptiness you may feel needs to be filled with something spiritual, that the material will simply no longer satisfy.

The lives of saints and sages from every spiritual tradition have been touched by this yearning. Indeed, it is a theme that comes up again and again in the stories of both the mystics and the everyday people that are told in this book.

But if you are a student of one of the Eastern philosophies, particularly Buddhism, you may be thinking to yourself right now, "But isn't yearning the same as desire and isn't desire bad? Isn't it what holds us back?" And while this is true in the sense of what we usually mean when we talk about desire, the difference between this type of desire and the yearning I'm talking about can be thought of as the difference between an "I want, I want" that is being cried by an angry, demanding ego and a "You already have, you already have" that is being softly murmured by an inner, divine, and brightly burning flame. But because few of us really believe or know with our whole hearts that we already hold all the love and power we need within, this divine feminine fire has to keep propelling us forward along the path that will eventually lead to this miraculous realization.

She does this by making us yearn for exactly the traits and characteristics of the transformation she wants us to achieve. Nowhere are these characteristics and the power of yearning portrayed more passionately than in the life of Mahadevi Akka, an extraordinarily creative woman who lived in twelfth-century India. Today, more than eight centuries after her death, she is still revered in Southern India and held to be both a saint and a divinely inspired creative genius. In spite of the fame she holds in India, her story is virtually unknown in the West and needs to be told.

Mahadevi lived only until her early twenties, but she produced hundreds of poems—many as exquisitely beautiful and powerful as any poetry ever expressed in any language. Almost miraculously, over two hundred of these poems have survived. That they have is a testament to how extraordinarily revered she was, for she may not have recorded all, or even many, of them. She simply sang them out as she traveled the countryside. They were memorized, passed on, and eventually written down by those who venerated her.

These poems and what we know of her life paint a captivating picture of the process of transformation and its characteristics: she had profound mystical experiences of oneness and divine light and is believed to have developed siddhis. Her divinely inspired creativity is legendary and thought by some to include glimpses of divine revelation. And as she progressed along her path her desire to make the world a better place became so strong that she joined a radical spiritual and social reform movement that was striving—in the twelfth century no less—not only to abolish the caste system but also to treat women with equality.

Of course Mahadevi's experiences lie somewhere towards the far end of the continuum described in the last chapter. Because of this everything about her life is intense and extreme. Still, in her we can see ourselves—yearning to become more spiritually fulfilled, longing to know our true selves, aching to ease the suffering we see around us, and wanting passionately to find a way to express all this in both our creativity and the way we live our lives. Because of this, Mahadevi has much to teach us—especially about how this type of yearning is an expression of Shakti's power, how we *already* hold this power within us and how our learning to simply "be" with this mighty force can be the key to conquering all the fear that holds us back.

Mahadevi's life began in the part of India now known as Karnataka. The village she was born in was called Udutadi and, although it no longer remains, ruins suggest it was near what is now the city of Shimoga. The location of the village becomes significant for a number of reasons, one of which is simply the astounding beauty of the area that Mahadevi grew up in. Karnataka's white sand beaches, craggy cliffs and inlets are backed by lush green hills that rise and grow higher until they become the heavily forested mountains known as the Western Ghats. This mountainous area is characterized by soaring peaks, rich valleys, rushing rivers, and cascading waterfalls. The forests are thick with teak, sandalwood, mango and coconut trees. The beauty of these forests clearly influenced Mahadevi's writing and her poems are alive with the creatures—parrots, cuckoos, monkeys, elephants and tigers—that roamed them.

Although the stories about the childhoods of saints are so glorified over time that it is hard to separate legend from reality, it seems likely that Mahadevi was in fact a remarkable child. She is said to have been gifted in the arts and languages and to have been adept in both her native Kannada and Sanskrit by the age of six. Around this time she also began to reveal an unusually devout nature. This side of her continued to develop, and when she was about ten she declared openly that she would dedicate her life to God.

Certainly Mahadevi was born into a deeply religious family. Her father, Nirmala, and her mother, Sumati, were Shaivites. This meant they were worshipers of Shiva rather than Vishnu—the two manifestations of God revered in what were then, as they are now, the two main branches of Hinduism. Shiva is a fierce God. He is often pictured with his hair wild and matted, his body smeared with ash, dancing in frenzied abandon on a cremation ground in the black of night, crunching on the bones of the dead. In this guise Shiva is known as the cosmic Destroyer. Although the image of a berserk god destroying the universe is a terrifying one, Shiva is good. For what he destroys is the world of misery and suffering that exists around us. In this way, he shows us that this world is, in one sense, nothing more than an illusion and leads us to the realization of our oneness with the ultimate divine reality.

Thus the word "shiva" also means benevolent. And it was this aspect of Shiva that Mahadevi worshiped and that was the focus of the great yearning that literally ruled her life. For Mahadevi longed not just to worship Shiva with her whole heart and soul, but to become his bride. In Hindu sacred stories, Shiva's divine feminine counterpart is given many names, for instance Sati and Parvati. All of these are understood to be manifestations of the cosmic divine feminine, Shakti. Although Mahadevi did not refer to Shakti in her writings, her great yearning was to become one with Shiva. In this, she succeeded. As the Hindu scholar Dr Siddhayya Puranik says, rather poetically, near the end of her life she *becomes* Shakti.

While Mahadevi spoke of her love for Shiva from an early age, her parents didn't even begin to realize how profound her commitment was until she reached marriageable age, probably sometime during her mid-teens, and they began to search for a husband for her. There was no shortage of suitors—for the one thing all Mahadevi's biographers agree on is that she was extraordinarily beautiful. As Mahadevi's parents presented these eligible young men to her one by one, she refused them saying she loved only Shiva, whom she had given the name Chenna Mallikārjuna—a term often translated as My Lord White as Jasmine.

Given the social structure of the time, Mahadevi's defiance was unheard of and her refusal to marry brought hardship on her family. An unmarried daughter was considered a great liability. A daughter that no one wanted to marry would have been bad enough but one who refused eligible suitors was a disgrace.

Her parents continued to plead with her to accept one of the young men, but she remained steadfast, saying that she longed only for Shiva and would have none other. In her poems she tried again and again to communicate the power of this longing and how she was—quite beyond her own will—consumed by it. In one poem to Shiva, she cries:

> Four parts of the day
> I grieve for you.
> Four parts of the night
> I'm mad for you.
>
> I lie lost
> sick for you, night and day,
> Oh lord white as jasmine.
>
> Since your love
> was planted,
> I've forgotten hunger,
> thirst, and sleep.

The power of this yearning and the transformation it was generating in her led her to extraordinary levels of defiance for her time and place. Even though all evidence says she had a happy home and loved her parents very much, in her poems she railed against her mother's interference and rejected her:

> O mother you must be crazy,
> I fell for my lord
>   white as jasmine,
> I've given in utterly.
>
> Go, go, I'll have nothing
> of your mother-and-daughter stuff,
> You go now.

Eventually she began to claim that she was not just in love with Shiva but betrothed to marry him. After this she became even more steadfast in her refusal to accept any of her suitors. Why, she asks her mother, in one of her poems would she possibly want one of "your husbands who will die and decay" when she was already joined to her exquisitely beautiful and immortal Lord White as Jasmine. In another poem she described being completely consumed by him:

> He paralyzed my will
> O mother; ravished my body, made my joy
> worthy of him; he has possessed
> My entire being: I am now
> The beloved of my lord white as jasmine.

Unfortunately for her parents, Mahadevi's refusal to conform to custom was soon to have even more serious consequences. Late one afternoon Mahadevi's village stirred with excitement. Prince Kaushika, the ruler of their land, was on his way home from a hunt in a nearby forest and would be coming through their village as he returned to his palace. To pay their respect the villagers lined the road through the village and waited upon his arrival. When he finally appeared, it was almost certainly with all the pomp and circumstance that befitted traveling royalty in twelfth-century India: the prince and his companions resplendent in their colorful silks, riding horses and elephants with bejeweled halters and brocade saddle blankets, followed by a large retinue of servants waving fans and carrying the spoils of the hunt on long poles on their shoulders.

When he passed Mahadevi, the prince drew up his horse and stared down at her. From the little bits and pieces we know about her appearance, it's easy to imagine what Kaushika must have seen when he looked down from his horse: a slender seventeen- or eighteen-year-old with large brown eyes, thick black hair hanging far below her waist, and shining mahogany skin that was probably flushed a little at being singled out by the prince.

Although the prince returned home that same evening, Mahadevi's image stayed with him. Deciding after a time that he must have her for his own, he sent a convoy of attendants to Mahadevi's parents bearing gifts and asking them for their daughter's hand in marriage. Fully expecting the family to gather up their belongings and joyously make their way to the palace, he eagerly awaited their arrival.

His wait, as you have probably already guessed, was a long one. Rich, handsome, powerful he may have been, but Mahadevi would have none of it. To her he was nothing more than any other slowly decaying mortal. And worse, he was an unbeliever, a heathen who did not worship Shiva. Still, it's not hard to imagine how her parents must have begged her to accept the prince. The marriage would not only have lifted them into a far higher standing, attachment to the royal family would have provided a level of safety, security, and comfort they could only have imagined before.

Over the next while the prince continued to send delegations and gifts and Mahadevi's parents continued to plead, but she was immovable. Eventually her parents began to relent. They were, after all, good Shaivites, and they must have been concerned about letting their daughter marry an unbeliever. By that time it must also have become clear to them that Mahadevi was truly consumed with her longing for union with Shiva and that she really did believe she belonged only to him. Reading the poem below, in which she pours out her longing for union using the imagery of the Hindu wedding and the bride who waits at the alter, it is easy to see why they eventually gave in to her:

> I've bathed in turmeric,
> Put on cloth of gold,
> Tied a silken gown around;
> And cried
> "Come, Lord, come, oh husband, come –
> Your coming is a birth to me!"

> And crying still
> I scan the roads to see if you,
> Oh my lord white as jasmine,
>   will come.

> My mouth is parched.

But even with Mahadevi's whole family united against him, Prince Kaushika wasn't about to give up. He was still determined to have Mahadevi for his own, and he had had enough of trying to tempt and cajole her into acceptance. His ego battered and his temper blown, he dispatched guards to Mahadevi's home and took, not her, but her parents into custody. He then passed a message to Mahadevi that both her mother and father would be killed if she did not comply immediately with his wishes.

Mahadevi realized she had no choice but to give in, and she

finally allowed herself to be taken to the palace. Once face to face with the prince, however, she made it clear she was not beaten. Unbowed she stood before him and told him she would marry him only if he granted her three conditions. First, he had to convert to Shaivism. Second, he had to allow her to feed and converse with any wandering holy men who came begging at their door. And third, he must promise to never interrupt her meditation. If, she said, he broke these three conditions she would consider herself released from the bonds of marriage and free of him.

Kaushika readily agreed. Mahadevi's parents were released from prison, and the wedding took place in short order. It wasn't long, however, before it became apparent to Mahadevi that the prince's commitment to her Lord Shiva was in name only. She considered the first condition broken, and began to bide her time, waiting for him to break the other two. His second transgression came some months later. Mahadevi had allowed a group of *jangamas*, the wandering holy men, into the royal courtyard. When Kaushika came into the courtyard later he saw Mahadevi sitting in a circle with them deep in conversation. Perhaps Kaushika was disgusted by the jangamas' appearance—the holy men were often not only naked, but filthy and smeared with ash like their Lord Shiva—or perhaps he was jealous of Mahadevi's passionate interest in their words; but regardless of the reason, Kaushika is said to have run into the courtyard, dragged Mahadevi out of the circle, and banished the jangamas from the grounds.

According to at least one source, Kaushika's third transgression fell hard on the heels of his second. One afternoon he is said to have crept into Mahadevi's room and spied on her as she sat cross-legged in meditation. Aroused by her beauty and radiance as he watched, he reached a point when he could no longer contain himself. He rushed to her, pulled her from her meditation mat, and forced her to have sex with him. Although this experience must have been horrific for her, she realized it was also her salvation. Mahadevi immediately declared that the three conditions of her marriage vow had been broken and that she was free. Kaushika felt such remorse at his behavior that he did not protest, and Mahadevi walked through the palace gates a free woman.

As she stood outside the palace, she stopped long enough to perform yet another act of defiance against her prince and her society: she ripped her clothing from her body. If the male jangamas could wander naked, so could she. For she was clothed, she later wrote, in the morning light of her Jasmine White Lord.

After leaving the prince's palace she was driven by a yearning so deep that she turned—not to the safety of her home—but towards a holy place known as Kalyana, located as the crow flies about 150 miles to the north. But the terrain that lies between the palace and Kalyana is scored with deep valleys and high peaks and rivers and in those days it was wild. The villages were few and far between; the land was covered with vast tracts of rainforest populated with snakes, wild boars, tigers, and other dangerous creatures.

None of this seemed to daunt Mahadevi. Barefoot, penniless, alone, and with nothing but her long black hair covering her body, she resolutely turned north and began her journey. Her body was on fire for her Lord White as Jasmine.

> Not seeing you
> in the hill, in the forest,
> from tree to tree
> I roamed
>   searching, gasping:
>   Lord, my Lord, come
>   show me your kindness!
>
> ...Give me a clue,
> Oh lord
>   white as jasmine,
>   to your hiding places.

Mahadevi's hope of finding union with her Lovely One in Kalyana must have been spurred by tales of wondrous happenings there. Kalyana was rapidly attracting a large community of Virashaiva followers and saints. The word Vira means "hero" in Sanskrit and "shaiva", or Shaivite as mentioned earlier, means "follower of Shiva". Thus a Virashaiva is a "heroic follower of Shiva". Although Virashaivism may have actually existed for close to two hundred years before Mahadevi's time, it was only just beginning to gain popularity. Even so it remained a radical splinter group passionately opposed to the traditional religious teachings and societal customs of the day. The credit for developing these revolutionary ideas goes to a holy man and great teacher named Basavanna.

Basavanna was born in 1106 not far from Kalyana, which in those days was the main seat of the huge Chalukya Empire. He spent his school years absorbed in spiritual study and had every intention of living the life of a celibate spiritual seeker. By the time he was in his twenties, however, tales of his wisdom had spread, and he was convinced by the prime minister of Kalyana to join the government there. Over the years, Basavanna's power grew, he became prime minister himself, and he used his increasing influence to spread the revolutionary tenets of Virashaivism. Centuries ahead of their time, these included a belief in the inherent equality of all humans, the need to abolish the caste system, and the need to wipe out the social customs that kept women from having the same rights and freedoms as men. Just how radical Basavanna's ideas were is evidenced by the fact that eight centuries after his death the caste system still functions, at least unofficially, in India and women of the poorer classes have in reality very few rights.

If Basavanna's ideas were revolutionary, Mahadevi was one of their most radical supporters. Down through the ages her biographers have repeatedly described her as one of the most outspoken proponents of these ideas. When she reached Kalyana, however, she was still an unknown quantity and had to prove herself in order to be admitted to Basavanna's community by being publically tested and deemed worthy. Because her questioner was none other than Allama Prabhu—a guru recognized in Southern India today as one of the greatest spiritual teachers and poets of all time—much of the inquisition has come down to us through the centuries. It is said that Allama began his questioning by stating that since such a young, beautiful member of their society must be married, all she needed to do to pass her test was to state her husband's name. Many of the crowd had probably already heard of Mahadevi's desertion of the prince and must have gasped at Allama's question. But Mahadevi didn't hesitate. She simply stated that her husband's name was Shiva, her Lord White as Jasmine. When Allama looked at her skeptically, she replied that all humankind was the "father and mother" who made this matchless match for her and who had prepared her for the wedding. They had smeared the holy turmeric powder on her body, bedecked her with golden bracelets, and placed her under a wedding canopy of fire. Then as the stars and planets looked on, a symbol of

Shiva that was painted on the palm of her hand rose up to become the groom and she, the bride, took him as her husband.

Records from Allama's life tell us that he continued to fire questions at Mahadevi that were virtually impossible to answer but that she never faltered and even challenged him back. Some historians say he dealt with her harshly not because he thought she might be unworthy but because he recognized her exceptional spiritual attainment and wanted to reveal it to the other members of the community. Be that as it may, Mahadevi would not have known this and probably felt a tremendous relief when Allama agreed not just to admit her to the community but to become her guru.

Mahadevi stayed as Allama's disciple in Basavanna's community for some time—probably a few years. Here Mahadevi truly found her home. Everyone in the community, regardless of gender or caste, was encouraged to think, to question, and to bring their ideas to group discussion. Mahadevi blossomed in this atmosphere of equality and freedom of thought and discovered a true sense of belonging and family. In her poetry from this period she called Basavanna her father, said she was the child of Allama, and called herself the infant daughter of the other saints. She also gave complete credit to Allama and Basavanna for the ever-higher states of mystical union she reached while living in the Kalyana community.

But like all saints, Mahadevi had her dark nights of the soul. Her union with Shiva was not yet permanent. One day she was Shiva's lover, another she was married to him, and on yet another she was left bereft, aching for his touch. In one verse she says the longing for her beloved was like that of a baby elephant—lost, separated from his herd, captured and taken far away—crying pathetically for his family and his beautiful blue mountain home.

Thus, in spite of all she had attained in Kalyana, Mahadevi kept longing for a union with her Lord White as Jasmine that would never end. Realizing that she must continue on her journey, she walked away from not only a loving community but one of the greatest gurus in Indian history and began another long, lonely trek.

Not only was this difficult decision the right one for her spiritual journey, it was also one that may well have saved her life. For shortly after she left, the attempts to oppress Basavanna's revolutionary ideas broke into open, violent persecution of the Virashaivas—a situation that was triggered when Basavanna, ever true to his principles, sanctioned a marriage between a woman of the highest caste and an "untouchable", a man of the lowest caste, who were in love with each other. When vigilantes heard of the wedding, they dragged the fathers of the bride and groom through the streets until dead. Shortly after this, Basavanna was forced to resign as prime minister and to return to his homeland. As soon as his replacement came to power, the new prime minister ordered the slaughter of thousands of Virashaivas. Those who were not massacred were forced to scatter; the idyllic community founded on equality and freedom of thought was crushed.

Although Mahadevi was safely away when the massacre occurred, she was traveling at a time when the hatred of the Virashaivas was reaching a fever pitch. Like all Virashaivas, she marked her forehead with ash and wore a lingam—a phallic symbol representing Shiva—on a necklace around her neck. This open declaration of faith combined with the message in the poems she was continually singing out almost certainly increased the amount of harassment she had to endure.

Probably still traveling naked, and certainly barefoot and with only a begging bowl, Mahadevi was headed to a mountain called Shrisaila, known as one of the mythical homes of Shiva. To reach her goal Mahadevi had to make her way across what is now the top of Northern Karnataka, probably again over part of the mountainous Western Ghats, across vast dry stretches of land, all the way into what is now Andhra Pradesh. But once there she did indeed find the fabled mountain Shrisaila and managed to climb it. From this point on very little is known about Mahadevi's life, but we do know that somewhere on the side of the mountain she reached the ultimate Realization that had been her goal. After this she remained on the mountain for the rest of her life, dying somewhere between her twenty-second and twenty-fifth year. The reason for her death seems to have faded into history.

According to legend, however, the moment when Mahadevi reached her ultimate union with Shiva came as she was walking up the side of the mountain and came unexpectedly on a kadali, or plantain, grove. After so many endless miles, the grove—with its towering vines, shimmering leaves, and heavy clusters of fruit—would have been an unimaginably beautiful oasis. It is easy to picture Mahadevi coming upon it and realizing she was finally at her journey's end. At that moment, it is said that the grove came to represent the entire material world for her and that, as she gazed upon it, she conquered it and all it represented. Her body, her mind, and all her passions dissolved into oneness with the kadali. She had finally arrived, she said, safe and sound to find Shiva, the Destroyer of the wheel of births, in this kadali grove. At that moment she felt her Lord White as Jasmine's boundless love for her rise up and engulf her; she became, she says, enfolded forever in the lotus of his heart.

One of the most valuable gifts Mahadevi has left those of us on the creative-spiritual path is a detailed description of her own experience of the awakening of kundalini-shakti and an unequivocal statement about how it affected her ability to express herself creatively. This poem is sixty-seven triplets in length—more than ten times the length of any of her other writings, and it is fascinating because Mahadevi's religion, Virashaivism, was not associated in any way with hatha yoga, Tantra, or indeed any of the aspects of Hinduism that were particularly concerned with kundalini. Still, she uses the very same symbolism and imagery yogis had been using for centuries to describe what was, and still is, referred to as the rising of the serpent power.

In this extraordinary poem, Mahadevi refers to this divine feminine force as a secret pearl that bestows wisdom. She tells us it awakened from the three glowing coils of light. The light traveled upwards through a central channel in her spine, turned her chakras to rubies and pearls, and lodged in her mind as a light that excelled a billion suns and moons combined. Upon seeing this light, she tells us, the nectar of Shiva's love poured down on her from a great pitcher in a luminous sky and filled her to overflowing. At that moment she was freed from life's pitfalls and, finally, found liberation. At the end of the poem Mahadevi refers to the nectar that filled her as the "precious juice of Grace". She then concludes the poem by telling us clearly why her Lord White as Jasmine filled her with this sweet grace: "So that I could write," she says, "the best I ever can."

Reading these words for the first time was a deeply moving experience for me. Not only had Mahadevi described in detail her experience of the awakening of kundalini—or as Dr Puranik puts it of "becoming Shakti"—she lets us know that there was a purpose to this. She was telling us she realized that, after having this profound mystical experience, she wasn't just meant to sit there basking in her blissful union with Shiva, she was to express this love—and to express it through her writing. She was being filled with sweet nectar, this precious juice, so that she could pour it back into the world. And by being able to write the best she ever could, she was being given the tools she needed to do it.

Even though few of us will ever, at least in this lifetime, reach the heights Mahadevi did, her story tells us that the potential for awakening this sweet "juice of Grace" lies within each and every one of us. If we open ourselves to it and allow it to fill us up, we too will be given what we need to express it.

Like so much on the spiritual path this is simple, but not necessarily easy. And, as I am sure you already well know, the thing that most often holds us back is fear. Not surprisingly, Mahadevi has a great deal to tell us about this too. Just imagine how much fear she—a teenage girl in a totally patriarchal society—must have felt at times doing the things she did: she defied not only her parents but also her society's most sacred values, declaring in both word and deed her right as a woman to determine whom she would marry and even whether she would marry. When faced with even the potential assassination of her parents, she still stood up against the prince and managed to force him to marry her on her own terms. And even when the prince finally released her from her bonds, she must have faced great opposition from his loyal followers who would have considered it a terrible betrayal. She then abandoned a life of ease and security for one of poverty and danger. In an act of complete defiance against her society, she symbolically claimed her right to do anything male spiritual seekers could do by throwing down her clothes. She then faced the world utterly alone. Imagine what her journeys must have been like. Barefoot, penniless and covered only in her long, dark hair, she traveled over treacherous mountains and stretches of parched land. In the villages men leered at her. In the jungles she slept alone at night listening to the tigers roar, the hyenas shriek, and the deadly wild boars rut in the underbrush. Her only possession was her begging bowl. But Mahadevi never—in spite of experiencing what must have been at times overwhelming fear—stopped following her yearning or expressing it.

For each and every one of us, the spiritual journey is characterized by this struggle between yearning and fear, and for those of us who yearn to express ourselves creatively, the struggle has special significance. Each time we lift a pen or a brush or begin a new song or dance, we have to overcome some degree of fear. There is really no secret why this is so. The creative process requires us to search for the most deep-down, hidden, vulnerable parts of ourselves, to turn them inside out, and offer them up for all the world to see. This frightens us, and so we stop.

Although few, if any, of us will ever experience this yearning to the degree Mahadevi did, it is essential that we come to understand it. When we yearn for something in our lives here in the West, we tend to focus on the *object* of our yearning. If we are aware of yearning itself at all, we tend to experience it is as a maddening itch that we need to soothe. And we believe the only way to get rid of this terrible sensation is to obtain the "thing" we're yearning for. Most of us already know that the hunger for excessive material possessions driving so many people today is in reality a desire to fill up the deep emptiness caused by the lack of spiritual fulfillment. But even those of us who know our deepest yearnings are really spiritual in nature tend to focus on the object of our yearning and to think of the yearning itself as something that needs to be *satisfied*. At some level, we think that finally writing that novel, for example, will make the *need* to write that has been driving us crazy go away—much like satisfying sex makes the immediate need to have sex go away.

In all this yearning to get somewhere, to do something, to obtain something, to reach some goal, we miss the point that the yearning itself is something. Mahadevi recognized this. She never ignored the yearning. On the contrary, she relished it. "I burn," she cried in one poem, "desiring what the heart desires." Mahadevi did not just embrace this all-consuming fire; she recognized it for what it really is: the divine feminine, the primordial power of the universe.

In the face of this primordial power, Mahadevi's fears did not stand a chance. And neither do ours. The fear that we are not good enough, not talented enough, not deserving enough—all the fears that block our creative expression—dissolve in the face of the primordial power. The trick is to realize that we, like Mahadevi, do indeed embody this power and then to become comfortable with the way this *feels*. We need, in other words, to come to a place where we can sit and quietly hold this great power in our bellies.

From years of personal experience and gathering the stories of others on this journey, I can say that it is almost impossible to become comfortable with all this unless you are not at least to some degree comfortable with your emotions. This means we have to be not just in touch with our emotions but deeply aware of their *physical presence* in our bodies.

Just how detached we can be from this was driven home to me when I was younger by a guy named Mike whom I had fallen madly in love with. We'd been going out for quite a while and, although he told me often that he loved me, I didn't have any real sense that this was so. One day when we were in the midst of yet another discussion about whether he really loved me something made me realize that he might not feel this powerful emotion the way I did, as an ache that rose up from my belly and a passion that filled my heart. So I stopped and said, "Wait a minute. *Where* is this love you have for me?" Clearly thinking this was the stupidest question he'd ever heard, he said, "What do you mean, *where* is it?" I answered, "You know, when you feel this love for me where is it? Where in your body is it?" Looking at me as if I were absolutely nuts, he said. "It's not in my body! It's in my head! Where else would it be?"

With the pervasive emphasis on the importance of "expressing our emotions" that has occurred over the last few decades, we might imagine that there aren't too many people left who believe like Mike that emotions are something we *think* rather than something we feel. But the truth is things haven't changed all that much. Much of Western society—particularly Anglo-Saxon society—still has a tremendous difficulty with emotional awareness.

Not long ago a major study on gender bias showed that, in spite of many parents' good intentions, one of the primary cultural messages little boys still receive is that it is neither all right to cry nor to express any of the sort of "soft" emotions—in other words, emotions associated with being a girl. As we've known for ages, when we suppress the expression of emotions it leads to the suppression of the ability to feel them. Of course this isn't just a problem for men. Many women have never learned to express their emotions and many others have been forced to suppress them in order to succeed in male-dominated professions. The same is true for many little girls, especially those who are being taught to be "tough" so that they can compete and succeed in school, sports, and eventually the professional world.

And even of all those women who *are* comfortable with emotions, very few are comfortable with the feeling of wild, surging power. The same study on gender bias showed that while girls were being taught that it was generally all right for them to feel emotions and express them, this did not include either powerful emotions or negative ones: society still believes that little girls and women are supposed to have sweet, gentle emotions.

Thus we find ourselves as a culture in a situation where a great many people—I'd even go so far as to say the vast majority of people— have trouble either with all emotions or at least with strong, powerful emotions. Ironically this is occurring at exactly the time in history— if great thinkers like Marion Woodman and Gopi Krishna are correct—when we are being called on to become intensely aware of the great passionate power of the universe as she manifests in both our minds and our physical bodies.

Mahadevi was the epitome of a person who was able to live fully with her great yearning. Although her attainments may make her seem far beyond us, she was just a person. And we can learn from her that when we allow the divine feminine into our lives she is able to begin consuming the fears and doubts that block our creative expression and hinder our spiritual growth. Beyond this, the process of transformation she engenders will grace us with the very tools we need.

Creating a Protected Space

One of the most amazing things about Mahadevi was the way she continually managed to be in the space she needed to be in. This can be seen in the way she made her way to the spiritual community in Kalyana and again when she journeyed to her sacred mountain. But it was also true when she was forced to live with Prince Kaushika—for even then she set out the rules and boundaries that created an environment she could survive in.

Having a safe space is essential for creative expression. Part of this can be as simple as setting up a corner of the house where you can work uninterruptedly. But you can also use techniques like creative visualization to create a safe, protected mental and emotional space where you are free from that harsh inner voice of criticism that so often plagues us and hampers our creativity.

Countless variations on techniques like this have been tried and proven to work. But the most effective I've been able to come up with for my workshops is one that uses the seven colors of the rainbow. I think one reason it works so well is that, as myth and legend tell us, the rainbow is a powerful, numinous symbol, and the mystical nature of the number seven—from the seven notes of the musical scale to the seven chakras—is embedded deeply in the collective unconscious.

1. Have pen and paper or whatever tools you want to use close at hand. Then begin by using the creative visualization technique described in the previous exercise—or one you prefer—to breathe in radiant life energy and fill yourself with white light.
2. Continue to breathe in this sparkling, luminous white light and see it not only filling you but creating a protective bubble of light around you. Sit for a moment in this peaceful light.
3. With your next inhalation, breathe in the color red. As you take a few more slow, measured breaths, see this vibrant color filling your lungs, then spreading outward until it flows through your entire body. Colors, of course, have meaning, and red is associated with energy. See it filling your body with a calm, peaceful, purposeful energy. Then, see it moving outward and forming a protective bubble around you.

4. Next, breathe in the color orange. Orange is associated with joy and other positive emotions. As you breathe in this color, feel your emotions becoming positive, affirmative, and peaceful. As you breathe in and out slowly a few more times, see this glowing color fill your body and then flow into your protective space. As it does, you will see the orange light move outward and form an outer shell for your protective space.

5. Repeat this process with each of the remaining colors of the rainbow— each one filling your space and then moving to the outer rim. With yellow you will feel your mind becoming still and calm yet alert, with green you will feel yourself flooded with healing energy, and with blue you will feel unconditional love. Purple is the royal color and associated with the spiritual search; violet with spiritual fulfillment—these two spiritual colors lead the way for the white light to flow once again into your space.

6. As the white light returns, you will notice that it is even richer, thicker, more radiant and opalescent than before—ready to flow upward and outward, as it did in the Creativity Exercise in Chapter One, inspiring your creative work.

Creative visualization is simply "seeing" with your mind's eye the way you do when you daydream, imagine, or bring pictures to mind. Not all people are, however, visually oriented and for some this technique brings about not so much mental pictures as sensations, impressions, or fleeting images. Keeping your mind focused in creative visualization or meditation takes a great deal of practice, and unwanted thoughts and worries do sometimes intrude. When this happens don't try to resist the thought or force it out of your mind. This just gives it energy. Instead, imagine that your mind has a trapdoor and see the intruding thought floating out of your mind, just like it floated in.

CHAPTER THREE

The Great Battle Between Yearning and Fear

The morning I first began writing this chapter one of those weird and wonderful "coincidences" occurred that happen so often on the spiritual path. I'd rewritten the beginning about ten times—not improving it one whit—because I was stuck. In the same way that poets sometimes say a rhythmic pattern will begin to pound in their heads long before any words or even the subject appear to them, this chapter had already developed its own cadence, and an insistent beat was saying, "Next you need a story, a modern day story, next you need a story." Searching through the interviews I'd already done, I couldn't find anything that was exactly right. I needed a story from an ordinary woman that would build on Mahadevi's experiences described in the last chapter and show how our deep, powerful yearnings can overcome our fears today just as they did for her all those centuries ago. But the story I needed was nowhere in my files.

Then the phone rang. It was my sister-in-law Christine, who had just returned from the Association for Research and Enlightenment in Virginia Beach where she'd taken a course at Atlantic University called "Deepening Awareness of Self and Others".

Christine was overwhelmed with emotion and bubbling with excitement at the same time. "This course," she cried, "was exactly what I needed!" Not surprisingly the story that unfolded turned out to be exactly what I needed too. Although it wasn't clear until later, Christine was in the midst of a transformation in her consciousness that was emerging out of an inner battle between her deep spiritual longings and her fears.

A few years ago, Christine, a single woman in her mid-fifties, took early retirement from teaching, a profession she loved deeply. "The reason I left teaching," she says:

> ...was to create a space in my life. My life had become very, very busy, and I needed the space to explore other parts of myself. I wanted to discover who I really was, to discover my essence. I wanted to take time to walk in the woods, to meditate. I wanted to feel more connected to God. I also wanted to explore my love of art.

Christine was clearly experiencing a deep spiritual longing—one that took the form of a need to express herself creatively. In order to do this, she applied to a very prestigious art college and was thrilled when she won a spot in the school. But she was also afraid that her work wouldn't stand up to that of the gifted young people she'd be studying with.

During the summer between when she left teaching and would begin her art classes, she threw herself into repainting her condo. But as the summer drew to a close, she became aware that she was beginning to feel a vague, pervasive fear. She also began experiencing unusual sensations that moved from her neck down to her heart, and she became afraid that something was wrong with her heart. "After a short time I became filled with fear," she says. "I found it difficult to sleep at night. I would toss and turn all night. Finally I decided to seek out a therapist to help me deal with this."

One of these fears concerned driving on busy highways. Although she'd been plagued by this fear for some time, she had not faced it. She just shrugged it off and, instead of driving on highways, found alternate routes, caught rides with family members, and took buses and trains in order to avoid highway driving.

Christine's family and friends were baffled. We couldn't imagine her being afraid of anything, especially something like driving. In fact, she has been one of the most intrepid women any of us have ever known. Taking breaks in teaching over the years, she traveled completely on her own around most of the world. On one trip she took the Trans-Siberian Railway across Russia. On another she'd spent a year traveling around Mexico. She spent more than a year in Asia, at one point walking up rice terraces so remote that a whole village threw a celebration in honor of having a foreign visitor. Christine also made three trips to India, where she traveled the country and spent a total of close to two years living in ashrams, meditating, and studying yoga.

Over the years Christine had also been fearless in her exploration of her inner landscape. While living in the ashrams, she often looked the dark side of her psyche in the face. At home she explored her soul through Jungian analysis and years of intensive dreamwork. She often used her artwork to express herself, never hesitating when she needed to look at her negative emotions or let them show in her paintings.

So here was Christine—a woman who had not only had the courage to face her inner demons but who had also flown in rattle-trap planes in Russia, taken broken down buses over perilous mountain passes in Central America, and ridden with maniacal drivers on treacherous Indian roads—terrified at the thought of driving on a relatively civilized North American highway. Clearly something was wrong; some area of Christine's psyche still needed to be explored. But her family kept quiet, having faith that at some point she'd reach this conclusion on her own. Then, as so often happens when something in our psyches is left unexplored for too long, Christine's body forced her to look at it.

After attending the art school for a semester, Christine decided not to go back after the Christmas holidays. She had come to the realization that art school and all the assignments were keeping her just as busy as teaching had and that it was preventing her from creating the space in her life she needed. She had also become aware that her art was really a means of spiritual exploration and expression for her and that she didn't need the formalized training the school offered. Instead of continuing at the college, she said, she was going to paint on her own. Family and friends applauded her decision but were surprised over the next several months when she made no move to begin.

By the middle of January, Christine explains:

> I finally had a lot of time on my hands. I had wanted this, but now I was afraid of the emptiness. At times I tried to fill the space with shopping, watching videos, and so on, but some of the time I did try to stay with this emptiness. I started to meditate again, but it didn't seem to work for me. About this time I started experiencing really excruciating pains in my stomach.

Christine's pain became worse. It was often so excruciating she couldn't sleep at night. Bathed in sweat, she'd lie awake afraid that she was going to die. Beyond this she was gripped with an almost debilitating fear of the pain itself. She and her family had watched her father die of stomach cancer when he was only fifty-four. His pain had not been properly controlled and he suffered a horrendously painful death—a situation made even more tragic by the fact that he had been complaining of severe pains in his stomach for almost two years that the doctors had repeatedly told him were psychosomatic.

Christine immediately began a series of tests. Blood work, ultrasounds, colonoscopies, and myriad other examinations revealed that Christine did not have cancer. Assured that tests for the detection of cancer were vastly more sophisticated than they had been thirty years earlier when her father had died, she began to search for other explanations for the pain and explore them in therapy.

Although she was aware on one level that her father's having had cancer increased her own fear of having it, on another level she seemed to miss the possible direct connection between her father's pain, her pain, and her fear. Gentle hints like "Gee, Chris, have you talked to your therapist about your dad and what he went through?" were met with an oh-I-dealt-with-that-years-ago response. Finally, Christine's brother, my husband, got into the act. Not one to put much stock in psychology, even he could see that something needed to be explored here. Bluntly, he said, "Really, Chris, have you thought about the fact that you just turned fifty-five and Dad died when he was fifty-four?" "No," she responded. "Well, you should," he said.

Since everyone had seemed so insistent about all this, Christine decided during her next therapy session that she would spend a few minutes talking about her dad and the obvious relationship between his having cancer and her worrying about it. But as soon as she began to talk, she began to cry. She spent the next hour reliving the horror of her father's suffering and her anguish that no one had believed he was really sick. "I spent the entire time sobbing," she said. "I couldn't believe that I had this much pain inside after all these years."

Christine's fears were, of course, much more complex and involved than simply a fear of dying the way her father had. She discovered that her fear of driving was related to, among other things, a loss of control and powerlessness she had felt as a child when she had been sexually abused by a friend of the family—a horror that was compounded years later when she was traumatized by being raped. The terrible powerlessness Christine had felt in these situations was joined in her subconscious with the helplessness she had felt as she watched her father suffer, and both contributed to the fear she experienced. "But one thing I realized," she says:

> ...was that I was very different from my father. My father had said if he couldn't eat what he wanted then he didn't want to live. I realized I was not my father. I did want to live and I was willing to make changes in my diet if that was what I needed to do to live. I became aware of what I could control. I would do what was in my power to control these things, and I would surrender the rest to God. If I had to die a painful death, so be it.

Thankfully, this was not to be. After the session with the therapist, Christine's stomach pains virtually disappeared. She listened to her body and discovered she no longer wanted to fill it with the unhealthy foods she'd been eating and that had caused her to gain a great deal of excess weight over the years. As she did this the weight began to melt away. She reached a level of health she hadn't known in years. She says:

> I began to listen to my body. My body knew what it wanted to eat. I gave my body a voice. Also, I was no longer unconscious. When I

was still teaching I was so busy, it had been easy to be unconscious. I filled my self with so many things from the outside that I never had to look inside. I filled my body with food instead of feeling the emptiness and other emotions.

But once I was able to give my body a voice, I was able to express my feelings through art and therapy at a deeper level than I had before. I sat with the emptiness. I lived with the loneliness. I observed the anger I'd had against my mother and had suppressed for years. I discussed this anger and the guilt I felt about it with my therapist. I allowed myself to simply observe the anger and guilt. I allowed myself "to be with what is". I became able to express my anger to my mother in honest, appropriate ways. Over the next several months my relationship with my mother became better than it had ever been.

"Through all this," Christine adds, "I yearned to be filled with the oneness with God I had felt at times when I had been in India. I yearned to get to my essence—to get to the very core of my being—to find the essence of my self that exists at the deepest level of my soul."

This longing was never far from Christine's consciousness. Ironically, the whole time Christine had been preoccupied with fear on a physical level, this yearning had been propelling her forward. She was exploring deeper levels of her psyche, healing her relationship with her mother, and coming slowly but surely to a place where she would be able to overcome virtually all of the irrational fears that were hindering her life and blocking her creativity. The key to this progress was Christine's increasing willingness to allow herself, as she has told us, to simply be with her negative emotions—her emptiness, her loneliness, and her anger. But before she could have the profound experience in Virginia Beach that would wipe away much of her fear, she would also allow herself to experience her positive emotions—the passion and personal power inherent in her yearning—and become comfortable holding these in her body, too.

The pattern Christine followed on this part of her journey is common for most of us who have been working towards ever-greater self-awareness. Taking part in therapy and other practices aimed at shedding light on our inner selves, many of us have taken a long hard look at our negative emotions. In spite of this it is still quite rare to find people who are able to allow themselves to *fully* experience the intensity of their emotions or who are able to experience how these emotions manifest in their bodies at the very deepest levels. And this remains true in spite of the fact that the rallying cry for most therapists and self-help teachers over the past few decades has been "Get in touch with your emotions" and "Learn to express them!"

Over the last few years I've thought a lot about these two expressions. Because my graduate work involved working with emotionally disturbed children and adolescents, I had quite a bit of training in psychology and counseling, and because of this I believe wholeheartedly in the importance of emotional expression. But I've noticed something very interesting about the phrases "getting in touch" and "expressing" when used in this context. Neither of them implies any kind of *sustained* contact with these emotions. "Getting in touch" is a phrase that implies quick communication. When we call someone and say, "I'll get in touch with you this afternoon." we mean we'll call again but be on and off the phone in a jiffy when we do. In the same way, when we talk about getting in touch with a negative emotion it generally means we take the time to discover the emotion and to recognize it for what it is. Once this is done, however, we generally do whatever it takes to get rid of it as quickly as possible.

When we talk about "expressing" our emotions it implies this same lack of sustained contact—we want to get the emotions out of our selves, out of our bodies as soon as possible. If we're angry about something, for instance, we need to "get it off our chest" by telling the person who caused the anger or by pouring it out to someone who will listen or, failing these more effective options, by pounding a punching bag.

These are often very appropriate actions to take. However, they do not allow us the time we need to actually *feel* our emotions for any amount of time. This is one reason—in addition to the cultural conditioning mentioned in the last chapter—that we never have much of an opportunity to become aware of emotions in our body.

While all this is important for our general psychological health and well-being, it has a very specific significance for our creative growth: if we are going to allow our yearning for creative expression to grow, to expand, to blossom into the tidal wave of passion that washes away the obstacles created by our fear, we have to be able to hold that passion in our bodies—and we can't do that unless we have learned to *sit with* our emotions. This is another one of those tasks on the spiritual path that is simple but not easy, even for people who are really comfortable with their emotions.

I have learned a great deal about this from a friend of mine named Beverley. She is one of those rare people who really walks the walk. Her spiritual journey began many years ago when she was drawn to studying *Vedanta*, or the wisdom of the Vedas, the great Hindu religious texts. When Beverley started down this path, she didn't do it by half measures. She gave up a lucrative and secure position with the government as a writer and moved to an ashram in Pennsylvania where she spent ten years learning Sanskrit and studying the Hindu texts in their original language. When the time seemed right to her, she left the ashram and went to live on her own in a quiet rural area.

Beverley continues to advocate the life of simplicity she learned from her studies and to live it. She makes a just-adequate living writing and teaching yoga. Her home is a simple cottage. She has few possessions; she grows her own vegetables and barters with local organic farmers for food she can't raise herself. A dedicated grass-roots activist, she works tirelessly for causes that promote peace and environmental awareness.

All this makes Beverley sound like a paragon. But she would be the first to laugh at this description of herself and tell you how far she still is from reaching her spiritual goals. Still, it's clear that Beverley practices what she preaches a good deal better than most of us do and that, especially now that she's in her seventh decade, she is someone with some wisdom to share.

A few years ago I was listening to her speak at a conference when a bit of that wisdom had a profound influence on my life. After speaking eloquently for about an hour on the Vedic teachings, she said that if you had to take just one small bit of knowledge from all this philosophy, it would be this: "Be with what is as it is."

You may well have encountered this phrase and know that it means sitting in the present with whatever the present holds—without pressure from the past, without worry about the future. It means being at one with the present moment. In terms of our emotions it means being at one with what you are *feeling* in the present moment. If you are feeling jealous, for instance, you simply sit with the jealousy.

You feel it. You don't judge it; you don't try to get rid of it; you don't try to justify it; you don't plot what you are going to do about it. In other words, you don't *think* about it! You let your mind become absolutely still, and you just feel it.

If you happen to have been working on "being with what is" for any length of time, you know that this is one of those spiritual concepts that you can spend your whole life striving to truly realize. It can even, the great gurus tell us, lead to enlightenment. And "being with what is" in terms of sitting with our emotions is especially difficult. This is particularly true for those of us here in the West when it comes to sitting with negative emotions. This is because we find them intensely uncomfortable. We are also afraid that allowing a negative emotion to exist might mean we are somehow condoning it and this, in turn, might mean we would never do anything to get rid of it or to correct the problem that might have triggered it in the first place. But "sitting with" an emotion doesn't mean we never do anything about it. It simply means that when, and if, it is necessary to *do* something this action arises from and flows naturally out of the core of our inner wisdom.

Sitting with positive emotions tends to be easier for us, at least when they are relatively mild. The problem comes, as we mentioned in the last chapter, when the positive sensations we feel hold great power. But sit with this great power we must, for this is the key to the transformation of consciousness and, in turn, to the awakening of our creative spirit.

For Christine much of this became clear during the intensive course she took at Atlantic University. It included breath work, body work, active meditation, and other exercises designed to help the participants get in touch with their fear, anger, sadness, and other emotions and, most importantly, reclaim their own power.

During the course Christine was indeed able to reclaim this power. This profound transformation occurred, not surprisingly, when Christine experienced the divine feminine within her body. "I was," she says, "able to express a power so deep within my belly that it filled me with joy." Although this significant moment was triggered by the exercises Christine did during the course, it was ultimately brought about by the work she had done over the years—doing yoga, keeping fit, and honestly exploring her inner landscape—and it simply could not have happened if she hadn't been making the effort she had to become aware of both her positive and negative emotions and to learn to sit with them.

When registering for the course, participants had been asked to name one issue they wanted to deal with. For Christine, the choice was obvious. She wanted to deal with the debilitating fears that were still controlling her life.

The day before Christine had the profound experience of the divine feminine and the realization that this cosmic power existed in her own body, she had been thinking a great deal about her fears and was beginning to realize how intricately they were related to personal power. She explains:

> I had been having difficulties with issues of power for a long time, in particular with disowning my personal power. I was afraid of this power, and I was afraid of the abuse of power. By a strange coincidence the day I started art school was 9/11 just before the first plane hit the towers in New York and I was having issues around how this was related to the abuse of power. But I was also becoming more conscious of how power was affecting my life. It was becoming clear to me that the loss of my own power was translating into my fear of driving on the highway. And I was also beginning to think that my inability to control what I had no power over—for instance, when and how I would die—may have been contributing to my fears in general and more specifically to the pains I was experiencing.

With these realizations fresh in her mind the next day, Christine participated in an experiential exercise using dance and movement. The exercise began with breathing exercises and a meditation that was focused on kundalini-shakti. The meditation was followed by music, and the participants were encouraged to dance in any way that the music inspired them to move. Christine describes the experience like this:

> I couldn't believe how I moved my body during this dance. I felt this energy moving through my whole body and I felt such amazing creativity. At one point, I danced a powerful guttural dance with stomping feet and punching and thrusting movements—it was a dance of strength and power and came from deep within my belly.

At another point, I danced a dance of love.

The part of the dance when I became so energized and in awe of the sacredness and creativity moving through my body came right after I picked up a flowing scarf and began to twirl it to the sound of the music. Then I began to use it as a veil and dance with it in a sensuous, rhythmic manner. At some point "thought" no longer existed. An energy was moving me and I simply flowed with it. As I whirled and twirled, the dance picked up momentum and at times became very energetic. My movements were so fluid and graceful and my energy seemed boundless. As my arms and hands danced with a rhythm and movement unknown to me, it was as if I had become a dancer from the olden days in India.

At one point, I then dragged the veil along the floor and placed it on my head. The Virgin Mary came to mind and I felt as if I was wearing her veil. My dance became more serene and ethereal. Then I wrapped my head up totally with the veil and tied it at the neck. It seemed to me that this was a symbol of turning off the intellect and allowing the inner, intuitive voice to express itself. In this sense, it was very clear to me that it was the divine feminine energy that was moving through me.

The dance was like a cosmic dance—I had a sense of that cosmic energy moving through me and at the same time moving me. It was a dance of fire, and I was a sacred vessel. As this creative energy was moving through my body and creating the dance, I knew that I was one with it—and that I had found my essence.

I continued to dance until the music stopped. It was amazing because I have had so much trouble with my knees for so long that I haven't been able to dance at all for ages, but I just danced and danced. I seemed to have boundless energy. Most of the other people were out of breath, and that much exercise would normally have made me very tired and breathless, but this dance energized me and left me in awe.

After the dance I went outside and walked through the garden. As I wandered, I was consumed with awe and wonder at the divine sacred place I had just entered—my body.

When Christine first told me about this experience she kept stressing how clearly she experienced the energy that was moving through her body as feminine and added, "I became so sensual as I moved; I did not feel sexy, I felt sensuous. It was such a creative energy, and it just seemed to move through me. I was a vessel—an *open* vessel for the energy to move through—and it was as if a cosmic energy was moving me."

On the last day of the course, the participants were asked to say a few words about how the course had helped them connect with their personal power. Going around a circle, each one did. But when it came to Christine's turn, she simply opened up her mouth and roared. The whole group, knowing how fear had been dominating her life, spontaneously burst into applause.

When Christine returned home, she continued to do the meditation and to dance. She also began to write in her journal again for the first time in months. Soon she was doing artwork again. It was clear to her that some new movement of energy had opened up in her body. After a few more weeks of working on her fears, Christine was able to drive her car on the highway for the first time in two years. Although this took a tremendous amount of courage, she says, "When I'd be driving and the fear would start to come back, I'd just focus on that feminine power within my belly that I had felt during the course. And—if there was nobody else in the car—I'd just open up my mouth and roar!"

Christine's yearning to absolutely, authentically know her true inner being—that wonderful roaring lioness within!—led her on a great adventure in facing and overcoming fear. Even right up to the time she left on her trip to Virginia Beach her fear of facing the fear itself was so intense she wanted to back out of the journey. But even though she *wanted* to back out, there was really no chance she would. Speaking with her on the phone just before she left, I could hear the fear literally making her voice quake even as she said the words, "I have to do this. I know this is what I need right now." Like great waves pounding a cold, hard stone to sand, the yearning was breaking down the fear.

In the last chapter we looked at how this yearning is a manifest-ation of Shakti, the creative force of the universe. Another way of looking at this force is to see it as the active power of divine love. This struggle between divine love's irrepressible drive to move us forward and the fear that blocks this great cosmic thrust is at the heart of both our spiritual and our creative journey. In fact, according to some great thinkers these two opposing forces represent the only two emotions that actually exist: love and fear.

The idea that the two great emotions are not love and hate, but love and fear was brought to Western attention by a minister named Emmet Fox. Born in Ireland in 1886, Fox was deeply influenced in the early 1900s by a movement that began in England called "New Thought". He was able to take the ideas of New Thought—an extremely intellectual set of concepts—and make them easy to understand. Out of this he developed a spiritual philosophy that stressed the power of thought and prayer, the all-pervasiveness of divine love, and the reality of God's abundance. After moving to New York in the late 1920s, Fox became the leading proponent of these ideas in the United States. By the 1930s his teaching became so popular that he often packed Carnegie Hall.

Of course Fox wasn't saying that the only two emotions we ever *feel* are love and fear; he was saying that negative emotions like greed, anger, jealousy, and even hate all arise out of fear. In other words, we feel negative emotions not because we are hateful people, but because we are, at some level, afraid. For example, we might feel greed because we are afraid we won't have enough, anger because we are afraid of being hurt, or jealousy because we are afraid someone else has something we can't ever have.

Whether you agree with Fox's idea that love and fear are the two principle emotions in general, it's easy to see that they are the two main forces at work in our creative journey. On one hand, a bursting love fills our bellies and we want to pour this passion out into our writing, our music, our dance. And on the other, there is this nagging fear that says we can't.

Scores of books have come out in the last ten years about the blocks we experience to our creativity, but when we boil each and every one down to their essence we find a hard, black lump of fear. Although many of the techniques expressed in these books for overcoming these blocks are excellent, the fact remains that if we want to get to the real crux of the matter, the ultimate means of overcoming our creative blocks is to learn to sit with the intensity of our yearning. We can then, like Mahadevi and Christine, allow this passionate cosmic creative spirit to lead us where she wants us to go. This is allowing the active power of divine love into our lives. Once there, Fox assures us, this power can overcome any obstacle. Interestingly enough, this is exactly what St Hildegard tells us in the next chapter about the cosmic power of Sophia as the embodiment of divine love.

About the time I started writing this book I had an experience with yearning and fear that demonstrated how this power can overcome the most daunting creative stumbling blocks. The events that led up to this rather unusual spiritual experience began when I first tried to move from the research phase of creating this book to the actual writing stage. At this point it had been almost five years since I had written a book, but before that I had published a book practically every year for almost nine years. Looking back on this it seems to me that moving so rapidly from one book to the next kept me from having the time to ever have to face my fears. This time, however, there had been lots of time for the fear to get a real hold on me, and for weeks after all the research was done, I had a terrible time beginning to write.

Although I was aware that I was afraid, it wasn't until later that I discovered how deep and how pervasive this fear was. Much of it was fear that I just wasn't capable of writing the book I wanted to write. As the information I gathered piled up I became increasingly afraid I didn't have the ability to boil it down into a manageable book. But through all this I didn't have the one fear that plagues most authors: the fear of creating something you love so much and then not finding a publisher. I was sure I had not just a publisher, but a wonderful one. That little light shone at the end of even the very bleakest tunnels I found myself in.

And then one day, that light went out too. The editor of my last book, who had steadily encouraged my work on this one, suddenly decided to leave the publishing business. The problem with this was that, because I had felt so sure of her acceptance of the book, I had never submitted a formal proposal to her and consequently did not have a contract with the publishing house she worked for. For several weeks after she had left, I was frozen. I couldn't write at all. Great waves of depression and anger would sweep over me, creating an ever-spiraling tension.

For some days I tried to sit with these negative emotions. When I managed to do this for a long enough period of time the depression would seem to dissolve and, as if it were some strange shape-shifting creature, reform itself into its true nature, which was fear. The same thing would happen when I sat with the anger. It would just dissolve and I would feel a cold lump of fear in its place. As I was able to sit with the fear itself for increasing amounts of time I began to feel how it had insinuated itself into virtually every part of my body. A tightness had slithered under the skin of my legs, arms, and belly. It had made itself a permanent home in my back and, like some great boa constrictor, was squeezing the life out of my shoulders, my neck, and the back of my head.

Diametrically opposed to this was a great force nesting in my pelvis and rising up to my heart. It was an aching, a longing to begin writing again—not just the articles and short pieces I'd done over the last few years when most of my time was occupied with research—but to be writing something really significant.

The morning the experience occurred I had been overwhelmed by an intense emotion many of you must have felt, especially when reading the morning paper or listening to the news during that very vulnerable time just after you have awakened and have not yet armed yourself with the defenses you need to face the day. On that particular morning I happened to read the story of some innocent children who had been horrifically injured in a war-torn country in Africa. As soon as I finished the story I began to weep and the tears came back every time I recalled the graphic image that had been splashed across the front page of the paper.

Right after breakfast I needed to take the subway downtown for an appointment. As I stood crushed among the rush-hour commuters the image kept coming back to me and I had to avert my head to wipe the tears away. Even once the tears stopped, I was aware of those children and how, on some level, they represented suffering human beings everywhere. I was filled with a longing to do something, *anything* to help. Although this feeling has often motivated me, on this morning it became even more powerful than usual. At some point this deep emotion seemed to merge with the longing I'd been experiencing to be writing again. This extreme feeling continued as the subway car got closer to the city center.

Increasingly crushed by the people around me, I kept trying to suppress it so that I wouldn't start crying again. Finally realizing I was fighting a losing battle, I decided to stop trying to hold the emotion in and, instead, to try to just be with it as it was at that very moment. As soon as I did this I became viscerally aware of both the powerful yearning I was experiencing and the fear that had been so embedded in my body for so long. They appeared to me as two opposing forces, locked in battle. Although I'd been aware for a long time *intellectually* that this fear was hindering my ability to accomplish what I wanted, I had never been so aware of it physically before. I could literally feel the fear blocking the yearning—physically choking off the very energy that would "write" the book and help me, in a larger sense, to do whatever positive work I was meant to do with my life.

At that moment, standing in that overcrowded subway, my soul was completely open in its yearning. Suddenly my consciousness seemed to expand so that my mind, rather than being limited to the confines of my physical brain, felt as if it extended a few feet out around my head. At the same moment, the yearning I'd been feeling began to feel like waves that were rolling up my body and crashing against the rock-hard tightness of my neck and shoulders. The feeling was so forceful that for a moment I was afraid I was going to have some kind of mystical experience right there in the middle of the rush-hour crowd, and I had to laugh at myself thinking it would be fairly typical for me to have something so outlandish happen. But I needn't have worried. What unfolded next was not by any means a true mystical experience. It was, I suppose, however, some sort of visionary one because quite suddenly the image of an orange-clad Tibetan monk appeared in front of my mind's eye. Because my conscious mind seemed somehow larger than normal, this image was much larger and far more vivid than one from a typical daydream. The little monk was sitting cross-legged and laughing, his saffron robes fluttering in the wind.

Exactly what this vision was—a daydream, an archetypal image tossed out by my subconscious mind, or possibly even some brief glimpse into another dimension of reality—doesn't really seem to matter now. What does matter, however, is the effect it had on me. The moment this little monk appeared I was flooded by a feeling of being loved absolutely and without condition.

At that moment this symbol of divine goodness seemed to burn itself into my heart and mind. And as it did I had one of the strangest experiences I have ever had. The fear I had been holding so tightly in my body for so long just vanished. Its physical manifestation, the aching, the tightness, just slipped away and for the first time in weeks the squeezing-tight tension was gone. I looked up at my little monk. He was still there. Laughing, with his head thrown back, like he'd just heard the greatest joke in the world.

The Power Play Between Love and Fear

This chapter has explored the battle between yearning and fear and the ultimate power of yearning to, quite literally, conquer all. As the ancient texts on the divine feminine teach us, our deepest yearning is nothing less than the active power of divine love working in our lives. Looking at love in this way brings extraordinary meaning and depth to the time-honored phrase "Love conquers all."

In order to tap into this great power that lies hidden within, however, we have to be comfortable with holding our yearning in our bodies. We have to be comfortable with passion. We have to be able to sit with these passions—to simply feel them and allow them to be.

As we learned from Mahadevi in Chapter Two, this is the great secret to being able to allow our yearning to guide us in the direction we are meant to go. It is also the facility that lies at the very heart of creative expression.

When we are working with this idea in the workshops I lead, I some-times use the slightly corny expression, "No art without heart". The music of Mozart and the art of Michelangelo have lasted through the ages because these works of art move us; they awaken in us the emotions the creator was striving to express.

It makes no difference whether you are expressing your creativity for your own satisfaction and growth or in order to make it public as part of your professional work in the arts—your work will only reach its fullest potential when you can allow yourself to sit with your emotions before you begin to express them.

Before doing the following exercise you need to make a trip to your photo albums—or that big box of pictures you really are going to put in albums someday. Go through them until you find one that reminds you of a time when you experienced unconditional love—love that had no expectations or strings attached. It doesn't matter if you were receiving or giving the love.

1. Have this photograph along with pen and paper at hand. Then spend a few minutes looking at the photograph.

2. Begin with the simple pranayama breathing from Chapter One and the technique you learned in Chapter Two to create that safe, protected mental and emotional space where you are free from the harsh voice of criticism.

3. Continue breathing and focusing on the light within until you feel completely and deeply relaxed.

4. Bring to mind the photograph you hold. Allow yourself to sink completely into this time and place and re-experience it.

5. Sit with the emotions this triggers; hold them; experience them in your body.

6. When you feel ready bring your awareness back to the light that fills your body. See it rising up, pulsing with the beat of your heart, and then continuing to flow down your arms, out your hands, into the pen and onto the paper.

7. Begin to write by describing what is in the picture and allow your thoughts to flow from there.

8. Later you may want to use what you've expressed here as the basis for more writing or to create other art, music, or dance.

CHAPTER FOUR

A Supreme, Fiery, and Feminine Force

No sooner than the hard lumps of fear dissolved in my body did my ability to write return. The moment I could find a seat in the crowded car I pulled a notebook and pen out of my backpack and began to write. The great yearning I had been feeling for so long poured unimpeded out of my heart, down my arm, into my hand, and onto the page.

Over the next month, even though I spent only about forty or fifty hours actually working at my computer, I managed to write almost a quarter of the book. Meaningful coincidences, like the one when Christine called just when I needed her story, began to occur. Even more important for my peace of mind, the shape of the book began to emerge and before I finished one chapter I would know where I had to go with the next.

Finally after such a long, agonizing creative drought I was writing again. I was in that holy space where nothing exists but the creative energy that is pouring out of you and the work that you are creating. For me, as I'm sure for many of you, this is the place on my spiritual quest where I see things most clearly. It is the place where my hopes, my dreams, and my desire to do good for the world clash with my faults, my weaknesses, and my insecurities. It is the holy ground where the divine feminine energy rising in my body meets my ego head on and does battle. This battle was exactly what I had experienced that day on the subway.

Over the next few months every time I would become aware that the fear had crept back into my body—and creep back it did, for habits of a lifetime are rarely dissolved in one fell swoop—I would bring my consciousness back to the little monk. The moment I'd do this I'd have the sense that a river of love was flowing through my body and washing away the fear. In this sense I was right when I realized it didn't matter whether the little monk was a figment of my imagination or truly some being of light sent to help me on my way. What matters—at least from the Tantric perspective—were the powerful sensations of energy that were flowing through my body.

When I could hold this power in my body, when I could sit with it, and simply observe it, it became clear to me that sensations of flowing energy and the sensation of yearning were one and the same. And that it was no coincidence that this yearning—whether it was being experienced by a great mystic like Mahadevi or ordinary people like Christine and me—was expressing itself in an urge for creative expression. In order to begin to understand why this is so, we need to look in a little more detail at Shakti, the great creative force of the universe.

As discussed in Chapter One, according to Tantra, Shakti creates what we see as the material universe and then propels the evolution of this universe on its great journey back to the One. In the same way she propels the evolution of the individual. In the form of kundalini-shakti she lies coiled at the base of the spine, waiting for release so that she can travel up the spine, meet with Shiva at the crown of the head and propel the individual to the realization of divine oneness. But this does not mean Shakti herself is resting in the individual. In fact, the opposite is true: she is wide awake and is responsible for our thinking, feeling,

74

breathing, eating, digesting, expelling, moving, sleeping, dreaming—in short, every single activity we associate with being alive.

In not only Tantra but in every system of yoga and most Hindu philosophies, when Shakti manifests in this way she is called prana or, often, prana-shakti. Prana is given a variety of names in other traditions. In Chinese Taoism it is called *qi*, in Japanese Shinto *ki*, in the ancient Hawaiian philosophy of Huna it is called *mana*. Unfortunately, we have no word for prana in English. Researchers and others struggling with this idea over the years, however, have come up with a number of terms that try to capture the essence of this concept. They include bioenergy, orgone, universal life force, and life energy. While terms like life force and life energy are adequate, they fall far short of conveying what someone steeped in the yogic tradition would mean by prana. This force is referred to in one way or another in virtually every Hindu religious text. In most it is seen as the active principle underlying not just all living things but every thing that manifests in the world around us.

Generally when those of us on the spiritual path feel great rushes of "energy" in our bodies, it is the movement of prana-shakti. This is what Christine experienced in the power of the dance. It is not the same thing as the awakening of kundalini-shakti, but it is often related to kundalini awakening.

Prana is such a subtle force that it cannot be detected by even the finest scientific instrument, and yet it has been perceived by true mystics throughout the ages. Prana is not just life energy but is *intelligent* life energy. It is, in fact, intelligence itself. It is the energy of the mind, the energy of consciousness. It is the life-breath in a living creature; it is the fire in stars; it is the green force bursting out of plant-life in the spring. It is the vibrant force pulsing in every animate being—and every non-animate object as well.

Prana-shakti is also the creative force of the universe. It is the force that creates the universe—that propels all the myriad forms of existence into being. And because of this it makes perfect sense that when we feel her pulsing through our bodies, that when we become aware—even on the most deep subconscious level—that we too *are* prana-shakti, we feel the urge to create.

Evidence that this is so can be found in the fact that so many of our great creative geniuses here in the West—in spite of never having heard of such a thing as prana—describe something virtually identical to it in their writings. In *Talks with Great Composers*, Arthur Abell interviewed Engelbert Humperdinck, the composer of the opera *Hansel and Gretel* who was a close friend of Richard Wagner. According to Humperdinck, Wagner had much to say about this universal life force. Humperdinck says Wagner described this force as a "universal vibrating energy that binds the soul of man to the Almighty Central Power". Wagner went on to say that "this energy links us to the Supreme Force of the universe, of which we are all a part" and that anyone who could feel the "universal currents of divine energy vibrating the ether" could receive creative inspiration. Humperdinck continued that when Wagner was composing he would enter a meditative state that he called "the prerequisite of all true creative effort" and said that while in this state "I feel that I am one with this vibrating Force..."

In the same book, Johannes Brahms told Abell about having a very similar experience of a powerful, pulsating divine energy that he referred to as the "soul-powers within". He said:

> To realize that we are one with the Creator, as Beethoven did, is a wonderful and awe-inspiring experience...I always contemplate all this before commencing to compose...I immediately feel vibrations that thrill my whole being...These are the Spirit illuminating the soul-power within, and in this exalted state, I see clearly what is obscure in my ordinary moods; then I feel capable of drawing inspiration from above...[This] Spirit is the light of the soul. Spirit is universal. Spirit is the creative energy of the universe...

Whitman's works are filled with such references as he "sings the body electric". *Song of Myself* is replete with a pulsating force that "hums" through Whitman's being and unites the earth and all its creatures:

> Is this then a touch? quivering me to a new identity,
> Flames and ether making a rush for my veins,
> Treacherous tip of me reaching and crowding to help them,
> My flesh and blood playing out lightning to strike
> what is hardly different from myself...

The twentieth-century French Jesuit priest Pierre Teilhard de Chardin perceived this force in the rocks, stones, and cliffs of his native Auvergne and called it the "crimson glow of matter" and "the divine radiating from the blazing depths of matter". He even saw this pulsating, creative force as a feminine one. Much to the consternation of the Church, he even came to call it "the eternal feminine" and to write about it extensively. As can easily be imagined, his observations on this cosmic feminine principle were almost certainly one of the reasons Teilhard was eventually sent by the Church to work in the furthest reaches of Mongolia and live out much of his life there.

The most powerful descriptions of this universal life force in Western terms, however, are undoubtedly found in the writings of the twelfth-century Benedictine mystic Hildegard von Bingen. Her works are replete with references to cosmic forces that parallel both prana-shakti and Shakti herself. In fact, the first hint that the divine feminine force I'd been studying for so many years in the yogic tradition had a parallel in Christianity came to me through my research into Hildegard's life and work.

Interestingly enough it was Gopi Krishna who gave me the idea of looking into the life of Hildegard. About twenty years ago—when Hildegard was still virtually unheard of—a group of friends and I were getting seriously interested in how we could promote awareness of kundalini-shakti. Through a set of circumstances far too complex to describe here, we ended up having an opportunity to meet with Gopi Krishna and ask him how we could best do this. He suggested that one of the most valuable things we could do would be to examine the lives of the great mystics and divinely inspired creative geniuses from different traditions. He suggested that in doing this we would find startling similarities in both their mystical experiences and in their personal characteristics. What's more, he theorized we would find that these experiences and characteristics were exactly the ones the ancient yogis of India listed when they described the awakening of kundalini-shakti and how it affected the yogi experiencing it.

If this proved to be true, he said, it would help show that when yogis talked about kundalini, Tibetan Buddhists about *dumo fire* or *candali*, Kabbalistic Jews about *Shekinah*, Taoists about *jeng chi*, and Christians about the descent of the *Holy Spirit*, they were all talking about the same divine force.

To help us, Gopi later sent us a list of mystics and divinely inspired geniuses we could start doing research on. Fired with enthusiasm, my friends and I met to divide up the list and start working. I can still see that piece of paper. It had been typed with a very old typewriter on the flimsy, poor quality paper available in India in those days, and it had been creased and folded many times. Among the names listed were many well-known mystics: Ramakrishna, Krishnamurti, St Theresa of Avila, St John of the Cross, and Rumi. Then there was one person no one had ever heard of: Hildegard von Bingen. When we all agreed it sounded German, the chairperson of the meeting looked at me. "Well, Teri, you're the only person who knows any German, so I guess you get her." So I took Hildegard, bitterly disappointed that I didn't get to do one of the more interesting sounding mystics.

As fate would have it, my exploration of Hildegard's life and work ended up being one of the most profound influences in my life. It also set me off on my long search for the divine feminine as the creative force of the universe.

There's no need to go into Hildegard's life in quite as much detail as we did Mahadevi's for a couple of reasons. One is that her story has been told in *The Fiery Muse* and in great detail by medieval scholars such as Barbara Newman and Sabina Flanagan. The other is that the purpose here is not so much to look at her life story as it is to look at how the very Eastern concepts of prana-shakti and Shakti have been expressed in Western terms and how parallels to Shakti as the divine feminine can be found in the Christian tradition. Still, knowing something about her life is necessary in order to put her ideas on the divine feminine in context.

Before going on to her story, it is important to note that these two concepts—a universal life force and a divine feminine principle— overlap in Hildegard's writings. That this should be so isn't really surprising. The difference between prana-shakti and Shakti is an extremely subtle one. In fact, in one sense, there is no difference between them since absolutely everything in the universe as we know it *is* prana-shakti. That said, it is helpful to think of them in a simplistic sort of way as manifesting or functioning in different ways: Shakti is the divine feminine principle; prana-shakti is the universal life force and the "stuff" that the universe is made of; and kundalini-shakti is the divine feminine as she manifests in the human body and triggers the transformation of consciousness that can lead to mystical experience, paranormal experiences, and divine inspired creativity.

Hildegard's experiences with the mystical began at a very early age. Born in 1098, she was the youngest of ten children. Her home was in the Rhine River valley in what is now Germany, and she was raised in relative comfort, for her family was part of the minor nobility. From her own writings we know that Hildegard was an extraordinary child who began having visions at an early age. In her wonderful book *Sister of Wisdom: St. Hildegard's Theology of the Feminine*, Barbara Newman quotes a letter Hildegard wrote when she was seventy-seven to Guibert of Gembloux—a monk who became her secretary in the last years of her life. In it she says that even as a very young child she would feel as if her soul would rise up to "the vault of heaven" and expand out across the entire world. She also describes a vision of light that was with her constantly:

> The light I see thus is not spatial, but it is far, far brighter than a cloud that carries the sun. I can measure neither height, nor length, nor breadth in it; and I call it "the reflection of the living Light". And as the sun, the moon, and the stars appear in water, so writings, sermons, virtues, and certain human actions take form for me and gleam within it...

Along with these experiences of expanded consciousness and visions of light, Hildegard had paranormal abilities. One of the stories recorded about these abilities tells how, when she was about three years old, she looked at a pregnant cow and described to her nurse the exact markings the calf would be born with. In the introduction to her first book, *Scivias*, she explained that she told only a few select people about these early visions and concealed her "gift in quiet silence". Her family, however, knew about the occurrence with the calf and must have had some notion Hildegard was "different" in some way. In fact, Sabina Flanagan suggests in her book *Hildegard of Bingen: A Visionary Life* that Hildegard's unusual abilities may well have been the reason her parents decided, when she was still quite young, to dedicate her to God and offer her up to life in a convent. Although accusations of witchcraft were not particularly common in that time and place, it may well have been a worry for her parents.

Accordingly, when Hildegard was somewhere between the ages of eight and twelve she was taken to a nearby Benedictine monastery and given over to the religious life. Although this practice was not unusual in the Middle Ages—particularly since Hildegard was the tenth child and thus viewed as a "tithe" to God—the way in which it was done was unusual. Hildegard's parents didn't just send her to a nunnery; they had her enclosed in the cell of an anchoress—a woman who allows herself to be symbolically "buried alive" in commitment to God. This particular anchoress was named Jutta, and her story is made somewhat romantic by the fact that she was the beautiful daughter of a high noble family. The small cell in which she and, eventually, Hildegard were confined was attached to a Benedictine monastery in Disibodenberg. Over the years, Jutta taught Hildegard the religious observances, at least rudimentary Latin, and possibly even how to play a musical instrument called the psalter.

For all intents and purposes both Hildegard and Jutta should have remained "enclosed" in their cell for their entire lives, but events conspired to alter the situation. Although it is unclear exactly how this happened, it is known that an increasing number of young women were attracted by Jutta's story and came to join her. It can be supposed that the cell simply became too small and was, out of necessity, expanded over time until Jutta became the abbess of an official convent attached to the monastery. Regardless, these changes had all transpired by the time Hildegard was fifteen and took her final religious vows to become a nun.

Little else is known about Hildegard's life during these years in the convent; she must have distinguished herself in some way, however, because when the Abbess Jutta died in 1136 Hildegard was unanimously chosen as her successor. After this, Hildegard's life seems to have unfolded uneventfully enough for about five more years. She then had a mystical vision that literally transformed her consciousness. In the Introduction to *Scivias*, as it is translated in Flanagan's book, she described this as an experience of the "living Light" itself not just the "reflection of the living Light":

> And it came to pass in the eleven hundred and forty-first year of the incarnation of Jesus Christ, Son of God, when I was forty-two years and seven months old, that the heavens were opened and a blinding light of exceptional brilliance flowed through my entire brain. And so it kindled my whole heart and breast like a flame, not burning but warming...and suddenly I understood the meaning of the expositions of the books, that is to say of the psalter, the evangelists, and other catholic books of the Old and New Testaments.

According to Hildegard, this sudden change in her ability to comprehend these texts occurred in spite of the fact that she did not previously know how to interpret the words of the Latin texts, to understand the grammar, or to even know how the syllables of the words were divided. It also triggered one of the most phenomenal out-pourings of creative expression the world has ever seen.

Between her forty-third year and her death at the age of eighty-one, Hildegard produced what can only be called a monumental amount of literary, poetical, musical, medical, and scientific material. In total, she wrote three lengthy books on her visions, two books on medicine, a cosmology of the world, two biographies of saints, liturgical poetry, and the words and music to a cycle of over seventy songs. Hildegard even wrote the first morality play, a literary form that became the dramatic standard for the Middle Ages. Beyond all this, Hildegard expressed herself artistically by overseeing the work —if not actually doing some of the work herself—on a great many illustrations that depict elements from her visions.

A number of factors make this extraordinary output even more amazing. The first is that she spent much of her life in ill health and, as she said, "great suffering". The second is that she produced all this material in what little time she could spare from an astonishingly busy daily life. She was not only a nun who spent hours a day reciting the holy offices, she was an abbess—a demanding and time-consuming job in itself. She was also a healer with a tremendous knowledge of herbs and other healing remedies. Because of this—and because word of her visions spread—she had to deal with an ever-increasing tide of the sick and troubled who sought her out.

In addition, her time was taken up with writing literally hundreds of letters and meeting with many important people. She also made four lengthy journeys, each lasting many months, from the convent in order to preach—something that was completely unheard of for a woman of her day. She also spent a tremendous amount of time fighting social injustices and corruption; she became involved in a lengthy battle with the monks in order to break away from the monastery. Having done so, she then founded a new convent, built it up out of nothing, and founded a second convent some years later.

The other factor that makes her creative productivity so incredible is that she was probably not highly educated. The issue of just how well educated Hildegard was has become a matter of heated debate. Some scholars, particularly those who doubt her assertion that her creative outpourings were divinely inspired, claim she could not possibly have accomplished what she did without a good deal of education. All we know for sure, however, is that she knew how to read Latin and to write it, if not grammatically correctly, well enough to be understood. We also know that she needed the help of an educated monk named Volmar, who was also her friend and confidant, to assist her in writing down her visions, letters, and other materials. When Volmar died, other monks, including eventually Guibert of Gembloux, were needed to take on this task. Beyond this, she repeatedly claimed that she had been only "poorly educated".

Regardless of how much formal education she had acquired, Hildegard was also thwarted in her writing by tremendous doubts about herself. Women in Hildegard's day were generally not considered worthy of receiving direct communications from the Holy Spirit. Still, Hildegard did eventually come into her own. In 1148, a papal delegation was sent from a Synod being held at a place called Trier to investigate her. After returning to the Synod, the delegation presented the evidence it had gathered to Pope Eugenius. The pope, basing his decision on both the evidence gathered and the quality of her writings, decreed that Hildegard's visions were indeed genuine. He then gave her official sanction to write down and to make known the communications she received from the Holy Spirit.

Given all this, it doesn't seem much of an exaggeration to call Hildegard a creative genius. She continued to write, to compose, and to look after the illustrations of her visions until the end of her life; all while her daily life was taken up running the convent and founding new ones, battling the monks, and fighting corruption in both the Church and the secular world.

Hildegard's final battle for justice came when she was nearly eighty years old and received word from her bishop that a nobleman she had allowed to be buried in her churchyard was considered an unrepentant sinner and would have to be disinterred. Hildegard, claiming he had indeed repented for his sins, refused. The authorities were so angry with her they placed her and all her nuns under interdict—a punishment that banned them from singing, saying the holy offices, making confession, and going to Mass. Worse, it was also only one step from excommunication and, to her way of thinking, eternal damnation. Still, Hildegard refused to relent. She and her nuns lived under these terrible conditions for more than a year. Although she was proven right in the end and the interdict was lifted, this final battle proved too much for her and she died six months later.

Of all Hildegard's amazing contributions to art, literature, music—her most lasting may well turn out to be her contribution to theology. For, according to Barbara Newman, Hildegard was the first Christian to develop a theology centered around the divine feminine. And it is here we find her descriptions of the feminine life force that so clearly parallel the teachings on prana-shakti and Shakti.

It is important to understand, however, that she did not develop this feminine theology deliberately. She was not, as some have claimed, the first "feminist" nor was she in any sense a worshiper of the divine feminine. In fact, the main reason Hildegard was never excommunicated, accused of witchcraft, or burned at the stake, in spite of her open criticism of corruption in the Church, was because the basic theology of her writings fit well within the established Church doctrine of the day.

Regardless, strong strains of emphasis on the divine feminine do indeed exist in Hildegard's work, particularly in her writings on Sophia, a divine being that appeared frequently in her visions. When these strains are separated out of the body of her work and put together—as they are in Newman's brilliant *Sister of Wisdom: St. Hildegard's Theology of the Feminine*—we find that Hildegard was pivotal in the development of a tradition in Christianity called "sapiential theology". To understand the importance of Hildegard's contribution to these ideas we need to take a brief look at this tradition.

Without getting into an involved, academic explanation of what this term involves, sapiential theology can be described as a set of ideas that focus on the concept of "wisdom" as it is portrayed in the biblical books that frequently mention this topic and are, indeed, often referred to as the Wisdom books. These include Proverbs, Job, Ecclesiastes, the Book of Wisdom, and Ecclesiasticus. They are found in the Old Testament and the Apocrypha—a sort of appendix to the Protestant Bible that consists of a number of books that are still found in the Catholic Bible.

The word "wisdom" generally refers to a quality or an attribute. But when you look through the Wisdom books, you find that the Wisdom mentioned there sounds much more like some sort of a divine being than an attribute. This, as you'll see below, has created a number of problems for Judeo-Christian theologians over the centuries. One of the most pervasive is related to the idea that *nothing* can be "divine" unless it refers specifically to God, the Absolute. Today, of course, the word "divine" is often used—as I am using it in this book—to refer not just to the Absolute but also to anything that is extremely closely related to God or has God-like characteristics such as omnipotence, omniscience, and omnipresence. However, in the strictest Judeo-Christian terms, nothing can be divine that is in anyway different or separate from God. Over the centuries many theologians have explained away the problem of Wisdom appearing to be some sort of divine being by saying that it was not a being at all; it was simply a personification of God's wisdom.

The importance of all this to our understanding of the divine feminine is that the word for wisdom in Greek is *Sophia*. In Hebrew it is *Chokhmah*, which, like Sophia, is also a feminine noun. When you go back and read these parts of the Bible and plug in the name "Sophia" for the word wisdom—or find an older Catholic Bible which still actually uses the name Sophia in these passages—a very powerful picture begins to emerge, and it becomes clear that many of these passages sound like they are referring to a divine being and that this being is feminine. Over the last few decades many Jewish and Christian feminist spirituality movements have embraced the idea of Sophia/Chokhmah and begun to use references to her in their liturgy and rituals.

Although the majority of Jewish and Christian theologians throughout history have tended to treat Sophia/Chokhmah as a personification of God's wisdom, the idea that "she" was much more than this has surfaced many times. From well before the birth of Christ a number of Jewish mystical sects considered Chokhmah to be a divine feminine being. Many of these same ideas were taken up by Christian mystical sects in the first few centuries of Christianity. The teachings of these various Jewish and Christian sects have been lumped together under the name "Gnosticism". Although the gnostic teachings are far too complex to go into here, it's important to understand that the idea of Sophia as a divine being who was created by God—and according to Proverbs the first thing God created—has been around for a long time. The following passage from Proverbs is a good example of this.

In it, Sophia described her origins, saying:

> The Lord created me the first of his works long ago, before all else
> that he made.
> I was formed in earliest times, at the beginning, before earth itself.
> I was born when there was yet no ocean, when there were no springs
> brimming with water...
> When he set the heavens in place I was there, when he girdled the
> ocean with the horizon, when he fixed the canopy of clouds overhead
> and confined the springs of the deep.
> When he prescribed limits for the sea so that the waters do not trans-
> gress his command, when he made the earth's foundation firm.
> Then I was at his side each day, his darling and delight, playing in his
> presence continually
> playing over his whole world, while my delight was in mankind.
> [Proverbs 8:22-24; 27-31]

Over time the idea of Sophia as the first created being became lost in the Christian tradition. One reason for this was undoubtedly that the patriarchal Church fathers could not tolerate even the slightest suggestion that something feminine could be divine. In all fairness, however, it has to be said that a number of other forces also came into play. One was the rigid monotheism found in both Judaism and Christianity. Admitting that God might have had a partner, even if she was seen as secondary, hinted far too closely at polytheism and simply could not be allowed. It threatened the very tenet of "one God and only one God" that had made Judaism and, later, Christianity stand out from—and in their eyes superior to—the "pagan" religions that they were trying to replace.

The other factor in Sophia's loss of her divine position was related to the early Christian Church fathers' desperate need to find some reference to Christ in the creation stories in the Old Testament. Unfortunately for them, it simply didn't exist. So eventually some of these early theologians developed the idea that Christ was the incarnation of the "Word", or Greek *Logos*, that the Book of Psalms tells us God created first: "By the word of the Lord, the heavens were made." [Ps. 33:6] Over the years these theologians developed long-winded, tortuous arguments to support their positions and wrote reams of material on the idea that Christ was the Word. Many of them then went on to say that any references to Wisdom were in fact references to the Logos and were therefore actually references to Christ. (Anyone who wants to read more on the intellectual gyrations necessary to "prove" these positions can find it in the many scholarly works on what is called the "Arian controversy".) In spite of this, a few early theologians and Church fathers found ways—some as convoluted as saying there must have actually been two or three different Sophias—to refer to Sophia as some sort of divine feminine force created by God.

Over the centuries, the common people remained blissfully ignorant of all this theological controversy and continued to be moved by the power and lyrical beauty of the Wisdom passages. According to Newman, by Hildegard's day, many of these passages—such as the one from Proverbs above—had become extremely popular, and Wisdom was frequently portrayed in stories and art as a female allegorical figure who was often named Sophia. This, along with the discussions on Sophia in accepted Church doctrine, probably influenced Hildegard's visionary experiences of Sophia and, at least to some degree, her writings about this divine being. These trends were probably also one reason Hildegard managed to avoid being either banned or burned as a heretic.

Before going on to look at Hildegard's depiction of Sophia in more detail, it is also important to note that, no matter how powerful the image of Sophia appears to us in these writings, Hildegard was always careful to come back to the established doctrine that Christ was the incarnation of the Logos and that this incarnation was the ultimate purpose of all creation. Nonetheless, when you put all of Hildegard's references to Sophia together, as Newman has done, you come up with an image of a feminine being that is in many instances clearly omnipotent and in all cases divine.

Hildegard's writings on Sophia can be found in the three books she wrote on her visionary experiences. In the visions, Sophia appears to Hildegard in two main forms. In one she is generally called Sophia, *Sapientia*, or *Scientia Dei*. In the other form she is called *Caritas*. All these are Latin words. Sapientia is the equivalent of Sophia, Scientia Dei means "knowledge of God", and Caritas means "love". According to Newman, despite their different names, they all represent Sophia.

The first time Sophia appears in one of Hildegard's visions is found in Part III of *Scivias*, Hildegard's first book. In the original illustration accompanying this vision, she is called Scientia Dei and is depicted as a woman wearing a veil. She has been painted with glittering gold leaf and is set against a night-time sky filled with stars. One hand is raised in a gesture that suggests tolerance and mercy. Hildegard wrote that this image represents the "Knowledge of God" for Scientia watches over every one and every thing in heaven and earth. Hildegard describes Scientia as a being of a radiance that shines with "measureless splendor". She is as awesome and terrible as thunder and lightning, but as gentle as the goodness of the sun. The "dread radiance of her divinity" is so bright, that a human being could no more gaze into her blazing face than stare at the sun. Hildegard goes on to say that this radiant, divine being is also omnipresent for "she is with all and in all". She is also tender and "of beauty so great in her mystery that no one could know how sweetly she bears with people, and with what unfathomable mercy she spares them".

Sophia as this radiant, merciful, omnipresent divine being appears again and again in Hildegard's visions. One of the most powerful descriptions of her can be found in Hildegard's third book, *The Book of Divine Works*, where Sophia takes the form of Caritas, or Divine Love:

> I am the supreme and fiery force who kindled every living spark...As I circled the whirling sphere with my upper wings (that is, with wisdom), rightly I ordained it. And I am the fiery life of the essence of God: I flame above the beauty of the fields; I shine in the waters; I burn in the sun, the moon, and the stars. And with the airy wind, I quicken all things vitally by an unseen, all-sustaining life. For the air is alive in the verdure and the flowers; the waters flow as if they lived; the sun too lives in its light; and when the moon wanes it is rekindled by the light of the sun, as if it lived anew.

The first time I read these descriptions of Sophia and Caritas as she appeared in Hildegard's visions I was so deeply moved that I wept. They made me realize, for the very first time, that all the years that I had been chasing after the idea of Shakti as the divine feminine in Eastern traditions, a very similar concept existed in my own religion and I had never, not for even an instant, been aware that it was there.

As I did increasing amounts of research on the traditions associated with Sophia, I turned back to the Old Testament. Where before I had seen Wisdom as just an attribute of God, I replaced the word Wisdom with the name Sophia and a wise, but fiery and passionate, feminine counterpart to the divine masculine emerged for me. This personal discovery transformed my idea of Christianity and for the first time in years deepened my sense of connection to the religion of my childhood. What happened to me at that time was what has happened to many women who have been part of the feminist spirituality movement but remained within their own religious traditions: I found an aspect of God that I could identify with in a way I never had been able to before.

In addition, as I read, the parallels to Shakti, prana-shakti, and kundalini-shakti began to jump out at me, and I began to realize that my love of Shakti, my fascination with prana and kundalini, were not things apart from my roots or foreign to my traditions, they were simply ideas that had been lost, hidden, and buried along the way.

When I first read the passage below, my whole body was covered in goose-bumps for, if the words hadn't come from the Old Testament, I would have sworn I was reading one of the most beautiful, comprehensive descriptions of prana-shakti I had ever seen:

> In wisdom there is a spirit intelligent and holy, unique in its kind yet made up of many parts, subtle, free-moving, lucid, spotless, clear, neither harmed nor harming, loving what is good, eager, unhampered, beneficent, kindly towards mortals, steadfast, unerring, untouched by care, all-powerful, all-surveying, and permeating every intelligent, pure, and most subtle spirit.
>
> For wisdom moves more easily than motion itself; she is so pure she pervades and permeates all things.
>
> Like a fine mist she rises from the power of God, a clear effluence from the glory of the Almighty...
>
> age after age she enters into holy souls, and makes them friends of God and prophets
>
> for nothing is acceptable to God but the person who makes his home with wisdom.
>
> [Wisdom 7: 22-28]

Over time I became convinced that it is no accident that Shakti from the yogic tradition, Sophia from the Old Testament, and Caritas and Sapientia from the writings of Hildegard were all feminine cosmic forces. Although the One God is beyond gender, God manifests as polarity throughout the entire universe. And although masculine and feminine polarities are equally important, the *active power* of this divine manifestation is feminine. That she is this active power is underscored by the passage from Proverbs quoted earlier in which Wisdom describes her role during creation. In the translation that is found in *The Oxford Annotated Bible* she says not that she was God's "darling", but that she was by his side "like a master workman". As this cosmic force she is entering into us—holy souls that we are—and working through us. She is the creative force of the universe, and she is the creative force within each one of us.

This is why Christine experienced the creative power that surged through her body in the dance as feminine. It is feminine. And it is power. Look at Caritas' words, "I am the supreme and fiery force who kindled every living spark" and the description of Sophia as "the flawless mirror of the active power of God...She is but one, yet she can do all things; herself unchanging, she makes all things new..."

The power of this "supreme and fiery force" to make "all things new" is at the very center of our desire to transform and create. It is Wagner's "universal current of Divine Thought" that vibrated the ether everywhere; it is Brahms' "creative energy of the universe" that he called the Universal Spirit; it is the "flames and ether" that rushed through Whitman's veins. And it is the force that rushes through ours and that makes us yearn so deeply to create not just art but also a world in which we can come closer to oneness with the Divine.

Experiencing the Life Force

The imagery Hildegard uses when she talks about the supreme and fiery force that flames above the beauty of the fields and about the "air" being alive in the greenery and the flowers is so powerful that it seems she could actually see this pulsing life energy. Dylan Thomas gives the same impression when he talks about "the force that through the green fuse drives the flower" in the poem of the same name, and, in Fern Hill, about the air that was lovely and watery and fire green as grass.

If the ancient yogis had been familiar with these works they probably would have said that the writers had attained the siddhi of being able to see prana. And although you may well be a ways from arriving at this level, you can still become increasingly tuned into the life energy as it pulses around you.

There is probably no easier time to experience this than on an early spring day when the first flower heads are poking through the dark soil, and the tentative green buds are breaking out on trees and bushes. The pale, translucent green of these buds is a color that appears nowhere else. Looking at it, you can easily sense the life force pulsing through it—the force that through the green fuse drives the flower.

If you happen to read this on a spring day, go out now, experience this for yourself, and write about it. If you have to wait awhile for spring to roll around, do the following exercise. Have pen and paper handy so you can write about your experience.

1. *Breathe in the radiant white light and create your protective space as you did in the first two exercises.*
2. *Sit for a moment in the light that surrounds you allowing it to intensify around your heart and move upwards, filling your mind with light.*
3. *Slowly begin to allow images from childhood to flow into your mind. Then, move back in time until you find yourself in a yard, garden, or park on a spring day.*
4. *Allow yourself to experience once again how alive you felt—when the very air you breathed seemed to fill you with clear, clean life-giving energy and everything around you seemed to give off a radiant glow.*

5. *Next, begin to notice the details around you—how impossibly green the grass looks, how vibrant every tiny unfurling leaf on the flowers and hedges is...*

6. *Spend as much time as you want in this peaceful, life-giving scene and, then, when you are ready, slowly bring your focus back to the white light that surrounds you.*

7. *Sense the light intensifying around your heart again, then flowing upward and outward until it flows out your pen and onto the paper in your hand. Write about your experience.*

The Never-setting, Splendorous Sun

A few years ago a Danish woman named Britta contacted me after reading *The Fiery Muse*. A designer, she had heard I was looking for stories about creative inspiration for my next book. Her first letter captured my attention, and we've been in correspondence ever since. There was such a deep-down sweetness about her and such a child-like enthusiasm in the way she expressed herself that I came to treasure her letters.

Although it was clear from the spiky elegant handwriting in her first letter that she was schooled in another era and must be a senior citizen, I had no idea what her age might be. And she didn't tell me; she wanted, she said, to surprise me once she'd finished telling me her whole story in her letters. When she finally felt she'd answered all my questions, she sent me a picture of herself and asked me to guess how old she was before looking at the answer on the last page of her letter.

In the picture, she's standing in her backyard on an autumn day holding an extremely large oak leaf in each hand. A huge blue sweater covers her tiny frame, and her short, thick blondish gray hair falls around her face making her look like a pixie. Sunlight rims one side of her face but there also seems to be a source of light that glows from beneath her skin. Looking at that picture I saw such a calmness and serenity about her that I wanted to reach out and hold her.

Dutifully I tried to guess her age. I imagined she must be in her late sixties or, at the absolute most, seventy or seventy-one. I turned the page to see if I was right. "Ha!" I could almost hear her saying, "What do you think of that! I'm ninety!"

When I looked back at her picture not long ago and read again her letters with their freshness and innocence, it made me think of the letter, quoted in the last chapter, that Hildegard wrote when she was seventy-seven to Guibert of Gembloux in which she described the vision she called the "reflection of the living Light". To the words found in the last chapter Hildegard added:

> Moreover, I can no more recognize the form of this light than I can gaze directly on the sphere of the sun. Sometimes—but not often— I see within this light another light, which I call "the living Light". And I cannot describe when and how I see it, but while I see it all sorrow and anguish leave me, so that then I feel like a simple girl instead of an old woman.

Just such a simple girl, free from all anguish and sorrow, could be seen shining brightly just beneath Britta's skin. This picture of her confirmed what I had already gathered from her first letters to me: Britta had at some point in her life had a deeply transformative spiritual experience. In her correspondence with me Britta made it clear that this experience, along with her life-long spiritual search, was directly connected to her creativity and her artistic ability.

In some ways Britta's childhood in Denmark was idyllic. Along with her two older brothers, she was raised on a large, prosperous farm. She loved nature, and spent a great deal of time outdoors. When she described her childhood summer days, you could almost smell the heavy fragrance of apples ripening in the orchard and feel the breezes lifting the scent of new-mown hay from the fields. The idyll was spoiled only by her relationship with her mother, who never hugged or kissed Britta and repeatedly told her how bitterly she had wept when she learned she was pregnant. In general, Britta's mother ignored her and left her to fend for herself. This, combined with the fact that Britta had few friends to play with, meant that she spent most of her time alone as a child. However, she did feel loved by her father, a quiet and gentle man, and she also found great joy in working with her hands.

Her talent for handiwork was discovered by accident when she was about six years old and her mother sent her, for completely practical reasons, to learn stitching and embroidery from a neighbor. Britta grew to love the color and feel of the fabrics and became excited by the element of design in the work. By the time she was twelve she was sewing summer dresses for both her mother and herself, making beautiful embroideries, and knitting clothes as well.

When she finished school at seventeen her parents wanted her to go on to obtain a higher academic degree. But she refused, saying she wanted an education in dressmaking and design. Soon after this she left the farm for Copenhagen where she worked and took classes in art and design in the evenings. By her second year in the art school, she was taken on as a part-time teaching assistant and began to win prizes for her work.

Around this time her spiritual yearning was also becoming stronger. She began to read many books on philosophy and was intrigued by descriptions of Eastern saints like Ramakrishna. Still, her spiritual focus remained on the Christian teachings of her childhood and, over time, she became increasingly drawn to the story of the life of Jesus.

By the time World War II broke out, Britta had married and, during the war, had her first child, a daughter. Five years later she had a son. As for most Europeans the war years were difficult and, for Britta, the years after were even harder. Her husband, a zoologist, couldn't find work, and Britta supported the family with her dressmaking and design for many years.

Even though Britta's life was filled with the difficulties of raising her family and surviving in post-war Europe, her spiritual longings were never far below the surface. By the early 1950s—when she was about forty—she reached a point where she found herself extremely frustrated with the lack of compassion and caring she saw in the world around her and equally dissatisfied with what she saw as her own inability to live a truly Christian life.

At this time she began reading the New Testament and became even more deeply fascinated with the life of Jesus. She continued reading but realized it was difficult to interpret the true meaning behind many of his sayings and came to use the "Sermon on the Mount" as a kind of guidepost for what her behavior should be. Even though Christ's words were hard to understand, she struggled to follow them. Of this she said, "I could see my own faults and I worked hard on myself for a long time."

After about two years of this, she mentioned her difficulty in understanding the Bible to a friend who suggested she read a book called *A Search in Secret India* by Paul Brunton. Born in 1898, Brunton was an Englishman who left a successful career as a journalist to live among the yogis and mystics of India and came to be known as a mystic in his own right. After practicing meditation and studying Hindu philosophy for many years, Brunton felt compelled to try to explain his experiences in ways that Westerners could understand. His many books expressed the idea that the Eastern teachings, especially those on meditation and the inner spiritual quest, were not strange esoteric concepts but practices that could fit well into our Western lives. Through these books and his lectures Brunton became a major influence in bringing Eastern ideas to the Western world.

When Britta read *A Search in Secret India* she felt spiritually uplifted by the message of the book. Some time after this she heard that Brunton was coming to Copenhagen, and a friend of hers who knew him arranged for her to meet with him. "At that time," Britta wrote, "I was very shy about doing things like that, but I wanted with my whole soul to meet him as I wanted to know what spiritual life was all about." When they finally met, Brunton talked to Britta about some of the Eastern paths she could follow. "But I told him," she says, "I wanted to go the way of Jesus. Then he told me, 'Then you will have to have Jesus in your thoughts all the time.'"

The two then prayed for a short time together. As they did Britta felt as if she was lifted out of and over her body. But this mild out-of-body experience frightened her a little and, at the time, she even wondered if it had been caused by some kind of hypnosis. Brunton seems to have realized Britta had been strongly affected by the meeting, as he made sure she felt she could get home safely by herself, then walked her down the stairs and into the yard and watched after her until she was out of sight.

When she was almost home, she had another strange experience that made a life-long impression on her. As she was walking down the street she suddenly felt overwhelmed by a negative sensation. It was almost, she says, as if some dark force was racing around inside her. Frightened by this sensation, she thought about what Brunton had told her and began to focus her thoughts on Jesus. Immediately, the negative feeling disappeared and she was filled with a feeling of peace and joy. She described this saying, "But I took Jesus by the hand and then darkness was all gone!" This experience served to confirm for Britta the validity of the advice Brunton had given her.

Over the next while she said, "I did as Paul Brunton had told me and I came closer to Jesus; I worked hard on myself and had Jesus in my thoughts all the time." By working "hard on herself" Britta means that she was trying to eliminate what she saw as the sins and shortcomings in her life. Soon after this she went through an ordeal that lasted several days in which a "film" played continually in her mind that showed her all the sins she had committed in her life. As the film ran on she repeatedly asked for forgiveness and when the ordeal finally ended she felt completely cleansed.

Although Britta's emphasis on sins and her view of herself as a "sinner" made me uncomfortable, her attitude—at least the one she had at that time in her life—fit within the context of how so many Christians have interpreted the teachings of their religion over the years. Still, I can't help but think that Britta's "sins" were probably fairly minor transgressions in the cosmic scheme of things. On the other hand, the kind of "working on" herself and striving to improve herself that Britta did is an essential part of the spiritual journey. Beyond this, the sense of great cleansing that she experienced was an extremely significant one, for it set the stage for the deep spiritual experience she would have that would utterly change her life.

For another couple of years I continued to work hard on myself and I had Jesus in my thoughts all the time, as if he were part of me. And

then one night when I had gone to bed and done my evening prayer
—the Jesus prayer—I asked for the Holy Spirit.

It was not something I had planned or had been thinking about
doing. It came of itself—as if it were the most natural thing to do!

Then I waited without thinking. My brain was absolutely blank
—I was just kind of listening. And then suddenly I felt energy starting
at the lowest part of my spine—going slowly up my spine—but
when it reached my head—I suddenly got afraid and then it didn't
go further!

At that time I had no idea what had happened to me—but
nothing else happened that night—and after some time I slept.

The next morning when I woke up I felt as if I were in another
world—and for three days after this I was in an intense state of
peace, love, and happiness. I felt sometimes as if I were embracing
the whole world. I was filled with love. And after this I was not the
same anymore. For example, I was not able to say anything that was
not absolutely true. I could, to a certain degree feel what people were
thinking when I talked to them, and I could tell if they meant what
they were saying or not. In the same way I could get answers from
within on certain questions I had, especially if they were spiritual
ones. I also felt more concern about other people, and I felt for a long
time as if I loved everybody. This experience was, I think, not
something that just "happened". It came out of hard concentrated
work and a deep, deep desire to learn some of the Truths of what life
is all about.

This experience changed Britta's creative life equally—if not even
more—dramatically than it changed her spiritual life. First, she says,
her "talent for painting improved immensely". Up until that time, she
explains, the only way her artistic talent seemed to express itself was
in her fashion design and dressmaking. Her attempts at other types
of artistic expression had not been particularly successful. When she
was about fourteen she had tried taking a class in ceramics but had
found her work primitive. "It was," she said, "not alive!" The same was
true, she claimed, of several attempts she made at painting, and after
a time she gave these types of artistic endeavors up and made a
decision to just stick with her fashion designs.

After her spiritual experience, however, there was a great change in her ability. One of the most startling occurred when she attended an exhibition of drawings by Picasso that was held in Copenhagen not long after her experience: "When I came home I took some big sheets of paper and started to draw some of the pictures from memory. As I did, some of them came as easily as if I had them before my eyes. And they looked just like Picasso's! They were alive!"

As surprised and delighted with this unexpected increase in her artistic skill as she was, she was far more astonished when she suddenly developed the ability to write poetry. Although Britta had never had a talent for writing, she suddenly found that beautiful poetry was flowing into her mind. "The words came to me," she said, "out of nowhere—and if I didn't write them down immediately they would disappear into thin air." She took to carrying a notebook and pencil with her at all times so she could capture these wispy bits of inspiration before they could vanish like so much smoke on the wind.

Over the last four decades Britta has continued to express herself creatively through her artwork, and she has never abandoned her spiritual work on herself. Through all these years, Britta has also remained certain that her experience of the Holy Spirit triggered a great transformation in both her creative ability and her ability to understand Christ's real message. A good deal of her spiritual search has been focused on trying to understand exactly what happened to her during that experience and why it had such transformative power.

Britta's instinct to continue to look for answers to this question was a critically important one, for this type of transformation of con-sciousness is at the very heart of the spiritual-creative quest in which so many of us are involved.

Not long ago Britta—at the age of ninety!—read a book that contained a description of the awakening of kundalini-shakti and its upward journey through the chakras. Afterwards she wrote me and told me how excited she was to read this book on kundalini because she felt that it described exactly what had happened to her when she felt the Holy Spirit rising up her spine.

Although it makes no real difference whether Britta uses the words "Holy Spirit" or "kundalini", looking at her experience in terms of kundalini has a distinct advantage. The reason for this is simply that age-old yogic texts describe the experience and what can be expected from it in great detail and, in this way, present a framework that can provide us with a tremendous amount of insight into these types of transformative spiritual experiences and how they relate to our creativity.

Within this context Britta's experience would be described as a type of "partial" awakening of kundalini. A "full" awakening is an extremely rare occurrence that results in *enlightenment* or *liberation*. In Tantra and hatha yoga this state is called *jīvan-mukti* and the rare saint who has attained it a *jīvan-mukta*. Britta would be the first to tell you that the transformation she experienced, profound as it was, was far from jīvan-mukti. To clarify this difference between a "full" and "partial" awakening, in fact, some contemporary researchers in the field have begun to use the term kundalini "rising" rather than awakening. This is a useful term because it conveys the notion that the awakening of kundalini is not just an experience but a process that often lasts a lifetime. It also fits in well with the idea expressed in Chapter One that these types of experiences occur along a continuum. While Britta's experiences were not as earth shattering as those of people like Mahadevi and Hildegard and while she did not become a saint or a creative genius as these two did, they were the same *type* of experiences.

If you look at Britta's story carefully you will see that it contains all the elements of a classic kundalini experience just as they are listed in Chapter One. First, the experience she had the night the Holy Spirit came to her was clearly an intense mystical one. What's more, during the experience itself she felt the energy rising upwards along her spine just as the ancient yogis have told us it does.

In yoga, kundalini-shakti and prana-shakti are said to move through the body along channels called *nadis*. Most schools of hatha yoga say there are 72,000 nadis; others say there are hundreds of thousands. But they generally all agree that these nadis carry prana-shakti throughout the body. They also agree that the three most important—and most significant in terms of kundalini rising—are located either in or running along the spine. Ideally, when kundalini rises it makes its way upwards through the central one of these three nadis, known as the *sushumnā*. The sushumnā is flanked on the right by the nadi called the *pingalā* and on the left by the one known as the *idā*.

As the energy travels upward it makes its way through six chakras —the wheels or vortices often called energy centers—that are located along the pathway. The first of these is the root chakra or *mūlādhāra* and is located at the base of the spine. This chakra is where kundalini-shakti rests, coiled three and a half times around the base of the spine, until she awakens. The second chakra, *svādhishthāna*, is generally said to be located near the genitals. The third is *manipūra* or the navel chakra. Next comes *anhāta*, the heart chakra. The fifth is the *vishuddha* chakra, which is located at the base of the throat. The sixth chakra, *ājnā*, is often depicted as being located behind the center of the forehead, an area sometimes known both in yoga and Tibetan Buddhism as the "third eye". Above these six chakras is *sahasrāra*, known as the thousand-petaled lotus. In some traditions sahasrāra is called the seventh chakra and is said to be located at the crown of the head; in others, it is believed to transcend the body and be located above the head.

Many yogis would say that the fact that Britta felt the sensation so clearly in her spine was a sign that she was indeed experiencing a kundalini rising and not just the prana-shakti moving through her body. In Britta's case, however, the rising did not reach the highest centers for, as she explained, when she felt the energy reach the top of her spine and move into the base of her brain, she grew afraid and the movement stopped.

This probably explains why Britta did not have the visions of brilliant, all-encompassing light that Mahadevi and Hildegard did. Still, light in general took on a new significance for her after her experience: she found that the world around her took on a certain radiance, and the imagery of light and fire appeared often in the poetry she later wrote.

The feelings that engulfed Britta as soon as she woke up the next morning are also characteristic of the classical kundalini experiences: she was filled with indescribable bliss, peace, and a feeling of deep love for and oneness with everyone and everything. In many Tantric teachings these feelings are associated with the idea that kundalini has risen to and "awakened" or "opened" the heart chakra. And, in fact, many texts emphasize the importance of the heart chakra in the process of kundalini rising.

Even though Britta's awakening was only a partial one, for her— as for anyone who has experienced anything similar—it was the most momentous experience of her life. However, what is even more significant than the experience itself is the way it changed her. As she said to me once in her straightforward way, "I woke up the next morning and I was a different person."

I can't emphasize enough that it is this *transformation* that is at the very center of everything we need to learn about our spiritual journey and our creative inspiration. One of the most important reasons for emphasizing the transformation rather than the experience itself is that many people, even those who are intensively pursuing a spiritual path, simply never have any type of remarkable spiritual experiences at all. This does not mean they are not having success in their endeavors or that they are in any way "behind" or less spiritual than someone who has had the type of experience Britta had—let alone the more dramatic kinds of experiences some of the women in this book have had. There are a number of reasons for this. One is that kundalini rising occurs so gradually in many cases that its workings are virtually imperceptible. According to many teachings this is, in fact, the ideal way to awaken kundalini for it avoids the pitfalls that can accompany any kind of cataclysmic change. Another is that some people are born with kundalini already awakened to some degree. Individuals like this might not have ever had, for instance, a sudden vision of divine light because an on-going experience of light has always colored their perception. Consequently, they would also have no idea they see things any differently than anyone else.

The old yogic teachings make it clear, however, that any person going through this process—whether they have any noticeable "symptoms" of kundalini rising or not—*will* experience transformation. These texts also make the characteristics of this transformation clear. And Britta's experience coincides with them exactly. First, she began to receive inspiration. This manifested, as you've already seen, in the remarkable improvement in her artistic ability and in the sudden development of the ability to write poetry. Second, her intuition became much more sharply honed and she began to exhibit a psychic sense; particularly, in her case, with the ability to tell instantly whether people were telling the truth. Next, her desire for material success was diminished even more than it already was, and her desire for spiritual attainment grew even greater. Finally, her ethical sense, her desire to help end the suffering of humanity, and her passion for social justice all increased. It's also interesting to look at St Hildegard's experiences within this framework—for even though there is virtually no possibility that she would have ever

THE DIVINE FEMININE FIRE

heard of the philosophies related to yoga, her experience, like Britta's, fits exactly into the framework of kundalini experience gleaned from the teachings of the Tantras.

In these texts the element that most clearly defines the rising of kundalini to the higher chakras is an extraordinarily bright vision of light, fire, or flame. Hildegard's description of her first mystical experience, quoted in Chapter Four, reveals that she indeed experienced this: "...the heavens were opened and a blinding light of exceptional brilliance flowed through my entire brain. And it so kindled my whole heart and breast like a flame..."

Hildegard gave this ineffable radiance the name "the living Light" and continued to refer to it throughout her life. Both the Tantric texts and the writings of the yogis who experienced the awakening of kundalini are replete with references to this light. One particularly beautiful example is found in a text called *Panchastavi* that was probably written about 800 CE in Northern India. The text begins with these words in praise of Tripura, a name used interchangeably throughout the verse with several of the more common names for Shakti and kundalini-shakti:

> May the Goddess Tripura, who is of the nature of light and sound, shining in the forehead like the lustrous (rain)bow of Indra, in the crown of the head like the luminous white shine of the moon, and in the heart like the never setting splendorous sun...
>
> [Canto I; v. 1]

Another similar verse says:

> The splendor, which shines like the cool rays of the moon in the head, like the coloured beams of a rainbow in the middle of the forehead and which kisses the heart chakra like a tongue of fire, that splendor, verily, is Thy own glorious Form, O Mother.
>
> [Canto II; v. 11]

In other verses, particularly those that make specific mention of the awakening of kundalini and its journey upward through the six chakras, we find more references to this light. One, for example, says kundalini-shakti cuts her way through the chakras "with the brilliance of millions of flashes of lightning". In another she is said to shine "with the brilliance of millions of suns" [Canto V; v. 11].

Although Hildegard didn't specifically mention the sensations of energy rising up her spine that the yogis so often describe, she did stress the effect of the light on her heart as well as her brain when she wrote that the light not only filled her entire brain, but "kindled her whole heart and breast like a flame". This is surprisingly similar to the lines quoted above from *Panchastavi* where the yogi said that the luminous light shone in his forehead "like the never setting splendorous sun" and kissed his "heart chakra like a tongue of fire". These references to the heart are consistent with the teachings of many Tantric schools where the importance of the heart and the heart chakra is often emphasized and where the spiritual seekers are instructed, during meditation, to hold the image of the Divine in both their minds and their hearts. One of the most well-known Tantric texts is, in fact, the *Kulārnava Tantra*, which means literally "Ocean of the Heart", and it refers to the spiritual practice it describes as the "path of the heart".

Hildegard also experienced the feelings of love, bliss, oneness, and peace that Tantras tell us are another touchstone of kundalini awakening. Her description of having all "sorrow and anguish" fall away quoted earlier provides a good example of this, and the full passage as it originally appeared in her letter to Guibert of Gembloux makes this even clearer:

> From my early childhood...I have always seen this vision in my soul, even to the present time, when I am more than seventy years old. In this vision my soul, as God would have it, rises up high into the vault of heaven and into the changing sky and spreads itself out among different peoples, although they are far away from me in distant lands and places...
>
> Moreover, I can no more recognize the form of this light than I can gaze directly on the sphere of the sun. Sometimes—but not often—I see within this light another light, which I call "the living Light". And I cannot describe when and how I see it, but while I see it all sorrow and anguish leave me, so that then I feel like a simple girl instead of an old woman.

A remarkably parallel description can be found in a text on Tantra and alchemy from the eleventh century called *Rasarnava*, which means literally "Ocean of Mercury":

Perfect beatitude, unalloyed, absolute, the essence where of is luminous-
ness, undifferentiated,
    From which all troubles are fallen away, knowable, tranquil, self-
recognized...

This luminous essence certainly shone forth in Hildegard and made
her one of the rare truly holy men and women that have walked the
face of the earth—whether they were called great yogis or great
saints. In fact, in almost every way Hildegard is an example of what
Panchastavi called one of the rare "enlightened ones":

> Only a few, taking refuge in the dust of Thy lotus feet, became great
> poets, pure in heart, of great wisdom and noble deeds and won to
> fame which resounded in the three worlds, stainless like the moon,
> silk, milk or snow.
>
> [Canto II; v. 26]

After Hildegard's transformative experience of the living light, she
created exquisitely beautiful music and poetry. She brought great
wisdom to the world. She was certainly pure in heart, and she sought
—even though she remained a human being with faults and shortcomings—to become as stainless as the moon, silk, milk, or snow.

But Hildegard was a saint. And making a comparison between
her experiences and the Tantric teachings on enlightenment is not
meant to make less of the experiences of someone like Britta—or
the kinds of experiences people like you and I have most likely had.
On the contrary, the purpose is to remind us once again that these
experiences occur on a continuum: Hildegard's experience of the
Divine Light may have turned her into a firebrand who risked her
life for social justice, but it is no less significant that Britta, after her
experience of the Holy Spirit, said "I was not able to say anything
which was not absolutely true." and "My desires for material things
were changed automatically for desires for a more spiritual and
loving life—and to helping other people, especially."

All this points once again to the fact that these experiences,
different as they were in terms of intensity, were of essentially the same
essence. The same is true for people who are experiencing this transformation gradually. Not everyone has brilliant flashes of light or dramatic risings of energy up their spines. The divine transformative

energy—call her Shakti or Sophia—is calling out to the vast majority of us with a quiet voice, increasing our desire to be closer to the Divine, our need to make the world a better place, and our hunger to express ourselves creatively slowly, but very surely, over time.

Mandalas—Hildegard's Circle of Life

The illustrations of Hildegard's visions are replete with circular images that the Swiss psychoanalyst Carl Jung would have called mandalas.* Jung "discovered" mandalas at age thirty-eight when he found his work in academia had lost meaning, left his university post, and began focusing on his inner life. During this time Jung kept a journal that contained his dreams, reflections, and sketches. Eventually he noticed that a series of circular designs he had drawn seemed to reflect his state of mind.

Fascinated, he began to research circular imagery and discovered it appeared in the sacred symbolism and ritual of many of the world's spiritual traditions. Calling these images by the Sanskrit word mandala, which means literally circle or orb, he came to see them as a mirror of the self and a container for the journey to wholeness or self-realization that Jung called individuation.

Although Hildegard wouldn't have called her circular images mandalas, they are certainly powerful images that rise up out of her own spiritual journey towards wholeness or oneness with the Divine. Creating just such a circular image for yourself is a perfect way to attune yourself to Hildegard and the message of oneness with the Divine she was trying to convey.

Although many circular drawings are considered mandalas today, strictly speaking, a true mandala contains four elements: the circle itself, a distinct midpoint, four quadrants or cardinal points, and some degree of symmetry. Also, in many traditional sacred designs the circle itself is contained within a square. In my workshops, I've found particularly vibrant mandalas can be made by using parchment paper and markers. Fine paper obtained from an art store works best, but even baker's parchment paper will do and any decent children's markers work well. When taped to a window, the finished mandala glows. A simple frame that makes it look even brighter can be made from black construction paper.

1. Have the materials for creating your mandala handy, visualize the white light and create your protective space as in the first two exercises.
2. Spend a little time surrounded and filled by the light. Then, open your mind and see what image, symbol, form, or color might come to you.

3. *Focus again on the light, allowing it to flow out of you and into your mandala—using the imagery you received as a starting point.*

Two good books on mandalas are Susanne F. Fincher's Creating Mandalas *and Judith Cornell's* Mandalas: Luminous Symbols for Healing. *Reproductions of many of Hildegard's illustrations can be found in Matthew Fox's* The Illuminations of Hildegard of Bingen.

The Breath of Wisdom

One of the most startling similarities in the stories of an ordinary woman like Britta and a saint like Hildegard is the striking change in both their level of awareness and their creative ability that occurred directly after their spiritual experiences. A careful reading of Hildegard's description of the "blinding light of exceptional brilliance" discussed earlier reveals that the experience quite literally transformed her consciousness. Immediately after this brilliant light flowed through her brain, she said, "I understood the meaning of the expositions of the books, that is to say of the psalter, the evangelists, and other catholic books of the Old and New Testaments." What's more, it was only after this experience that her extraordinary creative output began.

Although Britta's transformative experience and her subsequent creative outpouring were far more modest than Hildegard's, the relationship between them is just as clear. During our talks Britta frequently stressed that after her experience she was immediately able to see deeper meaning in the writings of the New Testament. This ability has continued to grow over the years and has helped her, she said, find an ever-deeper understanding of the New Testament message. The change in her creative ability was even more marked. As was explained in the last chapter, she developed a talent for fine art—as opposed to her commercial design work—and the drawings and paintings she did suddenly became "alive". She also spontaneously began to write poetry—something she had never had the slightest talent for before her experience.

If the relationship between these two women's spiritual experiences and the changes in their abilities were more than a coincidence, we would expect to find references to this type of occurrence in spiritual writings. And we do. The yoga texts, particularly the Tantras, overflow with just such references. Two of the loveliest are found in *Panchastavi*:

O Mother of the Universe, Goddess Tripura, the sphere of Thy surpassing beauty...becomes the means of granting...the talents of a poet to Thy devotees... [Canto II; v. 2]

He, Thy devotee, who perceives Thy form, like the white rays of the full moon...acquires the gift of limitless flow of words, rich with the ambrosia of sweetness and beauty of expression. [Canto II; v. 12]

The Tantras almost always use images associated with light like "the white rays of the full moon", "the never setting splendorous sun", and "a tongue of fire" when they are referring to changes in consciousness that result in new levels of understanding or creative ability. In fact, "light" has been used to symbolize new knowledge or wisdom and new ways of looking at things for ages. It's no coincidence that cartoonists have instinctively used the image of a light bulb to signify a "bright new idea" or that we say we want to "shed light" on a subject when we mean we want to come up with a new and different way of understanding it. It's also no accident that we use the words "enlightenment" or "illumination" to describe a transformation from a state of ignorance and darkness to one of grace and radiant understanding. This is the same reason we use the word "illuminati" to describe the greatest spiritual masters and geniuses the world has known.

One reason for this is undoubtedly that when the great seers and visionaries have written about sudden transformations in consciousness they almost always mention an experience of light as Mahadevi did in the poem where she talked about the "light excelling a billion suns and moons" that lodged itself in her mind and then went on to describe how this experience transformed her, making her able to write better than she had ever been able to before. And Hildegard stated very definitely that her sudden ability to understand the meaning of the Old and New Testaments occurred immediately upon having the "blinding light of exceptional brilliance" flow through her brain. A passage from the Tantric text *Rasarnava* paints a beautiful image of this connection between light and transformation:

> The light of pure intelligence shines forth into certain men of holy vision,
> Which, seated between the two eyebrows, illumines the universe,
> like fire, or lightning, or the sun.

The *Sat-cakra-nirūpana*, a Tantric text that was composed in the 1500s in Bengal by a yogi named Pūrnānanda, explains how these experiences of light and transformation are directly related to kundalini-shakti. This text was brought to Western attention in 1918 when it was translated by Sir John Woodroffe, an English civil servant who lived in India for many years and wrote under the pen name of Arthur Avalon. Thanks to Woodroffe's book, called *The Serpent Power*, the *Sat-cakra-nirūpana* became and has remained for years the best-known Tantric text in English.

Near the beginning of the text, Pūrnānanda described Shakti, saying:

> She is beautiful as a chain of lightning
> and fine like a (lotus) fibre,
> and shines in the minds of the sages.
> She is extremely subtle,
> the awakener of pure knowledge,
> the embodiment of Bliss,
> whose true nature is pure Consciousness.

The text goes on to say that Shakti, the divine feminine, shines with the "lustre of ten million Suns" and her awakening can turn a person into "a Lord of speech and a King among men, and an Adept in all kinds of learning". These same images and ideas are reflected in many verses in *Panchastavi*. One verse says:

> Those devotees, who see Thee clearly like the crescent moon, shining
> in the forehead, lighting from Its depths the sky of the mind, those
> wise men soon become seers...   [Canto II; v. 21]

But it is not just the Tantras and other yogic writings that describe this relationship between the awakening of the divine light and the transformation that brings about new levels of understanding and creative expression. An example of this same idea can be found in the early Judeo-Christian writings in the Old Testament Book of Wisdom where Wisdom—or Sophia—is described as a "spirit intelligent and holy":

> Like a fine mist she rises from the power of God, a clear effluence
> from the glory of the Almighty...She is the brightness that streams
> from the everlasting light, the flawless mirror of the active power of
> God and the image of his goodness...age after age she enters into
> holy souls, and makes them God's friends and prophets...
>   [Wisdom 7: 22-28]

If you look carefully at this passage, you will see that it is telling us that when Sophia, in the form of this radiant divine light, enters into certain souls she has the power to turn them not only into devotees to God but also into prophets—those individuals we see as having the deepest understanding of all.

Hildegard even described the sudden onset of "knowledge" and relates it to the divine light in one of the songs that is found in the collection of her music known as the *Symphony of the Harmony of Celestial Revelations*. This particular song is sung to the glory of the "Fire of the Spirit" and much of the song is dedicated to describing this fiery spirit and its powers. And although it seems she might have been referring to the Holy Spirit, she did not use this term and, instead, described this fiery spirit using exactly the same terms she had used to describe the divine feminine being, Sophia, in her other writings:

O fire of the Spirit, the Comforter,
life of the life of all creation,
Holy you are, giving life to the forms...
O current of power permeating all –
in the heights, upon the earth,
and in all deeps:
you bind and gather
all people together...
You are ever teaching the learned,
made joyful by the breath of Wisdom.

These last two lines are particularly important because the original Latin makes it clear that Hildegard was praising this "current of power" not because it teaches those who are already knowledgeable but because it is a force that actually *gives* them knowledge in the first place. Hildegard was saying, in other words, that this "spirit of fire" can educate and teach and that it can transform a person who has little or no understanding into one who does. Hildegard knew this to be true, of course, because she had experienced this transformation herself.

One of the most important things Tantra and the hatha yoga tradition have to tell us about these types of transformative experiences is that the transformation occurs not just in our minds but in our physical being as well. In this sense, we really are *embodying the divine feminine*. We are manifesting her—bringing her into being in the physical world.

Although it is not widely known, this startling concept is, in fact, at the very basis of all Tantric teachings and many yogic traditions. Just as Shakti exists as the core creative and transformative power of the universe, kundalini-shakti exists as the core creative, transformative power in each one of us. Kundalini-shakti is cosmic Shakti in microcosmic form; she is the divine feminine, firmly rooted and securely held in the container that is the human body.

As described earlier, when kundalini-shakti is released from her home in the root chakra, she travels upward and, eventually, reaches the crown. Although exactly what this involves is debated within different schools of yoga, virtually all of these schools agree that once kundalini-shakti reaches the brain she begins to transform it in some way. One school of thought pictures kundalini as a stream of radiant liquid light—a highly intensified, potent form of prana— that reaches and nourishes different parts of the brain and triggers higher levels of activity in these areas. According to this theory, the different "gifts" mentioned in the Tantric verses are the results of different areas being enriched. In other words, the person who becomes more intuitive does so because the areas of the brain that deal with intuition are being nourished; the person who becomes a poet does so because the areas that relate to language are being enriched and so on. In the case of the rare person who reaches jīvan-mukti, or liberation, the sahasrāra is not only reached, it is flooded permanently with the purest form of this potent prana.

A way of conceptualizing this that has helped me understand this process has been to think in terms of the brain as the organ of perception—and to realize that if this organ of perception is altered then the way we are able to perceive the world is also altered. This means, for example, that the mystic "sees" the light that is brighter than a million suns because an ability to see it has been triggered in his or her brain. It is important to realize that this light is real; it is, as the Old Testament says, the "effluence from the glory of the Almighty...the brightness that streams from the everlasting light, the flawless mirror of the active power of God". And the mystics' ability to see it is also real, physically real, rooted in the body and specifically in the brain.

It also seems to me that, just as our ability to perceive is altered, so is our ability to "receive". As our brain—and our consciousness along with it—is transformed, we are more able to receive inspiration from the Divine. We are more able to tune into the creative source of the universe and to act as a vessel that carries it out into the world.

Some schools of yoga describe a very specific area of the brain that is said to "open up" when the kundalini-shakti reaches the higher chakras. This area is called the *brahma-randhra*. *Brahma* here refers to brahman, the Absolute or universal divine power, and *randhra* means "aperture" or "opening". The brahma-randhra has been described as a hidden chamber in the brain that lies dormant until triggered into activity by kundalini. When it is fully opened and permanently nourished by kundalini-shakti, the yogi is said to reach illumination.

Regardless of exactly how any of this occurs, the scriptures of different religions, the writings of mystics, and the experiences of ordinary people like Britta make it clear that some sort of transformation of consciousness goes hand in hand with profound mystical experience. Stories like Christine's tell us the same is true for spiritual experiences that are even less dramatic. This has also been borne out by my own experience in meeting literally hundreds of people involved in different levels of creativity and spirituality over the years. In other words, this transformation of consciousness has occurred not just in the great mystics of the past but is occurring in everyone on the spiritual path today. In fact, Catholic priests like Teilhard de Chardin, Hindu philosophers like Gopi Krishna, and modern-day Jungian analysts like Marion Woodman would say that it is occurring in everyone. For some of us the process is intense and moves at a highly accelerated rate, for others it is far more gradual, and for others still it is virtually imperceptible.

The story of Wendi, a mother of two young girls, provides a wonderful example of this; it is one that many of us can identify with. Her spiritual and creative journey has been a slow one, sometimes moving steadily forward and sometimes falling back. She has had no dramatic spiritual experiences, no earth-shattering visions of light, no sudden or extraordinary increase in her creative abilities. In fact, other than joining a mainstream Protestant church when she was about fourteen, her journey wasn't focused much on spirituality at all. But she has grown greatly in psychological understanding and self-awareness over the years and has recently reached a place of calm, certainty, and creative strength that can provide inspiration to all of us.

Wendi was born in South Africa. When she was one year old, her family moved to Denmark, her mother's native home. They lived there until Wendi was six and then moved back to South Africa. Her family moved frequently, sometimes more than once a year within both South Africa and Denmark, and then just before Wendi finished high school, they moved to North America.

Wendi was a beautiful, creative, and talented child who loved to write. Often letting her creativity run wild, she invented imaginative, passionate stories. She dreamed of becoming an author one day. When she was twelve, however, her family was torn apart by an antagonistic divorce that caused her a great deal of pain and confusion.

The frequent moves in her childhood combined with this difficult divorce left her longing for stability and a sense of belonging. Although she developed excellent coping strategies and appeared outwardly to be fine, she lost touch with the child she had been, with her creativity, and with her dreams of becoming a writer. When she was nineteen she found—she thought—the security she craved in the person of a successful, well-established lawyer eight years her senior. Eventually they married and by the time Wendi was twenty-eight she was the mother of two beautiful daughters. By the time she was thirty, the marriage had failed. She says, "Somewhere along the line I realized that I had lost the connection with who I was and with the dreams for my life. I hadn't given myself time to grow up and truly discover what I was capable of."

For the next ten years Wendi struggled to find herself, succeeding in some ways and failing in others. She returned to university and obtained a degree in communications, found a job at an internationally respected financial services company, and rapidly began climbing up the corporate ladder:

> I moved into a small house of my own with my girls after my divorce, and tried to create a home that was an expression of who I am. I created a small lush garden that was the envy of my neighbors. But I was still rushing ahead by going back for a degree in communications and then following that with a full-time demanding job in public relations and corporate communications. I had attained my goal of becoming a "writer"—but somehow it didn't count. My career advanced quickly and before I knew it I was in a very stressful job that was in no way creative or aligned with my values...I was desperately unhappy with my work and really did not like who I was. I felt I was sacrificing who I was and my dreams for this great title and pay check. And I was.

Through all this good things were happening too. Her daughters were blossoming, and she eventually met and married a man whom she describes as someone who celebrates who she is and supports her desire to fulfill her dreams. Still, as the years passed she became increasingly aware that in spite of all the joy she was finding in her family, something was missing in her life. Occasionally she would take out the journals she had written in her teens, look back at that beautiful child who had been filled with such passion, intensity, and creative fire and weep because she had been left behind and, Wendi believed, lost forever. But of course the passionate spirit of that child was still alive and well— Wendi only needed to reach down deep enough to find it. Just about the time Wendi was taking the final steps necessary to make this reconnection occur, she wrote:

> How could I have lost her? I have been so sad for so long because I lost her. I have cried so many tears reading her journals, thinking her thoughts and knowing her dreams. Knowing she was gone. How lonely and alone I have felt. How abandoned and hopeless. How pointless. And how heartless it has been to try to go on without her. I have felt like half a person, like an empty facade, a shell moving blindly ahead. How uncomfortable I was in my skin because I wasn't all there. How awkward it has been trying to soldier along when I was half missing.

One reason Wendi was able to recognize how deeply she missed this passionate, creative side of herself was that she had never completely buried it. Even though she had lost touch with her creative urge for large blocks of time in her life, she was intuitively open enough to let it begin to rise up again and again—especially when she was in difficulty. She began writing in a journal as a child of twelve when her parents' acrimonious divorce threatened to overwhelm her. Although she stopped for several years during her first marriage, she began journaling again when she realized the relationship was seriously faltering. She even made a giant stab at letting her creativity flow when she was nineteen and dropped the science courses she'd been taking to concentrate on the arts. She says:

> Now I realize that I was desperately trying to connect with that creativity and build my life around that. I studied Fine Arts at university for eighteen months and then dropped out—it was just too difficult to reconcile my life as a nineteen-year-old student with that of being a partner in a relationship with a lawyer eight years ahead of me in lifestyle. I had gone in wanting to explore my creativity and understand where that could take me, but found it easier to abandon "me" than to question the bigger mistake I was making in my life.

When Wendi returned to university as a thirty-year-old who needed to find a means of making a living, she made what was at least a partial attempt at reconnecting with her creativity by choosing communications, a career path that would at least allow her to keep writing—even if it was not the passionate fiction she'd written as a dreamy young girl or the fine literature she longed to write.

About three years after Wendi had married for the second time, she took another major step on her path towards personal growth and self-awareness. Problems at work and general unhappiness with her job increased until she finally decided to do something about it and entered counseling sponsored by an employee assistance program. With the help of the counselor she began to delve deeper into her psyche and began to realize that many of the problems she found in the workplace were really difficulties that stemmed from issues within herself. As Wendi worked on these issues and took increasing responsibility for the state of her happiness, her situation at work improved. But more importantly, her meeting with this counselor and the hard inner work she did on herself set the stage—although she didn't know it at the time—for her reconnection with both her creativity and her spirituality. The next stage in this process occurred when, interestingly enough, the counselor recommended that she read *The Fiery Muse*. In a letter she wrote to me later she said:

> I was away from my work and surrounded by sun and warmth and my girls. The book was a revelation to me. I connected with your notion of spirituality and realized that it was something I had been yearning for, for a long time. I had chosen to be confirmed in a United Church when I was fourteen and loved the process, learning and meaning, but lost connection with it as a teenager. I had been hungry for a connection with something larger than myself for most of my life, and yet I had done little to fulfill that hunger.

About a year after this I happened to lead a workshop in the city where Wendi lived and had the pleasure of having her take part in it. During the workshop we worked on a series of creative visualization exercises that would help the participants create a space where they were protected from the harsh inner voice of criticism that so often plagues our creative work (rather like the Creativity Exercise we did in Chapter Two). In one of these exercises Wendi's unconscious mind created a lush, green, and quiet forest. The next day she wrote:

> I visited my woods again. I was there yesterday, standing at the edge
> of a path. In the dappled sunlight, warm breeze and rustling leaves I
> heard the birds again and could feel the calm. This time I moved
> forward to the protected glade and found a pool. Before it had been
> an empty meadow. Today, water. The light glistened on the water
> and I saw me. I've come to lead "me" forward.

Later in the day Wendi began to realize that the "me" she was leading
forward was none other than the passionate child she had abandoned
when she was twelve:

> I saw me today. I am at my core what I have always known...I stood
> tall and unclothed. So calm. Confident in my knowing and strength.
> I beckoned to that part of me that sat, small and hunched on that
> mossy bank. That girl was calm too. She knew that I had come. This
> image is one with me. I don't need to hurry. I don't need to worry. I
> don't need to be afraid. We are together now. As I sat on the rock and
> looked at her, standing tall and white on the dark water...I see her, I
> recognize her and I know her. We can move forward now. I can stop
> my frantic search, my running, my racing. She is here. She knows
> where we want to go. She's been waiting for me to find her. She's
> been patient and calm as I've raced, and hurried and worried along
> my way to her.

Although Wendi ended that day's writing with a sense of serenity
and calmness about the future, she did not know how she and her
inner creative spirit would choose the next path or find their
direction. The next morning she began her writing with even more
questions about where she would go and how she could hold onto
the serenity she had claimed:

> I saw me yesterday. Now what? Where from here? Why now? So
> many questions about what lies ahead...How do we move from this
> place of water and light? We stand in the warmth and shelter of this
> place of being. How do we move to the world of doing? The same
> gentle wood still surrounds us. The soft green paths lead in so many
> directions. The birds still sing. The leaves still rustle and all are
> oblivious to me and us...Do we have to leave this place of water and

light? Can we stay here with a purpose? Can we carry this light with us? Will it beat warm and bright in our hearts as we travel? Can we keep this feeling of calm and strength, strength and calm? How do we walk together? How do I use her voice, her energy, her creativity? How do I share her with the world? Present "her" as "me"?

Throughout the rest of the day Wendi continued to open up and reach deeper into herself for the answers. During the final exercise she had a visualization that she described in the following piece; when she read it afterwards there was not one person in the room who was not moved.

> I am me. I stand at the center of the pond. White light flows from my robe, from my fingertips and falls to glitter on the water. Soft ripples and movement below me. Calmness and knowing. I stand tall and strong at the center point of the woods around me...Maybe if I still my own questions, the quiet will talk to me and tell me what I need to know. Maybe if I stop my movements, my running and searching, maybe if I stand quite still my hand will fall down next to me and touch my answer...

Wendi described standing in this place of stillness for some time and then wrote:

> Light flowing onto me, through me and from me. I illuminate the soft green bank around me. Tall trees stand as my companions in this space, in this quiet. The birds and leaves murmur to me. They know me. They see me. I am one with them. We come from the same creator and are here to sing our songs together...I am aglow and still, save for my feet on the path. I will carry that light with me. I will illuminate my way...

Even though Wendi's hunger for spiritual growth and creative expression was from time to time buried in her life, it eventually rose up and led her to this place of calm and certainty. Although this was a visualization exercise and not a mystical vision like Hildegard's, it's no coincidence that at this moment of reconnection and realization she stands bathed in light.

Wendi's journey has been much like so many of our own. Although it has been devoid of dramatic kundalini risings and profound mystical visions, it has clearly been one of transformation. Over time her desire to become closer to the Divine and to express her creativity to its fullest potential has become stronger and stronger—and, along with it, her intuitive understanding of the world around her and how she needs to live in it has continued to deepen and expand. With this deepening and expansion has come an ever-increasing awareness of how the powerful transformative energy that surges through her is connected to Mother Earth and rooted firmly in the body. Wendi's first experience of this came when she was only a child. Interestingly enough, Wendi didn't recall this experience until fairly recently.

About six months after she wrote the above material, she enrolled in an eight-week workshop led by a former Catholic priest and a psychotherapist who also teaches meditation. The purpose of the course was to meet once a week and explore spirituality and spiritual experience from a "non-church" perspective.

During the first evening each of the participants was asked to tell a little about their own spiritual history and experiences. When it came to be Wendi's turn to speak she suddenly realized she had always carried with her a sense of spirituality—an awareness of being connected to the earth and to the universe in a way that was much larger and deeper than the limits of her self. Quite without expecting it, she found herself talking about a childhood experience that had been buried in her psyche for many years and only resurfaced at that very moment:

> It occurred when I was about eight or ten years old. We were living in South Africa at the time and would go and spend weekends in a small beach community, on the coast north of Durban, called Umdloti. I made a habit of rising early, at 5 or 6 am, with my father to go with him across the road to the beach to fish. He fished and I wandered along the beach lost in my thoughts and dreams. The sun would only just be rising and the beach was generally deserted except for a few ardent fishermen, like my father. On this one particular morning I sat down on the sand and watched as the sun started to rise above the horizon, far out into the Indian Ocean. I remember the cool surface of the sand, and how I wiggled my toes down into yesterday's warmth. My fingers idly caressed and filtered the sand. The ocean was calm and almost still—a strange phenomenon that

happens only during those early dawn hours. There were small waves breaking at the shore, but the rest of that mighty Indian Ocean lay almost as calm as a lake. I watched as the sun started to crest above the horizon. I remember feeling transfixed as it reached out one long finger of light that seemed directed at me and no one else in the world. It was blinding as it glinted off the water and straight into my eyes. I sat, a small hunched child who all of a sudden felt one with the earth and the universe around her. I could feel my connection to the sand, the air and the water. I could feel an energy rising within me to meet that great line of light. I remember thinking that this felt special, it felt like something bigger than me. In my eight-year-old mind it felt like the creator of the earth was speaking directly to me —showing me my connection to him and his place inside of me. I know I sat a very long time that morning feeling as if there was a flow of energy from me and to me—back and forth from the earth and from God. I felt filled with light and a sense of having experienced something special. Slowly the sun rose and that finger of light became wider until it engulfed the entire beach around me—and I felt released from its direct pull.

Wendi never told anyone about this experience on the beach, and it slowly slipped from her conscious memory. From the moment she was able to verbalize this experience, however, she realized that she has always known at some level that it was a moment of divine connection for her—a connection that existed within her and, at the same time, between her and a powerful cosmic creative force. Ever since the memory resurfaced, Wendi has been able to visualize that moment on the beach exactly as it happened. Each time she does, she re-experiences the pull and surge of energy once again in a very physical way. She feels the energy flowing from the cosmos and manifesting in her body.

Since she recovered the memory of her experience on the beach, Wendi has continued to express herself creatively and to do her spiritual work. She says her friends notice that she is calmer and more peaceful, and her family delight in the fact that she laughs more, takes more joy in life in general, and is quite simply a lot more fun. The change in herself that was at the core of all this was brought home to her not long ago:

As I stood on a busy downtown corner a couple of months ago surrounded by strangers and waiting for the light to change, I suddenly realized that I felt fully aware of myself. No longer did my body and skin feel alien to me. No longer did I feel uncomfortable and as if I didn't fit. I felt strong, proud and very feminine. In fact, I felt somehow divine. I felt as if there was a cord from the top of my head leading up into the sky connecting me directly with my creator. I realize that I now feel as if I carry an essence of that creator within me all the time as I move about my life. I see myself as divinely feminine now. I feel more powerful—and yet more gentle and caring than I ever have. I am even more sexual than I ever was. That moment on the street corner felt like a celebration and a confirmation of who I am and what I have come to know about myself.

Although Wendi wasn't particularly aware of it at the time, the intensely physical nature of these occurrences is extremely significant. In each of her earlier experiences, Wendi was acutely aware of the sensation being in her body. This awareness came together even more clearly as she stood on the street corner realizing for the first time that her body and skin were no longer alien to her.

Wendi had re-owned her body. This allowed her to take the next step—a realization that the divine feminine was not only housed in her body but was, in fact, one with her body. In doing this Wendi was experiencing—on a very physical level—a truth that has been known for ages but lost to most of us today: the divine feminine represents not just God but God-with-us—the Divine with us physically as well as spiritually. The Divine in the here and now.

Embracing the Process of Transformation

Chapter Six is about transformation. The personal stories and the information about Sophia and Shakti from the sacred texts are telling us that the divine feminine is gradually transforming us, gently propelling us along our spiritual path.

Embracing this process of transformation is essential both to owning the great power we hold within and to allowing creative inspiration to flow into our lives to the fullest. As positive as this process is, we may be unconsciously resisting it. This is because transformation implies change, and change is, of course, often painful. Being human, we quite naturally want to resist it!

The best antidote for this is becoming more deeply aware that Sophia is slowly but surely filling you with the breath of wisdom. The following exercise will help you see how this has been working in your own life.

1. Go to your picture albums—or photos stored on your computer—and pick pictures that include you at three different stages, for instance your childhood or teens, your thirties and now. If you're younger, just begin with childhood. (As always, it helps to pick pictures for these exercises that tug at your emotions.)

2. Arrange the photos chronologically in front of you, have writing materials handy, and enter that deep meditative space where you feel safe, protected, filled with light, and free from the harsh inner voice of criticism.

3. Allow yourself to go back in time and deeply reconnect with the person you were. While you'll be reminded of what was happening in your outer world at the time, the purpose is to focus on your inner world—who you were inside, independent of the success or failure occurring in your outer world.

4. Spend time in your deeply relaxed state with the first picture, considering your values, your attitudes, your beliefs, and feelings about yourself.

5. Bring your consciousness back to your inner light and, as you have learned in previous exercises, allow the light to flow upwards, concentrating and pulsing with your heart, and then to flow out your

hands, onto your pen and paper. Gently open your eyes and begin to note your impressions.

6. *Repeat this process for each picture, using a new sheet of paper for each one.*

7. *When you're done, compare these three stages. You will invariably find that your spiritual qualities, your inner characteristics, your level of awareness—the things that really matter!—are moving forward, improving with time. Sophia's breath is indeed bringing wisdom slowly but surely into your life.*

CHAPTER SEVEN

The Goddess Hidden in the Body

Myths and sacred stories from many traditions tell us about the embodiment of the divine feminine. Many of these tales have a great deal to teach us about how this power manifests in each of us as individuals and then pushes us onward in our search for spiritual growth and creative expression. One of the most powerful is the story that comes to us from Hindu scriptures of the marriage of Shiva and the divine cosmic Shakti who comes to earth in the form of the goddess Sati. This tale, as it's retold below, firmly supports the idea that the divine feminine represents "God-with-us"—the Divine that is one with us in the here and now.

When this idea first began to crystallize in my mind it occurred to me that, if it was indeed true, I should be able to find evidence of it in the Jewish and Christian traditions as well, and as you'll see in the material that follows this was indeed the case. Of all the discoveries I made researching this book this one had the most profound impact on me and my understanding of how the Divine works in our daily lives. For me, the experience of God has always been an extremely visceral one, especially since the first spiritual experience I ever had. As I explained in detail in *The Fiery Muse*, this experience occurred when I was about thirteen years old and was triggered by reading a letter from a spiritual mentor containing the words "God is love." This truth—one I had never encountered before—struck me with such force that it seemed to electrify my body. The sensation of physical energy was so great that I was compelled to run. Rushing to the pasture behind my house, I jumped on my horse without bridle or saddle and began to gallop through a storm that was raging across the desert. During this experience the waves of emotion and energy that were wracking my body seemed to radiate outwards until they made me one with my horse and then with the storm. Years later the similar but more intense experience that I described in Chapter One occurred while I was doing Tai Chi on the beach at dawn. For months after this waves of energy that originated in my pelvis flowed through my body. They burst orgasmically in my heart and sometimes near the base of my throat. During these experiences I was always intensely aware that the Divine was somehow with me.

By the time I had the latter experience I had learned that the process I was going through was somehow related to kundalini-shakti, but I hadn't even begun to understand how this might relate to the idea that the divine cosmic Shakti represents God-with-us. And I certainly had no idea that I would find scriptural evidence for a very similar concept in Judaism and Christianity.

In order to understand this more fully, we need to look in a little more detail at this idea of "God-with-us" as a concept. In Christianity the notion of a God that is "with us" stands in direct opposition to the idea of a God who exists somewhere away from us, above us, or far, far beyond us. In Christian theology these two differing views of God are expressed in the terms *immanence* and *transcendence*. Christian theologians have for centuries debated which of these terms describes the "true" nature of God.

The concept of the transcendent God is the one that has held the greatest sway in Christianity right up to modern times. This idea has encompassed a wide range of images, the most classic of these being an all-powerful bearded man in the clouds who sits on a golden throne and dispenses judgment on the world below. While the majority of Christians today have replaced this image of God as a "man" or a "human being" with a much less limited one, the idea persists for many Christians that God exists somewhere "away" from us: God is in heaven and we are here on earth. This is the God we have to lift our eyes to when we pray. Inherent in this image is the notion that God is difficult to reach—an idea that became entrenched in Western thinking by the early Catholic Church's insistence that ordinary people needed priests to act as intermediaries between them and God.

In contrast to this, Christians who think of God as being immanent hold images of a divine being that is close and approachable. St Augustine once described the immanent God as "one in whom we live, and move, and have our being". Some Christians carry this view even further and say that God exists not just all around us but also within us—within our hearts, our minds, and/or our souls. The word immanent, in fact, comes from the Latin root that means "indwelling". Some form of this immanent God is almost always the one the mystics talk about when they try to communicate what has happened to them during their profound spiritual experiences—this is because they are invariably trying to describe a direct experience of God, and it is only an immanent God that *can* be experienced directly. This is certainly what happened to me during the experience that was triggered by the idea that God is love: at that moment the overwhelming love that I felt pounding in my breast *was* God—it was the Divine manifesting in me and flowing out of me. It was a Divine I could touch, feel, and be one with.

Although this direct experience of God was a far cry from anything the true mystics describe, it was what first nudged me onto the spiritual path and, eventually, into my search for Shakti, Sophia, and Shekinah. Imagine then my excitement when I began to research these great cosmic feminine forces and discovered that each represented "God-with-us" in one way or another. This discovery came to me quite by accident and, although there may well be scholars who have noticed and written about this amazing phenomenon, I had not then—and still have not—ever come across their work.

This notion of the immanent God being, in fact, a goddess is naturally found much more easily in Hinduism than in Christianity or Judaism. The story of the marriage of Shiva and Sati is just one example of this. Bits and pieces of this story have been told in many Hindu scriptures, some that date at least three or four hundred years BCE. As the years passed, the story became much more fully developed. By the time the sacred *Purānas* were written, the story was being told in great detail. One of the most elaborate accounts of it is found in the *Kālikā Purāna*, a text that was probably compiled sometime during the ninth century CE. In retelling this story I have relied mostly on this *Purāna*, but I have also added a few details that are missing from this version but common in other texts.

In this story the goddess Sati is a manifestation of the cosmic feminine divine, Shakti. Sati's story begins in the early mists of time when the gods Vishnu and Brahma have both taken wives but when Shiva—the third god in the masculine Hindu trinity—has not. Shiva, as an ascetic, spends his time meditating and practicing austerities; he has no interest in women or anything else in the material world. This ascetic behavior creates a number of problems for the other gods. First, they realize that unless Shiva, the most benevolent and auspicious of gods, becomes more directly involved in creation, the world will be bereft of all benevolence and good fortune. Second, the gods are worried about the psychic energy and heat generated by Shiva's intense practice of meditation and yoga. When this energy becomes excessive it drives Shiva to the frenzied dancing that shakes the universe, and the gods are afraid that Shiva might one day generate so much heat and energy that he will destroy the world.

Given these worries, Vishnu, Brahma, and the other deities come together to figure out what action they should take. After much discussion they realize that a wonderful solution to their problems would be to get Shiva to take a wife. A beautiful woman would distract him from his austere spiritual practices and bring him, so to speak, out of the clouds and down to earth where his auspiciousness is so badly needed. This would also have an added benefit: sexual dalliance with a wife would siphon off some of Shiva's powerful pent-up psychic energy.

After congratulating themselves on coming up with such a fine solution, the gods and goddesses suddenly realize they are now faced with an even bigger problem: where will they ever find a goddess who is worthy of the great god Shiva—or one who is seductive enough to tempt this tireless ascetic away from his yoga and meditation?

The deities finally decide their only hope lies in asking Shakti herself—who is identified as the primal force of the cosmos in the text—for help. Brahma volunteers to be the one to beseech Shakti because he is especially eager to see Shiva seduced by a woman. Known as the "Creator" god in the masculine trinity, Brahma is particularly concerned about the threat Shiva's increasing pent-up energy poses to all of creation.

Brahma begins to pray to her devoutly and asks a great god named Daksa to pray with him. He then speeds off to Shakti to ask for her help. Eventually the great goddess becomes convinced that the concerns about Shiva are valid and that her help is needed. She agrees to be born and take the form of a beautiful goddess who will eventually become Shiva's wife. She decides that her parents will be Daksa and his wife—but she sends a warning to Daksa that if he ever fails to show her the proper respect she will leave her bodily form immediately.

Brahma hurries back to the other gods, tells them the good news, and makes sure Daksa and his wife will be the new goddess's parents. They consent but, as we discover later in the tale, Daksa only does this with some reluctance. Although he is thrilled that the great goddess herself will be manifesting in his family, it has dawned on him that this means Shiva will eventually become his son-in-law. Secretly he feels that Shiva—who is known to dance in creation grounds, crunch bones, wear skulls, and smear himself with ash—does not behave as a great god should. Still, he keeps his reservations to himself, and in due time the most beautiful baby girl in all creation is born to him and his wife; they give her the name Sati.

As soon as she comes of age, Sati strikes out on her mission to seduce Shiva and convince him to marry her. Even though she is the most beautiful and alluring woman in the world, she rejects the idea of using her feminine wiles. Instead, she determines to attract Shiva's attention with the intensity and sincerity of her spiritual practice. With this in mind she begins to meditate, practice austerities, and worship Shiva with great devotion. Eventually Shiva takes notice of this devotion and appears before her. Shiva is greatly impressed by the depth of her devotion, the fortitude with which she has endured her austerities, and her extraordinary loveliness. Before long he begins to fall in love and for the very first time feels sexual desire. Soon overcome by these powerful emotions, he offers to grant Sati her longtime wish for marriage with him. She accepts but tells him he must make the proper arrangements for the wedding through her father, Daksa.

Reluctantly, Daksa gives his consent and at Shiva's urging the preparations for the marriage ceremony are arranged with alacrity. When the great day dawns, the gods and goddesses sweep in on the wind from the furthest reaches of the cosmos. Brahma and Shiva arrive in chariots followed by long retinues of joyous men and women who dance along beating on drums, blowing on conch shells, and clapping their hands. Sati shines in all her radiant glory, and the ceremony proceeds. On the earth below, fragrant winds blow, flowers rain down, and all who are ill regain their health.

When the ceremony is over, Shiva places Sati in front of him on the great bull he often rides and the two fly off to his beautiful dwelling place in the Himalayas. There they stay for twenty-four cosmic years, delighting each other with their lovemaking. Sati makes friends with some of the other goddesses, and Shiva continues to meditate and perform his ascetic practices but in a much more moderate way than before. He truly longs for nothing but Sati and he never tires of her. He brings her wild flowers, decorates her body with ornaments, covers her with lotuses, and combs her hair. Their love and passion for each other increases as time goes by.

Eventually, however, trouble enters paradise. One day Sati notices a commotion in the distant heavens near her father's home and goes off to see what it is. As she approaches she sees that every god and goddess in the universe is headed towards her father's home. What's more, as she looks around she sees that all of the human beings, animals, insects, and plants are on their way there too. Curious, she speeds to her father's to find out what is happening. There she discovers that Daksa is holding a great ritual sacrifice to honor *Brahman*—who is, as opposed to Brahma, the ultimate universal divine presence that exists as the Absolute. She also discovers that she and Shiva are the only two beings in the entire cosmos who have not been invited. When Sati confronts her father about this, Daksa finally reveals that he has never been very happy having Shiva as a son-in-law. He is disgusted by Shiva's appearance, his graveyard dancing, bone-crunching and other offensive habits. He calls Shiva a "skull-wearer" and says no one who wears skulls or who consorts with skull-wearers—in other words, Sati herself—is welcome at the sacrifice.

Sati is enraged at this affront to her and her beloved husband. She reminds him that she had warned him that if he should ever show her disrespect she would leave her body. When Daksa refuses to make amends, Sati begins to meditate and quickly amasses such tremendous heat that she bursts into flames and immolates herself. When the great blaze dies down, Shakti has returned to the heavens and Sati's remains lie back in her Himalayan home.

Just as he finishes his morning prayers and meditation, Shiva hears a great wailing on the mountain. He mounts his bull and rushes home as swift as the wind. He finds Sati's lifeless body and is overcome with grief. When he discovers why Sati has died, he becomes incensed. Fire and meteors fly from his eyes; his face flames like the sun at the end of time, and he rushes to Daksa's great sacrifice. In his fury, Shiva creates the most terrifying monster of all time. This great beast, followed by legions of other demons, begins to help Shiva destroy the sacrifice.

When the destruction is over, Shiva remembers Sati's body and speeds home. Wailing in anguish, he picks the body up and carries it through the heavens. As Shiva's hot tears fall they begin to flood parts of the earth below with scalding water.

Seeing this, Vishnu and Brahma become worried that Shiva's tears will soon deluge and scorch the entire world. They know he will continue to grieve as long as he holds Sati's body in his arms. They also realize it will never decompose naturally because of Shiva's great psychic power. The two gods beg him to let it go, but they can't convince him. When the flooding from Shiva's anguished tears worsens, Vishnu and Brahma realize they have to do something fast. Using the power of yoga to make themselves invisible, they enter into the body of Sati. As Shiva continues to fly above the earth, they cause bits of her body to fall.

As these pieces of Sati's body fall to the ground, they become embodied in the earth. Once the last of Sati's body has fallen, Shiva realizes what has happened and goes to join her there. Still grieving, he rushes to the place where her *yoni*—the Sanskrit word for vagina—has embedded itself in the earth. There, he turns himself into a phallic-shaped stone linga and sits beside her.

Over time Shiva's grief begins to lessen, and Brahma and Vishnu help him see the terrible destruction his sorrow has caused and that he must somehow overcome his grief. Brahma is able to ease Shiva's pain by letting him know that Shakti has promised to be reborn in one hundred years as the goddess Parvati and that she will marry Shiva again and bear him a son. This knowledge gives Shiva some solace, but he also continues to take great comfort from Shakti's "presence" in the earth.

The worshipers of both Shiva and Shakti were also meant to take comfort from this presence. Over the years detailed lists of exactly where the fragments of Sati's body fell to earth were compiled and recorded in the *Purānas* and other sacred texts. These locations came to be known as *pithas*. It is believed that at each of these places, Shakti established an abode and is ever-present there. The pithas are considered the holiest places on earth by many Hindus, especially those who worship either Shiva or the divine mother, Shakti. The holiest of all is the site near the town of Kamakhya in Northern India where Sati's yoni fell. It is important to realize, however, that Shakti's embodiment in the earth turned more than just the pithas into holy places; it made all of India and, by extension, the entire world into a sacred place.

This story tells us in no uncertain terms that Shakti is God-with-us—she is the immanent Divine, the Divine that is embodied within each one of us. The very same is true of Shekinah—the divine feminine in the Jewish mystical tradition known as Kabbalah. My first inkling of this extraordinary similarity between Shakti and Shekinah came when I read a passage in Gershom Scholem's book *The Mystical Shape of the Godhead: Basic Concepts in the Kabbalah* concerning how in Hasidic Judaism—an extremely orthodox tradition with a strong mystical strain—Shekinah is believed to be quite literally embedded in the earth in Israel. For some Hasidic Jews this means that surrendering a piece of Israeli land is quite literally like chopping off one of Shekinah's arms or legs and casting it away.

In many other Jewish traditions Shekinah is believed to dwell, if not in the land itself, then at least with the "Community of Israel". Known in Hebrew as the *Kenesseth Ysra'el*, this is the collective body of Jewish people wherever they may be. Thus, Shekinah has long been held to be "present" in a very immediate sense with Jews everywhere just as Shakti dwells as the divine spark in all children of creation.

In order to understand more fully how Shekinah relates to Shakti
—especially in terms of the embodiment of the Divine—it's necessary
to look at how this concept has developed over the centuries, first in
mainstream Judaism and later in Kabbalah. Because it is almost
impossible to understand Shekinah without exploring this development, this chapter contains quite a bit more research material than
any other part of the book.

One of the best places to begin this exploration is in the work of
Gershom Scholem. An eminent Jewish scholar who was a professor
at Hebrew University in Jerusalem until his death in 1982, Scholem
was the first mainstream Jewish scholar to do serious academic
research on the history and teachings of Kabbalah. Scholem explained that centuries before Shekinah came to be associated with "the
feminine face of God" as it is so widely today, the term referred
simply to the presence of God. In fact, the word Shekinah comes
from the Hebrew word for "indwelling" just as the English word
immanence comes from the Latin for the same term. In early Jewish
texts this divine presence was usually depicted as being in places like
tabernacles or temples and was often described using phrases like
"the radiance of the Shekinah" or "the wings of the Shekinah".

According to Scholem and other Jewish authorities, these types
of references to Shekinah as God's presence are the only allusions to
Shekinah found in the traditional Jewish texts, the Torah and the
Talmud, and are indeed the only ones found in any other early
mainstream Jewish texts. This means there is absolutely no indication
in Jewish biblical scripture that Shekinah was seen as being anything
more than an attribute of God—a sort of radiance that signified his
presence. This radiance was not seen as separate from God in any
way, nor was there any hint that it was feminine in any sense other
than being a noun of feminine gender. And it is important to respectfully realize that this is still the view held by much of official
Judaism today.

Over the centuries, however, an image of Shekinah as a divine
feminine being slowly emerged in both Jewish mystical tradition
and fairly widespread popular Jewish opinion. During this slow
evolution the questions of whether Shekinah was separate from God
and, if so, still divine, and whether this being was in fact feminine
remained central to the debate about the true nature of Shekinah. In

fact, these questions are still relevant to our understanding of Shekinah today.

Within the bounds of the early rabbinic tradition (mainstream Judaism based on the Torah, the Talmud, and the other official Jewish scriptures) Shekinah was clearly divine, but was seen simply as an *aspect* of God, one that was, as mentioned above, generally identified with God's presence or immanence. In another sense, Shekinah was associated with God's glory. The Hebrew word for this glory is *Kavod*; this term carries with it the image of the indescribably brilliant radiance that streams from the divine presence.

This narrow view of Shekinah began to change gradually as more and more references were made to her over the years in the rabbinic texts known as the Midrash and the Haggadah. (These are, respectively, a collection of interpretations by different rabbis on the laws and customs found in the Old Testament and a body of legends, anecdotes, and parables that elucidate the religious and ethical principles of Judaism.) During the Middle Ages Shekinah became increasingly personified in these writings. While these parables and anecdotes technically adhered to the idea that Shekinah was not in any way separate from God, the imagery being used—for instance, conversations between Shekinah and God—made Shekinah *seem* more and more like an actual separate being. Eventually, this began to present a problem for Jewish theologians that was much like the one early Christian theologians had had with Sophia: if Shekinah was in anyway separate from God, she couldn't be divine since the rigid monotheism of Judaism demanded that there be one and only one divine being.

According to Scholem, in order to get around this problem Jewish philosophers eventually began to refer to Shekinah not just as an aspect of God but as a separate being—a creation of God's that had its own free will. Unfortunately, in gaining this somewhat more separate identity, Shekinah lost some of her divine nature. Still, many philosophers over the next few centuries kept Shekinah in a very elevated—if not strictly divine—position.

One far-reaching and very beautiful description of her was written by a great medieval Jewish philosopher named Saadiah Gaon. He said that Shekinah was the same as the light first created by God. Saadiah said this light was the radiance of God; it was more sublime than the sight of angels and more enormous than all creation. When God's holy prophets saw this light, he said, they would know that the revelations they received were authentic and that they truly came from God. As Saadiah's opinions spread, Shekinah became increasingly accepted as being synonymous with the primordial light that was created at the beginning of time—much as Shakti is held to be—in spite of the fact that there was little scriptural evidence to support this.

This image was developed towards the end of the eleventh century by a famous Spanish rabbi named Judah ben Barzillai. He made the bold statement that Shekinah was not just a created being, this radiant creature was the *first* of all created beings. Interestingly enough, Scholem points out that ben Barzillai also equated Shekinah with the Holy Spirit:

> When the thought arose in God of creating a world, He first created the Holy Spirit, to be a sign of his divinity, which was seen by the prophets and angels. And He created the image of the Throne of his Glory, to be a throne for the Holy Spirit, called the Glory of our God, which is a radiant brilliance and a great light that shines upon all his other creatures. And that great light is called the Glory of God, blessed be his Name...And the Sages call this great light Shekhinah...

Other important medieval rabbis built on this imagery. One, Rabbi Moses ha-Darshan, who was from Narbonne, France, made an extremely important contribution by conceptualizing Shekinah not just as the primordial light but—again like Shakti—as the "primal matter of creation".

Thus, during the early Middle Ages, a picture emerged in mainstream Judaism of Shekinah as a created being that was probably God's first creation and certainly his most subtle and sublime. Still, this meant that Shekinah was distinct from God and therefore technically not divine. And there was still no reference to Shekinah being feminine.

During this same period the various mystical strains that would eventually provide the basis for Kabbalah were beginning to come together outside mainstream Judaism. Since that time this tradition has developed into a vast and enormously complex spiritual philosophy—one that is far beyond the scope of this book to describe in detail. Nonetheless, in order to understand how Shekinah compares to other conceptions of the divine feminine like Shakti, we need to take a look at a few of Kabbalah's basic tenets—with the qualification that Kabbalists from different times and places have interpreted each of these concepts in some very different ways.

According to the Kabbalah scholar Neil Asher Silberman, the two most important Kabbalistic sources for these concepts are the *Sefer ha-Bahir* (*Book of Brilliance*) and the *Sefer ha-Zohar* (*Book of Splendor*). The *Bahir* is generally agreed to be a collection of fragments from a wide range of times and sources that were ultimately compiled in Provence, France, sometime in the middle of the twelfth century. The *Zohar* appeared somewhat later. It was first brought to light in Spain in 1286 CE by a teacher named Moses de Leon. Although de Leon claimed—and some modern-day Kabbalists respectfully believe—the book was the work of an unknown author who lived many centuries earlier, most scholars believe that de Leon either wrote the book entirely himself or, more likely, wrote some parts of it and compiled others from earlier sources. Regardless of its exact source, the *Zohar* is an extraordinary work that, numbering some 1,700 pages, has provided the basis for Kabbalistic teaching for seven centuries.

It is in the *Bahir* and the *Zohar* that Shekinah finally emerges as both divine and feminine. Her incontestable divinity is based in this tradition on the fact that the Kabbalists never saw Shekinah as a "created being" who was separate from God the way the medieval philosophers did. Indeed, Shekinah was seen to be an integral aspect of the Divine. In this sense, she was held to be one of ten *Sefiroth*—often translated as "potencies" or "creative forces"—that Kabbalists believe form the very essence of the Godhead. Operating together through God's living force, these potencies maintain the universe, flowing not only outward into creation but also back into the Godhead.

Unfortunately for the Kabbalists, this dynamic picture of the Godhead stood in direct opposition to the very essence of traditional Judaism, where God is held to be immutable, unchanging, and unmoving. In order to get around this huge stumbling block, the early Kabbalists began to develop the concept that there were two "tiers" of the Godhead. The Kabbalists called the first of these levels *Ein-*

Sof, a term sometimes defined as the Oneness, the Infinite, or Un-differentiated Unity. This aspect of the Godhead was said to be, like the traditional God of Judaism, completely unknowable, unimagin-able, and immeasurable. As such, the Ein-Sof was beyond gender and was seen as neither masculine nor feminine. The second level was seen as God's dynamic, creative aspect—the one that thrust itself outward and expressed itself in creation and in world-main-taining activities. This, then, was the aspect of God that expressed itself in the ten Sefiroth. In one sense the Sefiroth were held to con-stitute the ultimate divine unity; in another, they were seen as inde-pendent "beings" that could manifest certain attributes, take shape, flow out, and animate creation.

Although different Kabbalists over the years have debated exactly how the Sefiroth function and what roles they play, they have remain-ed central to the teachings of Kabbalah right up to modern times. Often grouped in triads, the first three Sefiroth are *Keter* (Crown), *Chokhmah* (Wisdom), and *Binah* (Insight). The second group includes *Chesed* (Grace), *Din* (Judgment), and *Tif'ereth* (Mercy). The final triad consists of *Netsach* (Endurance), *Hod* (Splendor), and *Yesod* (Foundation). This ninth Sefirah, Yesod, is also frequently known as *Tsaddik*, which means "the righteous one".

These nine complete the picture of the creative forces that move in complex patterns flowing upward and outward, but also back into the Godhead. The nine are seen as basically, but not exclusively, masculine in nature. As the active, living force of the Godhead, they also represent the procreative force of the universe and as such flow towards and are united in the tenth Sefirah, *Malkhuth* (Kingdom). This tenth Sefirah is known more commonly as Shekinah.

Throughout the history of Kabbalah, two images have been used to portray this dynamic flow of the potent energies contained in the Sefiroth. One is the "Tree of Life", the other the "Body of Adam". The imagery of the Tree of Life comes originally from a passage in the *Bahir* where it says that God's creative forces grow into creation like a tree that is nourished by the waters of divine wisdom. In accordance with this, the Tree of Life is visualized as being upside down with the three highest Sefiroth, Crown, Wisdom, and Insight, forming its roots. The next six Sefiroth, Grace, Judgment, Mercy, Endurance, Splendor, and Foundation, flow upward and outward to form the

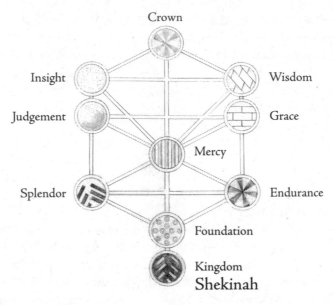

trunk and branches of the tree. In their role as the creative/procreative forces of the Godhead, these nine unite and flow into Shekinah. Here, Shekinah comes into her glory as the feminine aspect of the Divine. She receives the creative forces and gives birth to the world.

As Kabbalah developed and Shekinah became firmly identified as both feminine and still divine, she gradually began to appear in parables and metaphors in the archetypal feminine roles of daughter, virgin, bride, mother, and wise woman in more mainstream Jewish texts. Over time the imagery associated with Shekinah as the feminine aspect of God broke out of the bounds of Kabbalah and gained a widespread popularity among many traditional Jews. This trend has continued up to the present day. The fact that this has occurred even though there is no basis for it in traditional Judaic texts is, according to Scholem, evidence of just how extraordinarily powerful the image of Shekinah is. In another reference he even went so far as to say this provides strong evidence that this image of a Shekinah that is both divine and feminine answers a "fundamental and primal need" in the human soul.

In spite of all the power associated with images of Shekinah, especially the ones of her as the divine mother who gives birth to the material world, it is necessary to emphasize that Shekinah is seen as passive and receptive rather than active in Kabbalah. As the tenth Sefirah, she receives the divine emanations and creative forces of the upper nine Sefiroth. They flow into her and flow out of her into the created world. She gives birth to the world, but she is definitely not seen as the creative force per se or as the creatrix of the world. This puts her quite at odds with Shakti, whose very name means "power" and who is seen as the creative force par excellence.

In the early stages of my research into Kabbalah this perplexed me a great deal because Shekinah seemed so similar to Shakti in so many fundamental ways: she was seen as the primordial light and indeed the elemental essence at the very basis of all creation. She was the radiant divine light that told God's holy prophets their revelations were authentic. And beyond all this, she was seen as giving birth to the material world. How, I wondered, could she *not* be seen as full of power or, at the very least, active. As I delved into Kabbalah a little deeper I began to find answers to my questions. I came to learn that although Shekinah is most clearly identified with the tenth or lowest Sefirah, she is also associated with the third Sefirah, Binah. These two manifestations of the divine feminine principle are often referred to as the lower Shekinah and the upper Shekinah. Binah is not only active, she has an integral role in the very act of creation.

In *The Mystical Shape of the Godhead*, Scholem discussed the meaning of the upper and lower Shekinahs and in doing so answered my question about the active power of Shekinah even more clearly than I could have hoped:

> Two conceptions of the principle of femininity are realized and expressed in these images. As the upper Shekinah of the Sefirah of Binah, femininity is the full expression of ceaseless creative power— it is receptive, to be sure, but is spontaneously and incessantly transformed into an element that gives birth, as the stream of eternally flowing divine life enters into it. One might almost say, to use the terms of Indian religion, that the upper Shekinah is the Shakti of the latent God, it is entirely active energy, in which what is concealed within God is externalized.

Exactly how all this works becomes a little clearer when we look in more detail at the conceptualization of the Godhead that the

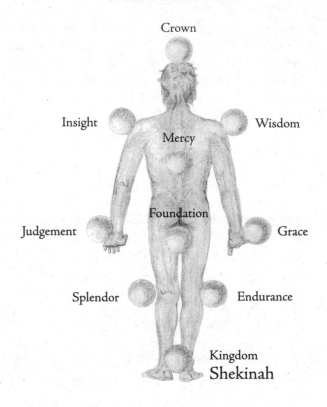

Crown

Insight Wisdom

Mercy

Judgement Grace

Foundation

Splendor Endurance

Kingdom
Shekinah

Kabbalists called the Body of Adam. In this image, the body itself—or more accurately the mystical shape of the body—is associated with the infinite, undifferentiated Divine and the Sefiroth are associated with various parts of the body where they function in virtually the same way they do in the Tree of Life. The three uppermost Sefiroth form the head, with Keter hovering like a radiant crown above Wisdom and Insight, which are seen to be the two guiding principles of divine thought. The right side—particularly the arms—represents God's merciful qualities and the left his sterner ones: the right arm is Grace, the left Judgment; the right leg is Splendor, and the left Endurance. Mercy, located somewhat close to the heart, provides the point of divine balance for these oppositional forces. All these creative forces meet in the phallus, the Foundation or the Righteous One. From this position, they are poised as the creative/procreative powers on the brink of flowing out into the universe.

They are completely powerless to do so, however, without the presence of the divine feminine, Shekinah. She forms the opening at the tip of the phallus on the mystical body of Adam. From this position, she fulfills her vital role in creation. She makes it possible for the creative forces to move from the spiritual realm into the material. But she does much more than this. She flows into the material world and remains there as the divine spark at the heart of each and every created thing.

In these upper and lower roles, Shekinah has a transformative function much like the one Shakti has. In her upper position, Binah, one of her most important tasks is to transform the pure undifferentiated divine Wisdom that is found in Chokhmah into a form that can be separated out and made to flow into the next six Sefiroth. In a similar way in her lower position, she transforms the pure undifferentiated light and life force of the Godhead by refracting it—almost as if she were a mirror. She then sends this less pure, reflected version of herself out into the created universe. Because this reflected life force is now less than perfect it cannot flow back into the Godhead.

This means that by sending herself out into creation Shekinah makes an unimaginable sacrifice: she allows a certain aspect of herself to be separated from the divine Oneness. Kabbalah makes it clear that this state of separation is agonizing for Shekinah and that she has spent the eons since our exile from the Garden of Eden yearning to be reunited with the Godhead.

But no matter how torturous this state of separation may be for her or how overwhelming her longing is, she never forsakes her place on earth or with the children of the covenant. She weeps with us when we are banished from Eden and from our homelands; she wanders with us in our long exile, and she wails with us in our grief. But as the immanence of the Divine she remains steadfastly with us, waiting for us to bring about divine union within ourselves so that she too can be wholly reunited with the Divine. Thus Shekinah is, like Shakti, truly God-with-us. She is the mother of the world, the embodiment of the Divine, and the living heart of God that beats within us and gives us life.

Kundalini-Shakti's Cradle

This chapter begins the exploration of the idea that the divine feminine represents God-with-us—God embodied not just with us on the earth but literally embodied within. This idea is, of course, clear in the traditions of Tantra and hatha yoga where Shakti is seen to be embodied in each and every one of us in her guise as kundalini-shakti.

In the story of Shiva and Sati, which tells us all this symbolically, it is no coincidence that the most sacred place on earth is the spot where Sati's yoni—her vagina—fell and became embedded. Nor is it a coincidence that this is the place where Shiva comes to rest, turning himself into a linga, a symbol for the phallus. The same is true for the fact that, in Kabbalah, the Shekinah is located at the tip of the phallus on the Body of Adam. All this imagery draws us to the relationship between sexual energy and the divine feminine as the creative force. It tells us this area of our body is not only sacred, it is the "home" of the divine feminine as she rests in our bodies. This is where kundalini-shakti lies, cradled in the pelvis.

As you will see in Chapter Thirteen, there is a clear relationship between kundalini, creativity, and sexual energy. Because of this, being comfortable with this part of your body is essential. Unfortunately, many of us—particularly women—are not. Some of us are still hampered by the notion, often subconscious, that anything to do with sex and sexuality is the antithesis of spirituality. Even more common, however, is a detachment that comes from forcing ourselves to ignore or "work through" all the pain associated with our pelvis and womb—from the misery of monthly cramps to the discomforts of pregnancy and the agony of childbirth.

The purpose of this exercise is to reconnect with this area of the body by focusing on it and allowing your mind to create an image that helps you identify with it as the abode of kundalini-shakti and, thus, the place from which all creative inspiration rises. This image might be anything from a cradle that holds the light of inspiration to a crucible filled with fire.

As an active meditation you might even want to physically create a symbol for this—model a small clay bowl you can burn incense in or weave a basket to hold bits of paper with creative ideas written on them. Directions for many projects like this can be found on the internet. One of my favorites *is for a basket that can be made out of old newspapers*—it seems so wonderfully symbolic to transform pages covered by such bad news into a basket that can be filled with light.*

1. *With pen and paper ready, sit cross-legged, if you are able, and enter that deep meditative space where you feel safe, protected, filled with light, and free from the harsh inner voice of criticism. Sit for a moment basking in this light.*
2. *Move your center of awareness to your pelvis. Be aware of the sensations of energy and movement that are normally not even noticed. If you become aware of sensations of sexual energy, sit with them comfortably and, after a time, see them being transmuted into light.*
3. *See your pelvis as the "container" that holds the power and potential of the Divine in your body. Ask for a symbol to represent this to you and allow it to rise up out of the light.*
4. *Write out a description of your symbol and how you interpret it. Later, draw or create your symbol if you like.*

* *To make this basket roll single pages of newsprint into very thin tubes. Mark the center of eight of the tubes and lay them out like evenly spaced spokes of a wheel. Pin the center to a piece of cardboard to hold the spokes until the basket starts to take shape. Starting a few inches from the center, begin weaving tubes of newsprint through the warp made by the spokes. Bending the spokes upward as you work to form the curve of the basket is made much easier if you wrap the first eight tubes around pieces of florist's wire—even a couple of pipe cleaners hooked together would work.*

In Body, In Spirit

During the time I spent in musty academic libraries, sometimes quite literally blowing the dust off books, searching out evidence for Shakti and Shekinah as the embodiment of the Divine in the earth and in ourselves, there was a little niggling question at the back of my mind about Sophia. For it was clear to me that if Sophia didn't have the same significance, my whole theory about how the Divine works in us and through us would simply not hold up.

But I shouldn't have worried. As soon as I had time to go back to the information I'd gathered on Sophia and began considering it with this question in mind, I found exactly what I was looking for. Many references to Sophia as the Divine-with-us can be discovered in the Old Testament. Some of the most beautiful are found in

Ecclesiasticus. Still part of the Bible used in Catholic churches, Ecclesiasticus is one of the books that was removed by the early Protestants and banished—along with a number of other books that refer extensively to Sophia—to the sort of "appendix" to the Bible that is known as the Apocrypha.

Ecclesiasticus was written by a Jewish teacher named Yeshua ben Sira, who lived in Jerusalem about 150 years before the birth of Christ. About twenty years later, Yeshua's grandson took the book to Egypt. In a Preface he eventually wrote to the book, the grandson tells us that upon moving to Egypt he found wonderful opportunities for education, became a scholar, and diligently struggled for several years to translate his grandfather's Hebrew manuscript into Greek—the language used there then— so that it could be published there. He goes on to say that he undertook this arduous task believing it was his duty to bring his grandfather's work to the world because it was a "legacy of great value" that contained deep insights and great wisdom.

This legacy of great value begins with a clear statement of how Sophia—called Wisdom in many translations—came to be embodied in the earth by saying that God created her before all else and then "infused her into all his works". This first passage of Ecclesiasticus then goes on to say that the Creator gave Sophia "in some measure" to every human being and to those who love God "in plenty". This description of Sophia being "with us" even goes so far as to say that she was not just created once at the beginning of time, she is in fact re-created when each human being is conceived and then grows with us in our mothers' wombs. This extraordinary description of Sophia ends by saying that the home she has built among us is everlasting and that she will keep faith with us for all time.

In another passage Sophia tells us how she swirled around the world like a mist until she finally came down and made her home in the earth. She then tells how she flourished in Zion:

> There I grew like a cedar of Lebanon,
> like a cypress on the slopes of Hermon,
> like a date-palm at En-gedi,
> like roses at Jericho...
> Like cinnamon or camel-thorn I was redolent of spices;
> I spread my fragrance like a choice myrrh...

I was like the smoke of frankincense in the sacred tent.
Like a terebinth I spread out my branches,
laden with honour and grace.
I put graceful shoots like the vine,
and my blossoms were a harvest of honour and wealth.

[Ecclus. 24: 10-17]

This beautiful passage becomes even more moving when some of the symbolism behind it is understood. The cedars that grew in Lebanon were renowned for their strength, their rich greenery, and the great height they achieved. Their roots were known to reach deep into the ground. En-gedi was a lush, verdant oasis located on the west side of the Dead Sea that was shaded by date-palms and blessed with both fresh flowing water and bubbling hot springs. A refuge from the scorching desert, it was widely associated with love and romance.

Jericho was also a place that had special significance. In biblical times it was known for the exceptional beauty of its "roses". These were lush plants we would probably call oleanders that had rich, rosy-pink blossoms and thick, gleaming evergreen leaves. Today in Jericho the vendors in the market stalls sell "roses of Jericho" that have their own special significance. They are a kind of dried tumbleweed that seems to miraculously come back to life when soaked in water.

In these images we find the very essence of Sophia as God-with-us. Her roots reach deep into the earth. From there she stretches upward and blossoms outward delighting her children with sweet scents and beautiful sights and sheltering them with her rich green branches. Here, scripture tells us, she remains in the earth and in the hearts of the children who love God.

But it is perhaps the last two verses of this passage that provide the greatest insight into Sophia. The phrase "the smoke of frankincense in the sacred tent" tells us that she is a fine, subtle spirit that pervades and purifies the holiest of places. At the same time, however, she is like a terebinth. In ancient days the terebinth was held to be a sacred tree. It was honored for its long life and venerated for the protection its great size and large spreading branches provided. People sought to have their loved ones buried beneath the terebinth because it was considered a mark of great favor, and people also often hid treasured objects in the earth beneath its roots.

These images of the terebinth and the smoke—one earth-bound and one ethereal—graphically portray the two sides of Sophia's nature. As the terebinth she spreads her protective branches and makes her home with us. As the incense-laden smoke in the sacred tent she is the subtle spirit who makes her home with God. In this way Sophia, exactly like Shakti and Shekinah, exists at once on both the earthly and the heavenly planes.

When I think back to the early days of my research and how worried I was that Sophia wouldn't represent the embodiment of the Divine in us and in the earth the way Shakti and Shekinah did, I realize this came about, at least in part, because I hadn't been thinking in broad enough terms. Because when I *did* think about it, I realized that this sense that the nourishing life force that is "with us" has virtually always been seen as the feminine. In the pantheon of gods and goddesses, the Roman goddess Ceres represented Mother Earth and was the source of the food that sustains us. Her counterpart, the Greek Demeter, was the goddess of the all-nourishing corn. In the cosmology of ancient China, the cosmic forces of yin and yang manifest as Mother Earth and Father Sky, and human beings are created by the first goddess, known as Nu Gua, who sculpts them from the mud of Mother Earth and blows the breath of life into them. Even St Francis of Assisi sang his praise to Mother Earth who "sustains us".

In these sacred stories we see again and again that image of Sophia who is with us physically, growing like the cedars of Lebanon and rooted deep in the earth like the terebinth, and with our spirits, as the all-sustaining life force. As we read how St Hildegard expressed it in Chapter Four, Sophia is the supreme and fiery force that kindles every living spark and makes all things green.

As I found more references like these in Hildegard's work and the Bible I began to wonder if Sophia wasn't then the same thing as the Holy Spirit. Eventually I discovered that many early Church theologians asked this same question and that a number of them came to the conclusion that the answer was yes. One of these was St Irenaeus. Irenaeus was born in Asia Minor about two hundred years after Christ. After traveling to Rome as a young man, he became a priest. Sometime after this he was sent to France and eventually became a renowned bishop. Around 202 CE he was martyred and was later made a saint. In his writings, Irenaeus seems to almost take it for granted that Sophia and the Holy Spirit are one. In one essay, for example, he said plainly, "...the Son and the Holy Spirit, i.e. the Logos and Sophia".

Another noted early theologian who had similar beliefs was Caius Marius Victorinus. Victorinus was born in Africa about a hundred years after Irenaeus. He also made his way to Rome and made a name for himself in the early Church as a respected theologian. His writings, too, contain clear-cut statements that equate Sophia and the Holy Spirit.

As soon as I came across the idea that Sophia and the Holy Spirit were the same, I started to ask myself if this could possibly mean that the Holy Spirit was feminine. When this thought popped into my head for the first time several years ago, it was another one of those "Eureka!" moments for me. I suddenly realized that, if the Holy Spirit was feminine, it would create a holy trinity that looked very different from the one I had learned in church. God the Father would represent the Divine that is beyond gender—just as it does now for most people in spite of the "father" imagery. God the Son would represent the divine masculine principle, and the Holy Spirit would represent the divine feminine principle. It came to me in a great rush that this was yet another instance of finding a parallel in Christianity to a Hindu concept I had identified with for so long: Brahman is the great cosmic divine force who is beyond gender and who then manifests as the cosmic masculine principle, Shiva, and as the cosmic feminine principle, Shakti. Once this realization came to me, I found that the Christian trinity had a balance and wholeness for me that I had never sensed before.

This notion of the Holy Spirit as feminine seemed so unique and exciting to me that for a while, I am slightly embarrassed to say, I thought I had come up with a completely original idea. It wasn't long, however, before I discovered that a number of early theologians had wrestled with this same concept. Victorinus, for example, not only said that Sophia was the Holy Spirit, he went so far as to say that she was the mother of Christ both in heaven and on earth.

Raised in traditional Christianity as I was, I found the idea that the Holy Spirit could be feminine incredibly liberating. Immediately I set out to find other theologians over the centuries who had been brave enough to claim that the Holy Spirit was feminine. One of the most fascinating facts I discovered on this journey was that in the early Christian Church in Syria the Holy Spirit was generally thought of as feminine until well into the fourth century CE. It seems the Syrian Church was so far from the reach of Rome that it had a good deal of independence and managed to interpret a number of Church rituals in its own way. Much of the symbolism involved in these rituals was based on the feminine images of the Holy Spirit found in the Bible, for instance where she hovers like a merciful, protective mother dove above the waters at the beginning of Genesis.

Continuing on this search, I eventually discovered a book that would have saved me months of work if I had only come across it sooner. This gem is called *The Divine Mother: a trinitarian theology of the Holy Spirit*. It was written by a Jesuit named Donald Gelpi. Although now basically retired, Gelpi is Professor Emeritus at the Jesuit School of Theology at Berkeley where he taught for many years. In *The Divine Mother*, Gelpi built a strong case for saying Sophia and the Holy Spirit are one and the same. One of the points he made is that, even if it can't be proven that they are the same, a careful analysis of all the biblical references to the two certainly proves that they *act* the same way. After providing many examples of this, Gelpi went on with unrelenting Jesuit logic to lay out his case for conceptualizing the Holy Spirit as feminine.

Consistent with this, Gelpi referred to the Holy Spirit as "she" throughout *The Divine Mother*. He also preferred to call her the *Holy Breath*. In the Old Testament and the books of the New Testament that were originally written in Hebrew, the word *ruah* is the word that is now generally translated as "spirit". In Hebrew ruah is the word for both breath and wind. When I first came across this, it seemed like an insignificant point, but I later realized that by using "Holy Breath" instead of "Holy Spirit" in his work Gelpi was not only being more accurate, he was getting across both the life-sustaining quality of breath and the sense of majestic power associated with wind—two points that are extremely significant when we come to consider the ways the divine feminine works in both our creative expression and our daily lives.

Once I had finished reading the reasoned and well-thought out arguments Gelpi expressed in *The Divine Mother*, I was convinced I was justified in thinking of the Holy Spirit as feminine and in considering the Holy Spirit and Sophia as one. Once I was confident of this, I went back to the Bible and looked at the references to the Holy Spirit in a new light. I really shouldn't have been surprised to discover how many characteristics she shares with Shakti. It was easy to see that she—like Shakti, Shekinah, and Sophia—represents the embodiment of the Divine within us; she manifests as divine light; she is seen as the universal life force, and most important for us here she is the source of transformation and creative inspiration in our lives.

Certainly I had no trouble finding references to the Holy Spirit as the Divine-with-us in the Bible where the Holy Spirit can be seen entering into prophets, descending on apostles, and dwelling with both individuals and communities. As Paul said in the third chapter of his first letter to the Corinthians, "Do you not know that you are God's temple and that God's Spirit dwells in you?" In fact, whenever God's immediate presence is being conveyed a reference to the Holy Spirit is made far more often than not in the Bible. As Gelpi put it, "It is through the action of his Breath that Yahweh Himself becomes present to his creatures."

The Holy Spirit also reveals herself as divine light in the same way that Shakti and Shekinah do. One of the most vivid examples of this is found in the Old Testament story of Ezekiel's vision of the fiery chariot. Ezekiel lived in the fifth century BCE during the time when the Israelites were living in exile in Babylon. One day when he was sitting among the other exiles near the River Chebar, he says the heavens opened up for him and he saw a vision of God. As he looked up into the sky he saw a mighty ruah coming out of the north. With this wind came a cloud that was flashing with fire and was surrounded by brilliant light. The cloud was illuminated with a radiance that Ezekiel tells us was like molten brass glowing in the heart of a fiery forge. Out of this cloud came four blazing cherubim. They were riding on four great whirling wheels—these wheels are the "chariot" that is referred to in the many songs and stories that are told about Ezekiel. The chariot was surrounded by radiance, light, and fire. It was moved, Ezekiel tells us, through the air by ruah—clearly by this point the Holy Spirit. This same spirit then enters into Ezekiel; it lifts him up, carries him away, and speaks to him—giving him a message of hope to take to his fellow exiles to make their life in Babylon more bearable.

The close relationship between images associated with light and

·the advent of the Holy Spirit found in the story of Ezekiel is also found in many other places in the Bible. Paul, for instance, is struck by a blinding light on the road to Damascus and is shortly afterward filled with the Holy Spirit, and the apostles are greeted with light and tongues of flame when the Holy Spirit descends on them during the Pentecost.

Many references can also be found that show the Holy Spirit is the subtle, all-pervasive life force just like Shakti and the other examples of the divine feminine. One of the most compelling illustrations of the Holy Spirit as the life force is found in Chapter 37 of the book of Ezekiel. In this passage the Holy Spirit picks Ezekiel up and carries him across the desert to a valley that is completely filled with dry, brittle, sun-bleached bones. The Lord then comes to Ezekiel and proclaims that He will clothe the bones with flesh and breathe the "ruah" back into them. First, however, he says that Ezekiel must prophesy over the bones and tell them all this is going to happen. Although Ezekiel doubts that he is capable of making such a mighty prophecy, he tries desperately. His first attempt falls short and the result is that the bones are covered with muscle and skin but they are not breathing: in other words, the bones look like people but they are not alive. There is no ruah in them. The Lord commands Ezekiel to try again, telling him that this time he should speak directly to the breath: "Prophesy, son of man, and say to the breath, Thus says the Lord God: Come from the four winds, O breath, and breathe upon these slain, that they may live." So Ezekiel tries again. This time he succeeds and says afterwards, "So I prophesied as he commanded me, and the breath came into them, and they lived, and stood upon their feet, an exceedingly great host."

In this vision of the Spirit as the life force that can turn a valley of dry, bleached bones into a mighty host, we see clear echoes of prana as breath, of prana-shakti as life energy, and of Shakti as the cosmic life force of the universe. Unfortunately, by the time the Bible was translated into Latin all this was lost. The feminine word ruah was replaced with the masculine noun "spiritus". Spiritus—and our word "spirit" that comes from it—have little of this sense of vital cosmic power. For us, a spirit is soft; it is ethereal; it is a mere wisp, a whisper. Lovely as these images are, they carry none of that sense of great rushing wind or of the mighty life-giving, life-sustaining breath of God—powerful metaphors for the way the divine feminine works in our lives, especially when it comes to transformation.

Gelpi, Jesuit priest though he is, even dared to say that the Holy Spirit—this feminine force—is *the* transformative spiritual force: "Transformation in the Breath," he says, "is transformation in the living reality of the Godhead."

Many biblical verses support this and, in fact, go so far as to reveal that the Holy Spirit effects the transformation of consciousness in virtually the same way that Shakti does. As we've seen in previous chapters, three of the main signs associated with this transformation are mystical experience, paranormal abilities, and divine inspiration—even inspired creativity.

Examples of each of these three abound in both the Old and New Testaments. For wonderful examples of how the Holy Spirit is related to mystical experience we don't need to look any further than the stories of Ezekiel and Paul that have already been told. Ezekiel's experience with the Spirit contains all the elements of classic mystical experiences described by the ancient yogis, including visions of radiant light, a sense of oneness with the Divine, and an overwhelming sense of divine power and love. St Paul's experience on the road to Damascus is much the same. He is struck down by a light so brilliant that it blinds him for several days. As soon as he realizes he has experienced the Holy Spirit, he is filled with love and bliss and with the realization that the Divine is alive in his heart.

More importantly, however, both of these men experienced a very distinct transformation of consciousness directly after the Holy Spirit came to them. The story of Ezekiel makes it clear that before the advent of the Spirit he was an ordinary man, afterwards he was a prophet. Paul, too, was turned into a great seer by his experience. And both were given the gifts known as charisms in Christianity—the paranormal abilities known as siddhis in yoga that were described earlier in the book.

In both the Old and New Testaments charisms are referred to as "gifts of the Spirit". Paul spent a good deal of time in his letters to the Corinthians explaining what the different types of gifts are, why people receive them in varying degrees, and why some people don't receive them at all. It is easy to understand why Paul would have needed to do this. The apostles and others who received these gifts were attracting a tremendous amount of attention and the people observing them must have been eager to have the same powers. One of the purposes of Paul's letters seems to be to chastise the Corinthians for being a bit too eager to receive the more sensational gifts. In this discussion, Paul carefully listed the different types of spiritual gifts. The more spectacular gifts in Paul's list, which can be found in 1 Corinthians 12, include the ones we would think of today as paranormal abilities. They include the gift of tongues, the gift of healing, the gift of prophecy, and the ability to perform miracles.

It is understandable that the Corinthians were wondering why they weren't all suddenly able to heal, prophesy, and perform miracles. Many of Jesus' followers, and not just Jesus himself, were given these gifts after experiencing the Holy Spirit. The book of Acts is filled with stories about the people who had these experiences and the wonders they were able to perform afterwards. Several of the stories are about Paul on his travels through what is now Turkey. In a village near the city of Konya, Paul came across a man who was crippled from birth and had never been able to walk. After looking at him intently, Paul made the command "Stand upright on your feet!" and as soon as the words were out of Paul's mouth, the man sprung up and walked. Later in Jerusalem, the disciples Peter and John performed feats similar to Paul's: they cast out unclean spirits, healed the lame, and knew intuitively when they were being lied to.

Some people who were not even disciples were given these miraculous gifts. Two of them were Stephen and Silas. Stephen, whose story is told in Acts 6-7, is described as being full of the Holy Spirit and is said to have performed many "signs and wonders". Unfortunately, his paranormal abilities gained him so much attention that he was persecuted unmercifully, and he became the first Christian martyr.

Silas' story, told in Acts 15-17, has a happier ending. A prominent member of the early Church in Jerusalem, Silas was chosen by the elders there to travel to Antioch—in what is now Syria—to help Paul with his mission. While there, Paul and Silas are thrown into prison. The two men pray and sing hymns until nearly midnight when the power of their combined prayers brings about a miracle: a great earthquake shakes the foundations of the prison, the doors fly open, the manacles on their hands and feet fall off, and they are freed.

In Chapters 12 and 14 of his first letter to the Corinthians, Paul was careful to set these paranormal gifts in context. He indicated—exactly as the ancient yogis did when writing about siddhis—that they are valuable only in that they could be used to further God's work and that they should not be sought after for their own sake. He then went on to indicate that the other gifts of the Spirit have a much deeper value. Interestingly enough, these are exactly the gifts we would associate much more closely with creative inspiration than with paranormal abilities. They include gifts that he called "wise speech" and the ability to "put the deepest knowledge into words". He explained this saying, "Now Brethren, if I come to you speaking in tongues, how shall I benefit you unless I bring you some revelation or knowledge or prophecy or teaching?" What he was referring to here, of course, is the type of inspiration experienced by saints like Hildegard and Mahadevi. Still, we need to keep in mind—as Wendi's story later in the chapter shows—that these gifts occur on a continuum and can come into play in our daily lives.

Just how closely these gifts are associated with what we think of today as creativity is shown in a particularly lovely chapter in Exodus. This extraordinarily important passage is one that seems to be rarely noticed and, as far as I have been able to ascertain, has never been considered in this light. It comes just after Moses has been given the stone tablets with the commandments written on them. The Lord has commanded Moses to build an ornate box, called an ark, to keep them in and to construct an enormous tent, called the tabernacle, where the ark will be kept and sacred rituals can be held. The Lord's directions for building the ark, the tent, and the paraphernalia for the rituals are exacting. The ark, the altar, and other objects are to be covered with gold that is carved in intricate designs. Other objects are to be wrought of gold filigree, silver, or bronze and are to be decorated with brilliantly cut gems. The curtains and veils of the tent are to be woven of the finest blue, purple, and scarlet linen and decorated with cherubim. The garments for the priest are to be of exquisite beauty.

For Moses and his people—in exile in a desert land—this must have seemed like an impossible task. But the Lord reassures Moses and tells him he will send the Holy Spirit to provide them with all the inspiration they will need:

The Lord said to Moses, "See, I have called by name Bezalel...and I have filled him with the Spirit of God, with the ability and intelligence, with knowledge and all craftsmanship, to devise artistic designs, to work in gold, silver, and bronze, in cutting stones for setting, for work in every craft...and I have given to all able men ability, that they may make all that I have commanded for you.

[Exod. 31:1-8]

In this truly remarkable passage we see how the Holy Spirit works—exactly as the ancient yogis tell us Shakti does—to fill us with divinely inspired creativity and transform us. Of course, it is easy to think that because these are biblical stories about transformation and its characteristics—mystical experience, paranormal abilities, and inspired creativity—that they only relate to great prophets and great moments in history.

But we only need to think back to Britta's story in Chapter Five to find an example of how this process is working in our modern-day lives: her personal experience of the Holy Spirit was a moving, mystical one. Immediately after it she became much more intuitive, with her dreams even occasionally giving her glimpses into the future. What's more, her artwork became far more creatively inspired, and she spontaneously began to write poetry.

Gelpi, too, makes this point. After giving examples of the Holy Breath being the author of transformation and illumination in the life of Jesus, he goes on to make it clear that she is also the source of inspiration for ordinary human beings. To illustrate this, he gives the example of Jesus telling a group of Christians who are about to face persecution not to worry about what they will say at their trials because the Holy Breath will give them the words they need and speak through them.

The sacred writings we have been examining in this chapter and the last one have really all been leading up to the idea being expressed here: the divine feminine can speak through us. But far more significant is the fact that she can speak through us *easily*—and she speaks through us easily because she is embodied within us. The epic Hindu tales we've looked at tell us Shakti is embedded in the earth and in our bodies, the lyrical writings from Jewish mysticism tell us Shekinah is God-with-us, the poetic passages from the Old

Testament tell us Sophia not only grows along with each one of us in the womb, she remains with us as the source of creativity and transformation for our entire lives.

But this is not a force that we only find in the poetic passages of sacred texts; this is not a force that makes herself known only to the great and gifted. This is a force that is present in our day-to-day lives—that is working her transformative magic in the here and now. And because she is embodied within us, this powerful transformative Holy Wind is *accessible*. She is as close as our next breath.

Wendi, whose story was first told in Chapter Six, provides a wonderful example of this, for she listens to the divine feminine and brings this creative power into her work every day. And that work is in a place that seems as far from the lush gardens of En-gedi as one can get—namely, the corporate world of North America.

As was explained earlier, Wendi's process of transformation has been a gradual, almost imperceptible one with no remarkable mystical experiences like Christine's or startling improvement in creative ability like Britta's. When we left Wendi in Chapter Six she had just had the revelation that she quite literally embodied the divine feminine—that she held this cosmic power within herself and that she could express it in her daily life.

At the time this occurred Wendi had a job she liked working in the communications department of a large, internationally respected corporation. She was in high-level management, had a prestigious title, and a salary to match it. But she found herself yearning for something more—a career that would allow her to be herself—the self she recognized as this divine feminine being. She also longed to do work that had more meaning and made more of a difference in people's lives.

Eventually Wendi decided to leave her job and try to find a career that would satisfy this deep yearning. "Doing this made no sense at the time, I was the mother of two girls, and my income was very much needed by the family. I was also leaving a job that had a lot of prestige and security." Still, she knew it was the right thing to do, and after a period of intense soul-searching, she entered a training program that would qualify her to work as a trainer and life-skills coach. Once she finished the program, she launched an independent practice. Although her practice has now become highly successful, from the moment she left her job right up until this success began to become apparent Wendi went through a very challenging period. No matter how difficult things became, however, her awareness of her connection to the divine feminine carried her through. Not surprisingly, her ability to make this connection was closely related to creative expression:

> From the time I left the corporate world and went out on my own, the one thing that carried me through all the literally paralyzing fear was my journaling. For me this was then and still is now a big part of my creative expression. And I still journal first thing most mornings. As soon as I wake up I turn on the light and grab my journal and start writing. It is stream of consciousness writing and it is all about being in a place where my day-to-day needs, my worries, and my fears cannot cloud my vision of what I am meant to be doing that day—my vision of myself, who I am, and what my purpose is. It is all about connecting with me and my core—and that core is the divine feminine.
>
> Doing the journaling is part of what maintains this connection to the divine feminine. It is also what keeps it clear and bright. This is important in my day-to-day life, but it is also essential in my work. As a coach I really have to be "me", and it is what allows "me" to show up in my work—it is what allows this divine feminine in me to be present in my work and out in the world doing that work.

For Wendi doing this work involves helping awaken this divine feminine spirit both in the lives of her individual clients and in the corporate world in general. "My work," she explains, "is really a kind of dance between my intuitive knowing—that divine feminine knowing—and the concrete world of structures, frameworks, and techniques that are related to the leadership, management, and business skills that my clients need."

Wendi says that she sees this intuitive knowing, which she also refers to as simply her intuition, as a direct expression of the divine feminine. "Another way to put it," she adds, "is to say that I see my intuition as the voice of the divine feminine. This is the way she speaks to me."

Wendi's ability to use her intuition has become the basis of much of her work with corporate executives and managers. "In my work I am always asking myself questions: Where is this client right now? What does he need? What is she asking for? How can I best respond to that?" The intuitive answers to questions like these help Wendi tune into her clients' needs on a very deep level and allow her to give them the specific tools they need to both accomplish more and become happier and less stressed in their work environment. "Of course," she adds with a laugh, "I don't tell my corporate clients this. It would sound *way* too woo-woo!"

Once she has used her intuition to establish what her clients' needs are, she then works to develop this intuitive knowing in her clients themselves. She does this by helping them get a sense of who they really are at the core of their being and come to trust this core. "This is really," she says, "just learning to trust themselves. This works because no matter who we are we have, at the very center of our selves, this divine feminine core."

When talking to Wendi it becomes clear that the way the divine feminine expresses itself in her work is multi-faceted and many layered. In addition to the way she uses her divine feminine knowing to work more effectively with her clients and, in turn, develop their own intuitive abilities, she sees developing feminine leadership skills in others as another aspect of this. In fact, much of the corporate coaching Wendi now does involves leadership training and helping clients to learn to make leadership decisions that come from trusting their inner core:

> In my work in the corporate world I have continually—both at my previous job and now—seen this world as being completely out of kilter. And I'm convinced the reason for this is that we are still seeing things solely from a masculine point of view. The approach we take to problem solving is based on the masculine model, and in general, the traditional masculine or patriarchal style of management is still the one found in the corporate world.

To counteract this, Wendi works to develop more "feminine" skills in the clients who take her leadership training programs. Sometimes referred to as the "softer" management traits, they include communication skills, relationship skills, problem solving that is based on people's needs, and of course, learning when and how to trust intuition.

In addition to helping develop more of these feminine leadership skills in both men and women in North America, Wendi is working on creating a program that will take this training to women in South Africa—the country Wendi was raised in and that she says is still where her heart lies. Part of this work would involve encouraging these women to recognize the strong inner feminine leadership skills they already have and helping them find ways to bring these skills out and apply them in the world they live in.

For Wendi, whether she is listening to the clear, bright voice she hears within, developing this intuitive skill in others, or encouraging them to become better leaders by learning to trust their inner core, she is helping bring that divine feminine that exists within each one of us out into the world.

It seems particularly appropriate to me that Part I of *The Divine Feminine Fire* concludes with Wendi. The way she has integrated the divine feminine into her life, connected with it through the creative expression she finds in journaling, and dedicated herself to helping it flourish in the world has been an inspiration to me.

Throughout Part I this cosmic creative force—call her Shakti, Shekinah, Sophia, or the Holy Spirit—has been revealed to be the Divine-with-us. We have seen many examples of how she, from the place where she is embodied within us, is able to change us, mold us, and inspire us. Ancient Judeo-Christian teachings tells us she can give us gifts that help us speak more wisely, put knowledge into better words, craft more beautiful works of art, and even see into the realm of the unseen. The Tantras tell us exactly the same.

In Part II we'll look in more detail at how this life force empowers our own personal enlightenment and at what it is we need to do to make ourselves as receptive as possible to the potential for personal transformation and creative inspiration that she brings.

A Clear and Bright Connection to the Divine Feminine Within

When Wendi described working to keep her connection with the divine feminine "clear and bright", I was captivated by the beautiful image and asked her to tell me how it had come to her. She surprised me by saying she had originally gotten the idea from a management training exercise. This particular exercise focused on keeping communication in relationships not just open but clear and bright.

The secret to accomplishing this, she discovered, often lies in becoming aware of our assumptions. And the key to discovering which of our assumptions might be misguided or false often lies in simply naming them. When Wendi started thinking about this in terms of her connection to her divine feminine core, she realized the same was true and, later, helped me develop the following exercise.

It is a simple one designed to help you examine your assumptions about the divine feminine and keep your connection to this source of creative inspiration and personal transformation as clear and bright as possible. Because the cosmic divine feminine is such an abstract concept, in this exercise you will use creative visualization to create an image of her that is one you can easily communicate with.

1. When you are seated comfortably and have a pen and paper ready, enter that deep meditative space where you feel safe, protected, filled with light, and free from the harsh inner voice of criticism. Sit for a moment basking in this light.

2. Begin to visualize or simply imagine yourself at a great age—an age where you have lived so long and learned so much that you have become a manifestation of Sophia, the divine wisdom within.

3. When this image becomes clear, see yourself sitting across from her, look at her intensely, and think of the many things you have always assumed about her. As these thoughts come to you, express them to her.

4. When you are done, sit for a moment, and then ask her what she has always assumed about you.

5. When she has finished, bring your concentration back to the light

that fills you and see it moving gently upwards and, as you have in earlier exercises, see it rising up, moving down your arm, and flowing out your hand into your pen and onto the paper.

6. *Write down your assumptions about Sophia. Write down her assumptions about you.*

7. *Later you may want to turn what you have learned in this exercise into a poem, a painting, a song, or some other expression of the Wisdom that lives within you.*

PART II

My Lover, My Longing

The story of Mechthild of Magdeburg provides a perfect bridge between the first and second parts of *The Divine Feminine Fire*. Her life and writings exemplify all the important points that have been touched on so far. In Mechthild we find a woman who intuitively understood the feminine aspect of the Divine and who was able to answer when the cosmic power that created the universe called her to be creative too. Mechthild knew that she was experiencing "God-with-us", and she knew—in spite of a Church that told her this was impossible—that this intimate, passionate relationship with the Divine *was* possible not only for her but for each and every one of us. This certainty allowed Mechthild to experience the great intensity of this force and to let the passion of her yearning carry her forward

on her spiritual journey in the face of what must have been tremendous fear. In this way Mechthild provides a link between the stories
that have already been told and the ones that follow. These are stories
of women who are, like so many of us, at various stages of learning
to understand their yearning to create and the transformation it
signals. They are also learning to be with the power of this yearning
and to stay with it wherever it takes them, to honor it, and—no
matter how overwhelming their fears sometimes seem—to allow
themselves to express it in their creativity and in their daily lives.

During her lifetime Mechthild managed to accomplish all this
and more. She was born about 1208 somewhere near Magdeburg, a
city in what is now the central part of Northern Germany. Certain
clues from her writings have convinced scholars that she was born
into a noble and probably affluent family. Although she didn't begin
writing until she was in her early forties, she had her first mystical
experience when she was only twelve and continued to have them
throughout her life. She later named these experiences "greetings"
and said that they came to her from her divine lover—a paramour
whom she depicted in the most passionate, erotically charged, and
intimate of terms. Early in her writing she described these greetings
in this way:

> God's true greeting...has such force that it takes away all the body's
> strength and reveals the soul to herself so that she sees herself re-
> sembling the saints, and she takes on a divine radiance...Then the
> soul leaves the body, taking all her power, wisdom, love, and longing...
> Then he draws her further to a secret place...
>
> This is a greeting that has many streams. It pours forth from the
> flowing God into the poor, parched soul with new knowledge, in new
> contemplation, and in the special enjoyment of the new presence. Oh,
> sweet God, inwardly on fire, outwardly blossoming, now that you have
> given this to the least...In this greeting, I want to die living.
>
> [Book I, 2]

By the time Mechthild was in her early twenties, her longing to continually "die living" in this greeting compelled her to leave her home
and move to Magdeburg, where she took up life as a beguine—an
extraordinary group of women who were not nuns but who formed
communities where they lived lives of chastity, service, and dedication

to God. Because the beguines lived neither in male-dominated homes nor in convents controlled by the Church, they are often referred to as the first women's movement in history.

Mechthild lived as a beguine for more than twenty years before she began writing. At that time she was, like Hildegard, in her early forties. Between that time and her death she produced seven "books" that were eventually combined into one large book that she called *The Flowing Light of the Godhead*—a work of both great spiritual depth and exceptional literary quality.

Mechthild remained a beguine until she was in her sixties when the general political climate—and almost certainly the threat of being persecuted for her mystical writings—obligated her to become a nun. The order she joined was a Cistercian convent in the town of Helfta. History tells us that there was a sweet irony to this move, for this particular convent was under the guidance of an abbess named Gertrude of Hackeborn. Gertrude was a poet and mystic in her own right, and the convent at Helfta eventually became what is almost certainly the greatest seat of women's mystical writing found in the Middle Ages. Mechthild lived in this convent until her death. Unfortunately, the date of this event is uncertain. Some confusion exists over the entry in the convent records, and it is possible that she died either in 1282 or in 1294. Thus she lived to be about either 74 or 86, either one meaning she had a long life for someone who lived in medieval times. Her longevity is especially remarkable because she suffered from various physical problems and general ill health for most of her life.

That Mechthild chose to spend most of her life as a beguine rather than as a nun is highly significant. It speaks to the independence of her spirit, to the deep sincerity of her quest, and to what must have been a great desire to do good. If she'd chosen to become a nun she, as a wealthy, aristocratic woman with a large dowry, could have dedicated herself to God and still lived a life of ease, comfort, and security. As a beguine she took a vow to live in chastity, poverty, and service. Although these vows were not "irrevocable" in the eyes of the Church in the same way nuns' vows were, the beguines themselves took them quite literally. The beguines lived with only the basic necessities and worked extremely hard, often in terrible conditions. Mechthild's writings indicate that she believed taking this more difficult path and the suffering it entailed would help ensure that she would continue to receive "greetings" from her divine lover. She tells us these experiences filled her with such all-consuming passion, such overwhelming love that she was willing to do anything and sacrifice anything in order to have them.

These few basic facts constitute most of what is known for certain about Mechthild. In a way it is unfortunate that we have so little specific information about her life. In another way, however, it seems fitting. For we can learn the most personal details about her inner life—and this was, after all, what mattered to her—simply by knowing what her life as a beguine must have been like and by reading her intimately revealing spiritual writings.

When Mechthild joined the beguines somewhere around 1230, the movement had probably been in existence for a good forty or fifty years. Written references to them can be found beginning in 1210. Over the next few decades they gained increasing respect and prominence, especially in the parts of Europe that were referred to as the Low Countries—a region that included much of what is now Belgium, the Netherlands, North-eastern France, and North-western Germany. Although some mistrust of this powerful women's movement always existed, for much of this period the degree of acceptance or persecution the beguines experienced depended on the attitudes of the local priests. The different popes in power during these years also held widely differing views, some very positive, on the beguines. By the second half of the 1200s negative feelings about the beguines were beginning to spread, and during this period the official Church position also became increasingly negative. By the beginning of the fourteenth century the beguines were being persecuted to some degree throughout most of the Low Countries even though scattered parish priests and monasteries continued to be supportive of them. Around this time some beguines were even burned at the stake. Eventually the Church decreed that all beguines would have to give up their "heretical" ways and go back to their families or join official Church convents. Shortly after this almost all beguine communities were dissolved or absorbed by the traditional monastic orders. Fortunately a few beguine communities managed to survive and, in fact, still exist quietly in Belgium today.

Looking back on the Middle Ages it's easy for us to assume that Mechthild and the beguines—as a movement of strong, independent women—were doomed to persecution from the outset. And while this is probably true, the situation wasn't as clear-cut as we might suppose. During this time period women in Europe had a few more rights than is generally assumed today. An unmarried woman could, for instance, own property. (A right that, once taken away, was not regained in most Western countries until the twentieth century!) Although a woman's husband assumed control of the property once she married, if he died it had to be returned to her, and she also inherited a portion—usually a third—of everything else he owned. Women also worked widely in the emerging trades and could own, along with their husbands, businesses like pubs and hostelries. If their husbands died, they became the sole proprietor of the business. Although women were not generally allowed into the tradesmen's guilds that were developing at that time, a few of the guilds actually allowed widows to take over their deceased husbands' memberships.

Thus opportunities did exist for a certain number of women to support themselves and for a few of them, particularly wealthy widows, to be in positions of influence and have authority over those who worked for them. Still, women were not independent in any real sense of the word, and they did not have any real power. A woman's choices were basically to marry, to remain at home as a burden on her father or her brothers, or to join a convent. During the twelfth century a growing number of women—whether out of true religious fervor or a desire to avoid marriage—began to flood the established convents. This soon became a financial burden on the monasteries that had to support these convents, and it became increasingly common for the monks to accept only those women who could bring large dowries of land and money with them when they joined. About this time, the Church was also becoming concerned that overseeing the growing number of convents was taking the monks away from their "real" spiritual duties and that having so many women—even cloistered ones—around might prove to be too much distraction for the monks.

The beguine movement, beginning as it did in this climate, seemed to most parish priests and to many in the Church hierarchy to be a perfect solution to the problem of having so many unmarried women on their hands: the beguines were committed to chastity so they weren't wanton; they were allied to the Church so they weren't heretics;

and—probably best of all—they were determined to support themselves and so would not be a burden on either their families or the Church. Of course, in those early days of the movement, the male Church hierarchy almost certainly never stopped to imagine what a group of women left to their own devices might accomplish.

Looking back on it, however, it is easy to see that this insistence on self-support was absolutely revolutionary. Mechthild and the amazing women like her gained a level of independence that was completely unheard of: they were not dependent on their fathers nor were they the property of a husband, and—since they did not belong to the established religious orders—they were not directly controlled by the Church. And for a good many years they got away with it! By the time Mechthild joined them, beguine communities were thriving. Some of these communities were as small as one house where a handful of women lived and worked together; others were entire walled-in, virtually self-sufficient "towns" within towns. Most of these were situated in the larger cities of Flanders and the Netherlands, and they generally grew up in the vicinity of those monasteries, frequently Dominican, whose priests and monks were supportive of their ideals. Some of these larger beguine communities contained scores of houses and came to control considerable amounts of property.

Because the beguines were dedicated to living Christ-like lives, they spent a good deal of time in prayer, but their primary goal was to be of service. They lived austerely and used their resources for charity. The beguines managed to build infirmaries, establish schools, and run leper colonies. They also worked in hospitals and cared tirelessly for the poor, often working in terribly filthy and disease-ridden conditions. Since the beguines working in this way in the outside community rarely charged for their services, other beguines stayed at home, spinning, weaving, making textiles and performing other money-making activities in order to make their charitable works possible.

When Mechthild joined the movement, the beguines were living in this way across the Low Countries. The next twenty to twenty-five years, however, was the period in which the tide of popular opinion and the Church's assessment of them slowly turned against them.

In the beginning this change in popular opinion was caused by the existence of women who were known as "singular" beguines.

These were beguines who chose neither to join a beguine community nor to live in a beguine house. Some of these singular beguines participated in charitable activities during the day and then returned home to their fathers or brothers in the evening. But some of them actually lived on their own in their own homes—something women, except for some widows, just did not do. The autonomy exhibited by these singular beguines made both the Church and the society at large uneasy, and before long the charge of sexual wantonness was being levied against some of these strong, independent women.

As time went on this distrust increased and eventually spread even to those living in the smaller beguine houses, which is the type of community Mechthild is believed to have lived in. Certainly, Mechthild was worried fairly early on about the effect stories about her visionary experiences might have if they were made public. In fact, this seems to be one reason she waited so long to begin writing about these experiences at all. At some point, however, she went to her confessor and began describing the visions she had been having for thirty years. The monk, convinced that God was speaking through Mechthild, insisted that she begin writing her experiences down and making them more widely known.

Although it is clear she longed to do just that, Mechthild agonized over the decision and repeatedly asked herself—just as Mahadevi and Hildegard did—how a simple, uneducated woman like herself could possible take on such a task. Although Mechthild stated briefly that she wouldn't have been able to begin writing if the monk hadn't been so insistent, she also made it clear she was writing because the Lord, her divine lover, told her to. Regardless of why she began or exactly how she got the courage to do so, once she started, nothing could make her stop even though opposition to the beguines was steadily increasing during the ten years in which she wrote Books I through V.

As this opposition increased so did the number and severity of charges against the beguines. Soon allegations ranging from hypocrisy and false piety to licentiousness and prostitution were even being laid against some members of the larger, well-established communities that were closely affiliated with the Dominicans and the other religious orders.

It is no coincidence these charges were becoming more common just when the beguines were becoming increasingly vocal in their criticism of corruption among the clergy and in the Church in general. Some beguines at this time were actually going into churches and claiming loudly that they could intuitively tell that the priest had had sex prior to offering mass. On top of this, the beguines were beginning to preach publicly about the meaning of the Bible—an activity the Church claimed exclusively for its priests.

Distrust of the women was also growing because it was not uncommon for the beguine women to have mystical experiences and to speak openly of them. As beguine scholar Fiona Bowie points out, the Church wrote and taught *about* God, while the mystics talked about a relationship *with* God. This distinction, subtle as it is, was a radical one for the times. The Church firmly held the belief that priests were the intermediaries between the common person and God. Although a few women mystics like Hildegard had come along and claimed they experienced God directly, they had almost always been members of an established religious order. That anyone, particularly any woman, was openly—and quite literally out on the streets—discussing the Bible, claiming to understand it, and sometimes even alleging to have spoken directly to God was considered fraudulent at best and blasphemous at worst.

These time frames for the general rise and fall of the beguine movement are very important in terms of Mechthild's life and work because they mean that she joined the movement when it was established and respected, began to write about the time the distrust of the beguines was growing, and lived—and continued to write openly —through the times of ever-increasing persecution. This information, combined with the autobiographical comments she occasionally made in her book, paints a fairly good picture of her character and what her life was like. An even better picture of the person she was, however, emerges from her writing itself, particularly the passages that relate to the "greetings". Mechthild told us these greetings continued for most of her life and increased in intensity over time. In *The Flowing Light of the Godhead* Mechthild tried in a variety of ways to express just how powerful these greetings were and how profoundly they affected her. In one passage in Book II, she wrote:

> The great tongue of the Godhead has spoken many mighty words to me. I took them in...and the brightest of lights opened up to the eyes

of my soul. In it I saw...and recognized the inexpressible glory, the incomprehensible marvel...the complete fulfillment, the greatest concentration of knowledge, bliss...unadulterated joy in the common union, and the ever vibrant life in eternity as it is now and ever shall be.

[Book II, 2]

In another passage, she described the greeting as a "sweet dew" that gushes out of the fountain that is the eternal, ever-flowing Godhead. Under this cascading force she lost herself utterly. Describing herself in the third person, she said:

In this most dazzling light she becomes blind in herself.
And in this utter blindness she sees most clearly.
In this pure clarity she is both dead and living...

[Book I, 22]

For Mechthild these were not mystical experiences that occurred in a vacuum, they were always seen in the context of a reunion with her divine lover. Much of Mechthild's writing about these visits from her Beloved is expressed in a literary form that was associated with a romantic tradition known as courtly love. In order to understand the subtle interplay between Mechthild and her Beloved it's necessary to know a bit about this tradition. Courtly love arose near the close of the twelfth century and flourished among the nobility and aristocratic classes during the thirteenth century. It was defined by an intricate set of rules and rituals that defined the way in which a nobleman or aristocrat, often a knight, was supposed to conduct an affair with a married woman. These affairs were quite commonplace and were basically a socially sanctioned form of adultery. Courtly love was able to flourish in part because the vast majority of aristocratic marriages in the Middle Ages were basically business contracts and were only rarely love matches. As long as there was no risk of breaking the provisions of the contract or of actually tearing the marriage apart, society deemed these affairs to be harmless.

The rules and rituals governing courtly love were celebrated and passed on in the songs of the troubadours. According to these strictures, the man would fall in love with a married or engaged woman of his own or somewhat higher rank. He would then begin to woo her. Over a considerable period of time he would write love poetry for her and perform heroic deeds that would prove his devotion. Although the nobleman would write and perform his heroics anonymously at first, as time went by he would provide clues so that the woman would begin to realize who her suitor was. Once the nobleman was fairly certain that his beloved returned his ardor, he would reveal his true identity and the two would pledge their eternal devotion. Eventually the two would consummate the erotic passion that had been building to a crescendo during the long courtship. The most stringent rule concerning this whole process was that the utmost secrecy about the affair be maintained.

The main literary traditions that grew out of courtly love and that were used by Mechthild were based on imaginary dialogues between the hopeful lovers. These dialogues were written in both poetry and prose. In them the lover often addressed the object of his affection as his "Lady Love". If the woman was more highly born than he was or if he wanted to emphasize how much above himself he placed her, the nobleman might call her his "Mistress" or his "Queen".

Several elements in the courtly love tradition made it a perfect vehicle for Mechthild to use in expressing her feelings and experiences: the long-unrequited erotic passion symbolized her insatiable yearning for the greetings. The eternal devotion of the two lovers represented her unquenchable love for God. The irrevocable requirement for secrecy reflected the way she had had to keep her own divine love affair hidden for close to thirty years before making it public in her writings. Even more importantly, however, the passionate interplay between the two lovers provided a perfect allegorical setting for Mechthild to reveal her awareness of both masculine and feminine divine forces and to emphasize—just as the courtly love tradition did—the elevated stature of the feminine.

Out of this framework of Mechthild's life, times, and work arises an extremely important contribution to those of us on the creative-spiritual journey today: Mechthild realized that she was undergoing a process of transformation and that this process was being triggered by a divine force. At some deep level she even recognized that some aspect of this cosmic force was feminine, and she was clearly aware it was related to her spiritual longing and her need to express herself creatively. She was also very aware that this force was working through her body.

Of course Mechthild, like Hildegard, would never have spoken about the "divine feminine" in so many words. Still, in the very first passage of Book I, Mechthild began by addressing a cosmic feminine force that she calls Lady Love. Although Lady Love is not God, she is clearly divine. She is pictured as being perfect, above all things, and even able to bend the Holy Trinity to her will. In the next few pages, Mechthild alluded in other ways to the femininity of this divine power. She called her "my Empress" and refers to her as a dove and a maiden. In a conversation between the Lady Love and Mechthild's soul that occurs in the first passage, it is revealed that Lady Love has coursed through Mechthild's body, purified her, given her sublime knowledge, and granted her heavenly freedom. In short, Mechthild made it clear that it is Lady Love that has transformed her.

In this first section Mechthild hinted at a passionate union with Lady Love. It occurs just as Mechthild's soul is complaining about all that she has suffered on her spiritual journey, saying that Lady Love has taken all her earthly riches and worldly honor from her, wracked her body with a strange weakness, and devoured her flesh and blood. After making these complaints Mechthild summoned all her strength and, using powerful language, called Lady Love a robber and demanded immediate recompense for all she has suffered. Without a further word, Lady Love complies and says, "Mistress and Queen, then take me." Mechthild responded that in this one moment of union she has been repaid a hundredfold for all she has suffered.

In the third section of Book I, however, Mechthild suddenly stopped typifying the cosmic divine as feminine. Although it's impossible to know exactly why she did this, it is certainly possible that Mechthild knew she was pushing the bounds of what she could get away with and simply decided to stop. Regardless, this changeover occurs when Lady Love is explaining to her what will happen when Mechthild has arisen from death. Lady Love says:

> Then I'll embrace you tightly
> And permeate you utterly,
> And I'll steal you from your body
> And give you to your Lover.

Mechthild responds by asking Lady Love to seal this promise and then says:

Be silent, dear one, and speak no more.
Dearest of all maidens, let all creatures, myself
    included,
Bow down before you.
Tell my Lover his bed is made ready.
And that I am weak from longing for him.

[Book I, 3]

When I read these passages for the first time, I had no idea Mechthild meant this command to Lady Love to "be silent" quite literally. But the moment I began to suspect this might be the last time Lady Love would speak, I began to comb *The Flowing Light of the Godhead* backwards and forwards searching almost frantically for another place where Mechthild identified the Divine with the feminine. When I was unable to find it, I felt let down and somehow forsaken. As I continued to study Mechthild's work over time, however, my disappointment slowly began to ebb and I was very excited to realize this change signified a momentous transformation. From this moment forward she began to see her own soul as the feminine counterpart to the divine beloved. This becomes clear in the passage that follows the one above. In it Mechthild described how her soul traveled to the heavenly court to meet with God. There he embraced her and the two of them were "united as water and wine". She then turned to nothingness and was transported completely out of herself. Mechthild then sang out one of her most beautiful poems:

Lord, you are my lover,
My desire,
My flowing fount,
My sun;
And I am your reflection.

From this point onward Mechthild identified her own soul with the divine feminine: the divine masculine becomes the Beloved and her own soul becomes the Lover—and it never loses its divine standing. Throughout Mechthild's writings, the Lover is treated as being equal to the Beloved. In this way, Mechthild is identical to Mahadevi who, as described in Chapter Two, *became* Shakti in her search for union with her Lord Shiva.

Although these passages make it sound like Mechthild underwent a sudden transformation, and she may well have, the rest of the book makes it clear that she was involved in a life-long process of transformation and that she knew it was being brought about by a divine force. This realization was an essential first step for her just as it is for us. We need to recognize that something is happening to us. We have to admit it. And then we have to understand that it is being triggered by the Divine. Otherwise we will be afraid of it. We will run from it and try to hide.

A good example of someone who has been able to come to this understanding is Anya, a woman I met in one of my workshops not long ago. A long-time environmental activist, she is the mother of two girls and two boys whose ages range from thirteen to twenty-three. She has been married to her husband, a doctor who practices in a rural area, for twenty-eight years. Anya's conscious understanding of this process and exactly what it is has been gradually increasing over the years. But right from the very beginning she had an intuitive awareness that something in her was changing and that it was being carried out by a loving and light-filled higher power.

The daughter of European immigrants, Anya was always interested in the spiritual. As a child she attended the Lutheran Church with her family and had what she calls an "active prayer life". Her first experience of the mystical occurred in the early 1970s when she was a teenager visiting cousins in Europe. Her cousins were very involved in the "Jesus movement" that was sweeping Europe at that time. Although she had a few reservations about some of the teachings, she became involved too and increased her prayers and devotions. One afternoon standing at a bus stop she was suddenly overwhelmed with joy:

> The whole world became bright as if bathed in a brilliant light like the brightest sunshine you have ever experienced, but thicker. When I got on the bus, it was filled with light and everyone in the bus was connected by it, as if they were held by it. There was no space between them and the light—it was like a continuum of water, living water but it was "light-water".

As she sat on the bus an intense love for everyone on the bus flowed out of her, and she came to the realization that we are all connected. Later in life she learned that this was an experience of what the mystics call "oneness" or mystical union.

Although the visionary experience of light didn't last longer than half an hour, the radiant love and joy Anya felt stayed with her when she returned home and started university. Spurred on by these feelings she became disenchanted with teachings that said Jesus was the only way and that anyone who didn't follow this path would be damned: "I had experienced the light and the immense love that must be God for myself. I knew that the love went to all on that bus, Christian or not, and so I couldn't imagine that any God could be less loving than I was capable of being."

Almost immediately after the experience Anya began to realize something was changing in her. She had always been an extremely shy person but she found she was now able to access her inner resources in a way that would allow her to temporarily overcome her shyness in order to act on matters that moved her. She gives an example related to the crisis with the Vietnamese boat people that was going on in those days:

> I was moved to tears and horror at the plight of these people, living on boats or in refugee camps. I joined the movement by calling the head office at the time and becoming a coordinator for my area. I gathered eight members of my family and friends and together we sponsored and brought over a family. Acting on this and other inspirations brought incredible joy. I wouldn't have had the courage to do this before the experience of oneness and the hope that it had forever kindled in me.

As Anya looks back on it now, she is able to see that these simple changes in her personality—the decrease in fear and shyness, the gaining of self-confidence and courage—were part of an on-going transformation being triggered by the Divine:

> I see that the Divine Feminine is the energy that rose in me—the energy that moves us to create with passion, and see everything as connected. This entity touched me, entered me and set me on fire with passion for Creation, for the world. She is the one who healed me and breathed new life into me with her desire and her love. She transformed me from a quiet, shy person into a person who could speak out for the Earth—an Earth I had experienced as being part of my own body.

It took Anya years to come to such a clear understanding of the process she had been undergoing, and it was not always easy for her. Like her, almost all of us have difficulty accepting—or even recognizing —that we are involved in a process of spiritual transformation. There are a number of reasons for this. One is simply that we have never been exposed to the idea that such a thing is possible. Another is that there is usually some part of us that doesn't *want* it to be happening: we know, whether consciously or not, that the path this process is setting us out on is a difficult one. One of the great truths relating to psychological and spiritual growth is that change is painful. Even if we don't consciously think this is so, we subconsciously know it to be true and, consequently, tend to resist change. Even when the change is taking us from something bad to something good, there is some re-calcitrant part of our psyche that struggles against it. A good example of this is found in people who remain in negative, unfulfilling relation-ships even though other opportunities might be open to them. And even if such extreme examples don't exist in our own lives, we can all think of destructive habits we don't break or unproductive ruts we remain in day after day simply because the old way is the comfortable way, it is the known way.

In Emmet Fox's discourses on fear he says that the unknown is perhaps the greatest of all our fears and that many of our fears are actually fear of the unknown in different guises. One of the reasons people sometimes stay in negative relationships longer than they should is that they don't know what life will be like when they leave. To some degree we all tend to do the same thing. We cling to the se-curity of what we know, and we resist what we don't know.

This natural inner resistance to change becomes compounded when we are forced to admit to ourselves that a divine force is triggering this transformation. Although this awareness is the one great truth that will steady us along the way and bring us the comfort when we need it most, it is often the one that is most difficult for us to accept. The very moment we begin to sense that the Divine is propelling us along, we begin to ask ourselves questions like "How could this be happening to me?" and "Why would God choose to touch someone like me in this way?" Interestingly enough, almost every person I interviewed for this book mentioned having feelings like this in spite of the fact that I never asked a question about it or raised the subject.

We are not alone in this. In their moments of doubt the great mystics have asked themselves the same questions. In her writings, Mechthild often hinted at how undeserving she thought herself to be and in some of her bleaker moments even called herself "worthless" and "utterly faithless". Hildegard repeatedly identified herself as "a poor little figure of a woman" and wondered why God would ask such an insignificant creature—and especially a feminine creature— to be the voice for his words.

While these moments of self-doubt are inevitable, we mustn't let them keep us from accepting the fact that the process we are undergoing is essentially spiritual in nature. As you are probably all well aware, one very practical thing we can do in this regard is to begin—if it hasn't been begun already—the psychological work we need to do to erase our feelings of inadequacy. Of course, the ultimate cure for self-doubt is the realization that we are one with God. And while most of us are probably quite a ways from truly realizing this—and instantly reaching enlightenment—we can, in the meantime, keep this great truth in our minds and hold it closely to our hearts.

But all our doubts don't come from a sense of inadequacy. Some arise out of a very sincere humility: it really is hard for us to imagine that the Divine is touching us in some extraordinary way. One antidote for this is, of course, the knowledge that this transformative process is touching everyone. As mentioned in Chapter Six, great thinkers like Gopi Krishna and the Jesuit priest Teilhard de Chardin have written volumes telling us that the consciousness of the entire human race is involved in a process of transformation that is propelling us ever nearer to union with the Divine. Teilhard described this in Christian terms and called it the Omega-point. He saw it as a coming together of human thought at a higher collective level that would result at some time in the distant future in a human race that was at once human and divine. Gopi Krishna described a similar process in yogic terms. He also believed that the whole human race was being propelled onward by the great cosmic power Shakti, gradually moving towards a state of enlightenment, and that some people today are simply experiencing a slightly accelerated version of this process. In terms of hatha yoga this would mean that an increased amount of kundalini-shakti—more, in other words, than what is normally required to maintain normal everyday life—is flowing through the body. (See Chapter Thirteen for more on this.) In many cases this is simply an increase in prana-shakti that is moving throughout the body as a whole; in other cases it is actually kundalini-shakti that is in a limited way beginning to make its way through the chakras and up the spine. In either case, Gopi Krishna for one would have reminded us that it is a very natural process and one that is being propelled by an all-knowing, all-loving divine intelligence.

This knowledge should help us to keep the process in perspective, to recognize it for what it is, to accept it, and to flow in whatever direction it wants to take us.

Your Yearning to Create

While Mechthild was far along in her process of transformation and the yearning that consumed her was—at least in its most apparent form—for union with her Beloved, the nature of her work indicates she also had a deep passion to express herself. Once she gave into the urging of her confessor and gave herself permission to begin to write, it was as if a creative floodgate was opened. Rather than simply being a recording of her experiences— which was really all her confessor directed her to do—her writing expressed an exceptional amount of creativity, especially given her time and place. For instance, she used a variety of literary forms that ranged from poems and dramatic scenes to essays. She also took themes from contemporary life, such as the courtly love tradition, and molded them to her purpose, and all this was done using language that was not only innovative but powerful, evocative, and exquisitely beautiful.

The following exercise is one that will help you tune into your own creative urge—the fire in your own belly—so that you recognize it more easily, respond to it more readily, hold it more comfortably and, most importantly, allow it to grow.

You have to wait to do this exercise until the next time you feel a strong urge to create something—be it a story, a song, a picture, or even a loaf of bread. Allow yourself to follow the urge and get to that point when you are aching to begin but when the paper, canvas—or whatever medium is yours—is still blank, silent, or still. Then, instead of beginning, stop and find a comfortable position and prepare to do a creative visualization exercise.

1. When you are seated comfortably enter that deep meditative space where you feel safe, protected, filled with light, and free from the harsh inner voice of criticism. Sit for a moment basking in this light.
2. Now begin to focus on the actual physical sensation of the yearning as it rests in your body. Where is it located in your body? Where does it seem to originate? Is it still or does it move or change? If it moves or changes, how does it?
3. Maintaining this awareness of your body as a physical container for this yearning, move deeper into the feeling. Go deeper still until you

sense the source of the yearning. Sit with this sensation, becoming more and more familiar with it.

4. *Feel it growing, rising up, and as it does allow it to turn into radiant white light that flows upward, surrounds your heart and, as in previous exercises, continues to rise up, flow out your arms and hands and into the creative work that you are longing to begin.*

CHAPTER TEN

A Fish Doesn't Drown, A Bird Doesn't Fall

Anya's intuitive understanding that the process she was undergoing was both natural and divine has helped her immensely over the years, especially in coming to terms with her second profound spiritual experience. This experience brought her to the realization that this process, though ultimately a spiritual one, is rooted firmly in the body and may be experienced in a very physical way. For the majority of us these physical sensations may be as gentle as the one Wendi described in Chapter Six when as a child on the beach in South Africa she felt an energy gently rising in her and flowing back and forth between her and God. For a much smaller number of people, however, these sensations can be quite powerful and very disconcerting. But even for these individuals such powerful experiences generally occur only rarely or for very limited periods of time.

Anya had only one. It occurred just after the birth of her third child. At the time she was experiencing such terrible back pain that she could barely lift her newborn infant. She was also suffering from post-partum depression, which went undiagnosed as it so commonly did until recently. Her husband, who was in his residency, was gone virtually all the time. She had no nearby family to help her with the baby or the other two children. One day the pain became so extreme she could no longer function. After a neighbor took her two older children, she took the infant to bed with her, collapsed in pain and despair, and was unable to move for the next few days. As she lay there gripped by pain and tears, she lost her will to live. She felt, she says, "inadequate—like a nothing". On the evening of the third day, she said a prayer from the bottom of her heart asking for help and surrendered, putting herself in God's hands.

At some time in the middle of the night she awoke from a strange dream. She heard a noise like a high-pitched tone and had the sensation that something in her brain had been switched on. She then began to have a visionary experience:

> I saw five colorful dials, or wheels, turning in the air—they were blue, pink, and red. And with them energy came, as if I was being turned on by the wheels. A magnetic pressure held me to the bed and I could not move. Then particles of energy raced through me—vibrating and tingling like a river of fire and flowing through me until I was burning hot. The feeling ran from the top of my head and through my body and my limbs, and circled back up again and again. My heart pumped with a strength and power that felt as though it could pump itself right out of my body.
>
> I felt as though my heart were a being unto itself but that it was powered by some other force—a force that had the power to give and take life. This was the force that had given me this life, this body, but it did not belong to me. I was not in control of it. My racing heart did not pump out of fear. It was being pumped by healing hands of love. I knew I would be all right, but as I felt the energy fill up my body, I was also aware that it held such incredible power that it could easily have killed me if that had been its purpose. I trusted it, and gave myself up to it. It kept increasing for a time and then subsided slowly, until I could move again. I heard a voice say clearly, "You are not nothing. You are mine." I felt it was the voice of Christ.
>
> When my heart eased, and my body slowly ceased its trembling,

I sat up, filled with wonder and joy. I woke my sleeping husband and recounted the story to him...When I awoke for the day, I was so enraptured with joy—and a new realization entered—my severe back pain was completely gone! I had experienced a profound healing, physically, emotionally, and spiritually. The world was again bathed in light. I loved everyone I met...

Understanding her profound mystical experience as an out-pouring of God's healing love provided Anya with part of the context she needed to trust what was happening during the experience itself and to flow where the spirit was leading her throughout the following years. Unfortunately, it didn't provide her with a complete framework—one that would allow her to be completely comfortable with what had occurred or with the energy as it has ebbed and flowed over the years. In fact, when she first wrote me describing the experience, she prefaced it by saying that she continued to wonder whether it might have been a brush with mental illness rather than a profound spiritual experience. These kinds of doubts plague virtually every person I have ever met who has experienced strong physical sensations on the spiritual path. When these people search for answers to their questions about what has happened to them they often find it almost impossible to find answers. Anya searched for years before she found someone who could help her put this profound experience into context for her:

> Once or twice I confided in a friend, but they didn't understand; it had no relevance for them. The church I belonged to did not have a place for me to share. The only comment I got was "Well, sounds like you've had a real experience." They had no advice about how to balance yourself, or deal with the reeling energy and overflowing love. Even when I told meditation teachers, the usual response was that they had no experience of what I was talking about and no explanation for it. One of these teachers did say that what I had couldn't have been a "real" experience of oneness, because if it had been people would have been drawn to me. I could not bring myself to tell him that, yes, people *had* been drawn to me because it felt like it was bragging...

When Anya was eventually introduced to the concept of the divine feminine, in the form of kundalini-shakti, she finally found a framework in which she could place this experience and indeed the entire transformative process she had been undergoing for years. Even before she came in contact with this information, Anya would have been reassured that what she experienced was not a nervous breakdown by seeing how many of the elements in her experience were similar to those found in the experiences of the great mystics. Spinning wheels, for example, are common in mystical visions. The illustrations of almost all of Hildegard's visions contain wheel-like shapes, and the vision from the Bible that we generally refer to as Ezekiel's "chariot" is, as mentioned earlier, not actually an entire chariot but simply four whirling "wheels" much like the ones Anya describes. Many mystics, including Hildegard, describe the feeling of being pressed down and unable to move. And as we've seen throughout the book, virtually all mystics tell of experiences of light and heat. In fact, Anya's description of the love and the river of fire she felt flowing through her body is strangely reminiscent of a verse in Book I of *The Flowing Light of the Godhead* in which Mechthild described the moment when her Beloved reveals his "divine heart" to her. During the vision, Mechthild gazed at the heart and described it as "red gold burning in a great fire of coals". As she was gazing at this burning heart, her Beloved picked her up and placed her in the middle of it [Book I, 4].

These comparisons between Anya's vision and those of the great mystics help provide a context for these types of experiences. In addition to this, the passionate, physical aspect of Mechthild's story is invaluable because it illustrates so clearly how the work the Divine does on our spirits is so firmly rooted in our bodies. Mechthild's story is also an inspiration because, in spite of how unremittingly visceral these experiences were for her, she did not try to avoid them. In fact, her writings indicate she not only allowed herself to experience the passionate intensity of this transformation, she embraced it.

One of the most powerful examples of this is found towards the end of Book II in a conversation she is having with her Beloved. She says she is weak with longing and begs him to come to her. The Lord, her Beloved, answers by telling her of his own love. She then cries out from what she calls her dank prison and accuses him of leaving her wounded and uncared for:

(I) am wounded to the death

By the beam of your fiery love,
Now you leave me, Lord lying in misery,
My wounds untended, in great torment.
[Book II, 25]

Her Beloved responds by telling her not to be so impatient and promising that there will be a time when he will give himself to her forever. Mechthild is clearly not satisfied with this and asks him where he will be when her eyes weep in loneliness, when her mouth remains mute, and when her body pleads with her. She goes on:

When my flesh wastes away,
My blood dried up, my bones torture me,
My veins contract,
And my heart melts out of love for you,
And my soul roars
With the bellowings of a hungry lion...
[Book II, 25]

But no matter how intense these physical sensations become, Mechthild continues to welcome them, revel in them, and even seek them out. In a passage in Book I she insists she is ready for more. In this verse she informs a messenger from heaven that she is no longer a child and that she has become a "full-grown bride". She then forcefully demands that the messenger take her to her lover. The messenger complies and takes her to a secret chamber that is hidden inside the Godhead itself. Now called the "bride of all delights", she finds an abode of love, a bed, and her Beloved waiting for her in the chamber. He is the "fairest of all lovers" and is indeed the Lord himself. The Lord then tells her to lie upon the bed and take off all her clothes, for nothing—no fear, no shame, no superficial virtue—can be allowed to separate them from each other. They then lie upon the bed and he tells her he will fulfill her all-consuming desire with his "limitless lavishness". After this, Mechthild tells us:

Then a blessed stillness
That both desire comes over them.
He surrenders himself to her.
And She surrenders herself to him.
What happens to her then—she knows...
[Book I, 44]

One of the reasons Mechthild was able to accept these sensations, even though she was sworn to a life of virginal chastity, was that the imagery of the Lover and the Beloved provided a framework for her. This framework gave her a context for understanding both the physical and the highly charged sexual nature of the images that came to her and allowed her to simply be with them. It easy to imagine that, without a context like this to place her experiences in, Mechthild might well have believed she was being "sinful" or "wicked" for having them. Fortunately, this imagery of the Lover and the Beloved was readily available to nuns and monks and was a very natural one for those who had mystical experiences to use. The Old Testament book The Song of Songs and its sensual descriptions of longings of the Lover for the Beloved were extremely popular in the Middle Ages. What's more, the Church had long been referring to nuns as "Brides of Christ" and the beguines saw themselves in much the same way. From this time onward various Christian saints and mystics, St Theresa of Avila and St John of the Cross for example, were able to use this concept of the Lover and the Beloved to frame and understand their experiences.

Unfortunately, this imagery wasn't really available for the common man and woman. The natural tendency to honor the human body that had been common in early cultures had long been lost: the Church had been busy for centuries telling people the body was "bad" and the "spirit" was good. For the most part any Christians who had profound spiritual experiences and felt powerful physical sensations during them would have seen these sensations as "lustful" and would have in many cases punished themselves for having them. They would have believed, as the Church did, that the body with its physical yearnings leads us away from God and onto the path towards damnation.

This attitude has been pervasive in our Western society right up to contemporary times, and as you are undoubtedly well aware, even now we are light-years away from having a healthy attitude towards the human body. Nearly naked bodies may be splashed all over billboards and bedroom scenes are played out on television during "family" viewing hours. But none of this is particularly healthy; none of it feels clean and natural. Rather there is something voyeuristic about it. It is permeated by the feeling that it is "naughty" and that we are "getting away with something" by viewing it.

Thus the idea that the body is bad and the spirit is good remains buried deep within our Western psyches. One of the most important steps we can take on the spiritual-creative journey is to make sure it is no longer buried in ours. This is essential to our being comfortable with the idea that our body is the container for our spiritual experiences and the vessel that receives and holds our creative inspiration. This is particularly true for people who have intensely physical experiences like the one Anya had but it also has significance for those who like Wendi have more gentle experiences.

It is a great misfortune for us today that the framework of the Lover and the Beloved that Mechthild and other mystics used has been lost to us and that a new one has not yet widely replaced it. As you'll see in Chapters Twelve and Thirteen, the teachings of Tantra can provide this type of a framework for us by giving us a deeper understanding of how the divine feminine spiritual energy works in the human body. One of the most beautiful things about Tantra is, in fact, the way it celebrates the body: since the body is created by Shakti, made of out of the essence of Shakti, and is indeed one with Shakti, it is held to be sacred. In this same vein the sensations that course through the body, for instance those of love and sexual yearning, are seen to be manifestations of our longing for union with the Divine. One reason this is so important, as we have seen from Anya's story, is that it can keep us from being frightened or overwhelmed by any powerful physical sensations we might happen to have. Another is that if we see our bodies as part of the spiritual process we will begin to listen to them more closely.

In *The Flowing Light* Mechthild certainly did this. In one truly remarkable passage near the end of Book I, she brought this home by personifying her body's physical senses and having a conversation with them. At one point she even gave them a severe talking to— telling them, in short, to settle down and accept any discomfort they might experience because the ultimate goal is worth whatever they might have to endure. But she also listened to them, heard that they were afraid, and reassured them by reminding them that what they were experiencing was totally natural and that they would not be harmed. This passage begins by Mechthild telling her senses that she is a full-grown bride who wants to go to her Lover. The senses reply:

Oh, Lady, if you go there
We shall go completely blind.

The Godhead is so blazing hot,
As you well know,
That all the fire and all the glowing embers
That make the heavens and all the saints glow and burn
Have flowed out from his divine breath...
How can you stay there for even an hour?

[Book I, 44]

In her reassuring response Mechthild tells them that God has created all creatures to live according to their natures and that it is her nature as a human being to go to God. In a beautifully poetic piece she reminds her bodily senses of this and at the same time indicated to her readers that as long as they follow their true nature they will not be harmed:

A fish in water does not drown.
A bird in the air does not plummet.
Gold in fire does not perish.
Rather, it gets its purity and radiant color there.
God has created all creatures to live according
     to their nature.
How, then, am I to resist my nature?
I must go from all things to God...

[Book I, 44]

After comforting her bodily senses in this way, Mechthild goes on to tell them not to be sad that she isn't taking their advice this time. She assures them that she will continue to listen to them and let them instruct her in the future—especially when she returns from this trip to visit her Lover in the very heart of the Godhead:

When I return I shall certainly need your advice;
For the earth is full of snares.

[Book I, 44]

In these few simple lines Mechthild gave a great volume of advice. As we all personally know, our spiritual journey through the material world is indeed beset by snares—blockades, detours, wrong turns, and obstacles of every shape and size. Mechthild was telling us that listening to our bodies, our physical senses and sensations, can help us avoid many of these pitfalls.

This is really what Christine was talking about earlier in the book when she said that she gave her body a voice. If we haven't already done so, we all need to give our bodies voices and then, as Mechthild advised us, to pay attention to what these voices have to say.

This is one reason "body work" has become such an important part of the contemporary spiritual movement. Often quite unconsciously people are drawn to getting massages, having Shiatsu done, participating in creative movement and dance, or taking part in any of the other practices available that work on the physical body. While these practices are often begun to improve physical health or overcome illness, many people eventually discover a direct relationship between the body work they are doing and their spiritual growth. One explanation often offered for this phenomenon is that body work can release certain blockages that prevent the flow of subtle energy—like prana or chi—through the body. These blockages might be caused by old injuries, unhealthy habits or even, some say, by deeply buried psychological issues and traumas that are held in the physical body as well as the subconscious mind. While Western science is slowly becoming more accepting of practices such as acupuncture and Shiatsu, there is no real agreement that something like prana or chi even exists and certainly no acceptance of the idea that psychological issues can be held in the body and block the flow of this energy. Still, there is an ever-increasing amount of anecdotal evidence that supports this. A good friend of mine who was a Shiatsu therapist actually went back to school and entered a four-year training program in psychotherapy because so many of his clients had deep psychological and spiritual issues arise during massages, and he wanted to become qualified to be of assistance when situations like this arose.

Christine also provided a good example of this earlier when she talked about the experience she had of divine feminine creative energy flowing through her body. As you'll recall this experience occurred during a weeklong course that involved a great deal of work with creative movement and body awareness. In describing events that led up to the experience Christine said that at one point she had felt as if a block had been removed from the base of her spine. When this occurred she felt a vibrational sound energy rise out of this area and travel upwards to her mouth. It made her feel, she said, as if the area around the base of her spine had opened up and was breathing for the first time. Her sense of this blockage was that it had been caused, or at least begun, by sexual abuse she had endured and been traumatized by as a child.

Regardless of what these blockages are or how they occur, they are very significant according to theories based on Tantra and yoga. (See Chapter Thirteen.) This is because the "energy" they are said to block is the life energy itself which flows through the body in the form of prana-shakti and, in some cases, kundalini-shakti. It seems obvious that we would want to remove anything that might be blocking the flow of life energy through our bodies. But in order to remove the blocks we need to be aware of them, and we are not going to be aware of them if we are not listening to our bodies.

The more comfortable you are simply sitting inside your own skin and quietly listening to your body, the more aware you will become of the sensations associated with prana flowing through your body. You will also become more aware of where you hold tightness and how that tightness—whatever it may be caused by—inhibits the flow of this life essence. On the positive side, you may also learn that there is a much greater flow of this energy in your body than you ever imagined. You may also realize that its flow is inextricably linked to your deepest yearnings and that it is gently pushing you towards goals that sometimes lead in unexpected directions.

An increasing ability to sit with and listen to your body is also necessary to generate ever-deepening levels of emotional awareness. This is true because, even if we subscribe to the Western scientific suggestion that emotions are nothing more than chemical reactions occurring in the brain, emotions generally come to us as physical, bodily sensations—obvious as it may sound, this is the reason we call them *feelings*.

Emotions and creative expression are inextricably linked in many ways. It has long been said that art is not great unless it is able to evoke an emotional response. When Violetta dies at the end of a good production of Verdi's *La Traviata*, you weep. If you have ever looked at a painting such as Botticelli's *Madonna and Child* you know you can't look at it without feeling some of that mother's love for that child. Great abstract art evokes emotions too; you can't look at Picasso's *Guernica* without feeling some of the wrenching inhumanity and horror that is caused by war. In order for these creations to evoke these emotions, their creators had to feel them.

But this emotional element isn't just a factor in "great" art; it is the ingredient that makes your creative expression important—whether you are doing it just for yourself or for others as well. Emotional content is what gives creative work meaning. Feeling emotions and letting them flow outward into the work is what makes others respond to it. This is why you often hear such wonderful words from people who are speaking at powerfully emotional events like funerals and weddings.

A while back I attended a funeral of a friend's father who had lived a long and wonderful life. For this reason the funeral wasn't as sad an occasion as some are. But when my friend's daughter, who had never shown any extraordinary ability to write or speak before, finished reading the eulogy she had written there was not a person there who was not weeping for her loss. The picture she painted of her Zaide was so vibrant we could see him gliding across an old outdoor basketball court, kicking up a storm on the dance floor with his beloved wife, and swinging his grandchildren through the air as clearly as if his life story was playing out on a giant screen behind her.

This surprising flow of creativity often occurs when people write speeches for weddings too—not ones where most of the guests are cynically wondering how long the marriage can possibly last, but the ones where the two people are joyously in love and wonderfully matched. You've probably noticed how a father who has never written a speech or spoken in front of a group in his life can stand up at a wedding like this and have everyone in the room laughing and crying at the same time.

Emotions are, in short, what give our creative work power. Just recently I went to an art workshop in a gallery with Christine. The idea of the workshop was to pick a painting we were drawn to in the gallery, meditate on it, and allow ourselves to become completely immersed in it. After this we went to another room and worked on a piece of our own—not one that copied the original piece in any way but one that flowed out of our reaction to it. After we finished our pieces we took them back to the gallery, laid them in front of the artwork we had originally chosen, and discussed what we had learned from the process.

When we got to Christine's piece, she was visibly upset. The original painting that Christine had picked was an abstract done in soft blues and greens with radiant white light seeping into it. Christine's piece was done in stark red, blue, and black. The gentle spiritual light from the first painting had been rendered as a gash of blue lightning slicing through the red and black. The lines had been drawn and the colors applied in the stark simplistic manner a child might use.

Even though the emphasis of the exercise was on the process and not the end product, Christine felt that in terms of technical artistic merit her piece fell short of the other pieces done during the exercise. But as soon as the other members of the group began commenting on it, it became clear they saw the piece much differently than Christine did. Words like "powerful" and "vibrant" were used to describe it. The entire group commented on the power, strength, and confidence that seemed to rise up out of it. No other piece done during the entire workshop evoked such a positive, emotional response from the group —not even when we all went back and created a second piece, including one by Christine that was technically far superior to the first one she did. This was because Christine had been in touch with powerful emotions while she was doing her artwork and she was able without any hesitation at all to go with those emotions and let them flow right out onto the paper. And people responded.

While this story shows that allowing ourselves to experience and be with our emotions influences the power held in what we create, it is just as important for the process of creation itself. The deeper you can go into your emotions, the deeper you can go into your art. The more in touch you are with your emotions, the clearer you will be about where your creative expression needs to go and what it needs to express.

One of the most important aspects of being able to allow ourselves to really "feel" our feelings is that it is a key to being in touch with our intuition. There is hardly anyone in the contemporary spiritual movement who doesn't recognize the importance of intuition. Although intuition isn't generally considered an emotion in itself, it is inextricably linked to our emotions and to how comfortable we are with experiencing them in a physical way. Just consider the expressions we use when we are talking about it: "I just had a gut feeling"; "I decided to go with my gut"; "I just felt in my heart it was the right thing to do"; "This feeling just came over me, and I knew I had to..." Following our intuition is thought of as following our hearts, and it is seen as the exact opposite of following our "heads". And it is one of the keys to true creative expression. There is a wonderful example of this in Wendi's story. It is also a good example of how our creativity can express itself in very unexpected ways.

For years Wendi had felt a deep longing to create a home that was truly an expression of herself. When she and her second husband got married, they bought a small home in an older area of the city on a lot that was full of large trees. When Wendi told her husband about her feelings about what she wanted to do with their new home, he was very supportive. Encouraged by this Wendi decided to follow what her intuition was trying to tell her regarding the house and to try to design the restoration herself.

When she wrote to me for the first time after taking the workshop she explained how she had created a vision of the home she wanted, worked with designers to get her vision down on paper, and then guided the building process every step of the way. When she wrote me again about a year later the restoration was complete, and she told me in a lot more detail about what a tremendous creative challenge the project had been for her and how much the house meant to her. This was particularly true she said because she had come to realize there was a connection between the way she had designed the house and the light-filled experience she had had on the beach as a child in South Africa. She wrote:

> I have just completed my first and most daunting creative challenge in my life—I have redesigned and rebuilt the home we bought when my husband and I were first married. I have struggled with my vision for the house—seeing parts of it and being able to tackle certain areas as they were revealed to me. Then we decided it was time to gut and completely rebuild the remaining eighty percent of the house. We are surrounded by beautiful old trees and face south into the enormous prairie skies and sunshine. I had always been compelled to break open walls to bring in the wonderful light that surrounds us. So we did it. I now have 15 windows in my bedroom alone! The living room and kitchen walls are all glass—letting the sunlight flow in all day long. Now of course, I understand where my need for light comes from and why I felt so compelled to open up my home and fill it with sunshine.

Wendi's intuitive desire to create a home that was full of light came before her recollection of her light-filled visionary experience on the beach. But because she was able to follow this intuition even though she did not know where it was leading, her new light-filled home was completed and ready for her to live in just when she was beginning to integrate her early experience of the light into her life. As time goes on the sunlight pouring through her windows will serve as a constant reminder to her that, at the very core of her being, she is one with God. Sitting in that sunlight she will also have the joy of knowing that following her intuition not only led to her creating just what she needed but also put her in touch with a level of creative ability that she had no idea she had.

None of this—the intuitive vision of what her home would look like, the passion to carry this vision to fruition, not even the recall of the lost memory of her experience on the beach—would have come about if Wendi had not been on a journey that was leading her to that place where, as she told us earlier, "I suddenly realized that I felt fully aware of myself. No longer did my body and skin feel alien to me. I feel as if I carry an essence of that creator within me all the time as I move about my life. I see myself as divinely feminine now."

Reading all this gives you a sense that Wendi has a very quiet but very deep passion running just beneath her surface. It also gives you a sense of the calm, collected way she is learning to trust this passion and flow with it. This fits with both her personality and with the gradual way her transformation is occurring. And many of you will be able to identify with it.

Others will find more to identify with in Anya's story. Her words paint a picture of a much more intense journey and far more tumultuous passion. Fortunately, Anya has generally been fairly comfortable with these strong emotions. This has allowed her to follow her inner intuition and learn to express her creative voice in a number of unique ways. Although Anya has always loved to play around with all types of art materials, she doesn't think of herself as an artist in any sense of the word. She also loves music and enjoys what she calls "fooling around" with the guitar and violin. But for the most part the ways in which Anya's strong intuitive voice has led her to express herself have not been ones traditionally associated with creativity. Anya's journey down this pathway was kicked into high gear directly after her second mystical experience:

> Right after my profound experience I was filled with longing to under-
> stand the Universe, and became enthralled by physics, wanting to find

an answer to the *sensation of* magnetism, the healing energy, and the profound experience of light. I read Einstein with understanding.

I immersed myself in a book by Carl Sagan and other prominent scientists. I became interested in stargazing and natural science. I had gained a new level of awareness intellectually and was able to remember and understand things that before I had not been able to. I felt as though my life, and all life had meaning and that behind everything was the source of our being—a loving powerful energy that could move hearts and mountains. Joy overflowed. I had a sense of curiosity and child-like wonder at everything in the natural world. With my new awareness, however, came also an ability to understand the plight of the natural world. I had a profound connection to nature, particularly to trees. I felt their strength and love, but also their sorrow. I needed to act—to find a way to ease the pain and express the beauty and love that all nature was singing to creation all the time, so that people hear it and become aware, like I had become. I had become a living container for this healing force. I thought many times that I could easily burst, or die from too much joy.

Anya's words "I needed to act" in the passage above are deceptively simple. This need was a raw, visceral cry that rose out of Anya's soul and spoke to her in a way nothing had before in her life. This was her inner intuitive voice telling her what she needed to do. She didn't need to listen to it for long before she became aware that it was telling her to focus her energy on the environmental movement. Once she set off down this pathway, creative inspiration began to flow to her. Although this inspiration has naturally ebbed and flowed depending on circumstances in her life, it has remained a powerful force in her life sometimes manifesting in more traditional creative outlets such as art and writing and at other times in providing her with a well of creative ideas for developing projects, increasing awareness, and raising funds for worthy endeavors:

> I had so much energy at the time that I was able to birth endless projects
> and involve and inspire others to help me in the work. I was aware of the
> sacredness of my task, and that it was not me who was doing the work—
> it was the fire within me that was a gift from the spirit that had come to
> me to bring light where I had experienced the darkness. People came
> from all around to help me achieve my goals. It was amazing.

With the help of a good friend, Anya used this energy to found a grass-roots environmental movement. The group, she explains, became the vehicle through which she was able to satisfy her "incredible need to act":

> The aim of the group was to deepen awareness of global and environmental issues...We got the town recycling program going, encouraged tree planting, had environmental fairs, hosted organic farming conferences, got involved on a national scale with a climate change project, and got involved in local schools. I think the undercurrent of all the work I did was to encourage others to get involved, and many amazing people with energy and talent came to help with the work.

One example of how this "fire within" led her was a project she came up with to increase environmental awareness. The idea for the project came to her when she realized one of people who joined their grass-roots group was a man who had been the founder of a café that had been locally famous for the folk music and poetry performed there in the seventies. Seeing this person in this new context gave Anya the idea of reviving the folk-music café for an evening. With the help of the former café owner and the other members of the environmental group, Anya managed to bring together a number of outstanding musicians for the event—it was successful beyond anyone's expectations and was, in fact, repeated for the next seven years. Although one purpose of the event was to raise funds for a good cause, thinking back on it Anya realizes it had even more impact in terms of building community and empowering others to take action. "The event really worked," she says, "to bring many people together in different ways, and brought much joy—and even more energy— we all received so much more than we gave."

Wendi's light-filled house and Anya's folk-music café are examples of the unexpectedly creative and joyful pathways the "fire within" can lead us along. But in order to be lead by this fire, we have to be able to sit with it. We have to allow ourselves to experience this spiritual force in our physical, earth-rooted bodies.

A Fish Doesn't Drown, A Bird Doesn't Fall

Now that you have heard the stories of mystics like Mahadevi and Mechthild and women like Christine, Britta, Wendi, and Anya it is time to tell your story—or at least begin to tell it. While this might well be the start of you writing a great deal, in detail, about your spiritual journey, the point here is to simply do an overview. It should start at the beginning of your spiritual journey—quite possibly in childhood with any special awareness or sensitivities you might have had—and then go on to describe the main highlights or junctures along the way.

One of the purposes of this exercise is to help you discover patterns that might emerge and see if there is a particular framework—a way of viewing your experiences—that fits your journey and helps you make sense of it. This framework could be any of a number of things. It might simply be seeing your journey more clearly as a process that is both natural and divine. It could involve finding a metaphor that encapsulates it, like Mechthild's imagery of the Lover and the Beloved. It could even be beginning to see it in terms of some more specific process like a gradual kundalini awakening or being descended upon by the Holy Spirit. Regardless, this exercise is essentially about discovering—or affirming—that you are a spiritual being on a spiritual path that is a natural, normal part of evolution and transformation.

Although this exercise is set up as one for writing, you might also like to try creating a mixed media collage to tell your story.

1. When you are seated comfortably and have a pen and paper ready, enter that deep meditative space where you feel safe, protected, filled with light, and free from the harsh inner voice of criticism.
2. Allow yourself to become increasingly aware that you are breathing in prana—the radiant life force.
3. Concentrate on this radiance until you are filled with an even richer luminous, resplendent white light. Stay for a while in this space allowing the radiance of the light to intensify.
4. Allow your mind to travel back in time until you come to the beginning of your spiritual awareness or your first spiritual experience.
5. Bring your awareness back to the light that fills you, see it flowing up-

wards, moving to your heart, resting there for a moment and intensifying with each heartbeat. Then see it flowing to your shoulders, down your arm, out your hand, into the fingers that are resting on your paper and holding your pen.

6. When you finish describing the first part of your journey, go on to the next highlight or significant occurrence. If this doesn't come to you freely—or if you have needed to take a break—repeat the beginning steps of the exercise.

I Must Sing, Dance, Hear, Tell!

The more we are able to be rooted in our bodies and see ourselves as the embodiment of the divine feminine, the more clearly we are able to hear the voice of this cosmic force as she calls to us. If you think back to the story of Britta, you will recall that she was primarily an artist, but that after her experience of the Holy Spirit she suddenly became able to write poetry. If she hadn't been listening, she would never have heard the voice calling out to her and offering up this surprising gift. The very first poem she received went like this:

Write, write, write,
The word I give you
Spread it with the wind
   out over the earth

Give it as life
to hungering souls.

At that time, of course, she had no way of knowing that it would be the first of many, many poems that would eventually come to her—especially since she had never written before and had never evinced any talent for writing. Only when she looked back on this particular poem much later would it become clear to her that she was being "told" to write down not just this poem but all the ones that would come. Britta was being "instructed" by the Holy Spirit to write. Over the next couple of years, it also became increasingly clear that she was being led not just to set the poems down but also to share them with others. Eventually she became aware that she *must* do this; she had to overcome any insecurity she felt about her ability to write or the quality of the poems and simply send them out into the universe.

Not many people get a message from the creative spirit as blatant as Britta's "Write, write, write!" There is, however, a long tradition among mystics of hearing voices that are just this clear. In Britta's case, there is an added significance to the fact that this was the very first poem she received. When she first sent this particular poem to me it was mixed in with a number of other poems, and I had no way of knowing that it was the one that had come to her before all the others. But just about the time I was beginning to put her story into the book, she sent me a letter in which she made a point of explaining that this poem was the very first one she ever received and that it came to her directly after her profound mystical experience. The moment I read this, goose bumps crept up my arms—for this was the same message Hildegard received immediately after the blinding vision of the living light she had when she was forty-two.

According to Hildegard's writings about her own life, she began to have visionary experiences of various types when she was a very small child and continued to have them her whole life. However, she kept very quiet about these experiences and told only a few selected people over the years. When she was young it appears that this included her parents, her nurse, and perhaps some of her older siblings. Later, it seems likely that the only people she shared these experiences with were the monk Volmar, a nun named Richardis whom she cared about very deeply, and possibly one or two others.

This all changed after the profound experience of the living light that she had when she was forty-two. Shortly after this, Hildegard heard a "heavenly voice" which called out to her saying, "O weak person...say and write what you see and hear." When she didn't follow the heavenly voice's instructions, it came to her a second time saying, "Speak therefore these marvelous things and write and speak those things taught in this manner." And again saying, "You therefore, o person, who receive these things not in the turmoil of deceit, but in the purity of simplicity, write what you see and hear."

After a good deal of initial resistance, which is discussed in the next chapter, Hildegard obeyed the voice. She began to say and write what she saw and heard in her visions and with this small step launched one of the most extraordinary floods of creative expression the world has ever seen.

Mechthild, too, heard the voice calling to begin to write—no matter what the consequences might be—but the voice came to her in quite a different manner. This voice, it seems, had been calling out to Mechthild quietly for some time, but she truly "heard" what it had been saying to her only after having a hideous nightmare. She described this dream in Book IV of *The Flowing Light of the Godhead*. The dream occurred, she said, in the twilight state just before sleep. In the dream she saw a devil fly over the earth. This devil was gigantic and horrific. Fiery sparks flew from his mouth and black flames covered him as he winged his way through the sky. Laughing with malicious glee and speaking in a raucous voice, he informed Mechthild that it no longer mattered that God had always been able to prevent him from tormenting her in the past, because now he was finding it increasingly easy to find hypocritical religious people who would torment her for him.

Mechthild defiantly replied that she would gladly suffer this torment if it meant that she would continue to receive the greetings from her divine lover. In this moment of open defiance, she also proclaimed that she had finally realized that the force of this love is so intense she could no longer keep silent about these marvelous greetings. In other words, she knew that she, like Hildegard before her, must say and write what she had seen and heard. But no sooner than this proclamation was out of her mouth, she fell into self-doubt, turning her attention from the devil to the Lord and begging him to tell her why he has chosen someone as weak and foolish as her for this task when he could easily have chosen a wise man or woman. At this, the Lord became extremely angry and demanded to know whether or not she was truly his. When she replied that yes, of course, she was, her Beloved said, "Shall I then not do with you what I want?" Mechthild knew that what her Beloved wanted is for her to write boldly about her experiences no matter what the consequences might be.

Overwhelmed and frightened by this experience Mechthild decided to seek the advice of her confessor, the Dominican monk Heinrich of Halle who later came to be a passionate supporter of her works. Trembling with fear, Mechthild unburdened herself and told him the story of her visions from the very beginning, and begged for advice. Heinrich listened and, much to Mechthild's surprise, responded by telling her to be light-hearted. Heinrich was sure that God had been watching over her and that he would undoubtedly continue to guide and protect her. Heinrich told her she not only had to tell people about her visions, she had to begin writing them down. In spite of her fear and self-doubt, Mechthild began. She knew in fact that she could not refuse because Heinrich was only verbalizing a message that had already come to her directly from the Divine.

Mahadevi's story gives us yet another example of how the divine voice calls us to creativity and is one that is easier for more of us to identify with. For Mahadevi didn't so much hear a voice as simply feel a need to express herself that bubbled up within her soul and flowed naturally out of her and into her poetry. That Mahadevi was continually responding to the call of this creative spirit is evidenced by the fact that more than two hundred of her poems are still in existence. This number is made remarkable by the fact that there wasn't a monastery system in medieval India like the one in Europe where a mystic's writings might have been preserved. This means Mahadevi probably wrote many more poems that were either lost as she wandered across India or never picked up by the oral tradition in the first place.

Although many references to exactly how the divine voice called her to creative expression may have been lost, the few places she does speak about it underscore how spontaneously it flowed out of her and how she knew without doubt that she had to express it. In one poem which was probably written soon after she came to live with her guru in Kalyana and was surrounded for the first time in her life by like-minded devotees, the creative spirit just seems to bubble joyously out of her. In this poem she cried:

I must sing, dance, hear, tell
Walk, speak

This joyous *must* that bubbled out of Mahadevi's innermost being is the same divine voice that told Hildegard to "say and write" and Britta to "write, write, write" and to throw herself even more deeply into her painting. It is also the voice that sent the frightening dream to Mechthild and awakened her to the awareness that the time had come for her to share her visions with the world. But of course this voice doesn't always shout quite so dramatically. For most of us it simply expresses itself in the longing to be creative that we have been talking about throughout the book—the kind of longing Wendi felt to take workshops and enroll in courses that would reconnect her with the writing she had loved so much as a child.

From the many stories told and the sacred writings that have been quoted so far in this book, I think that we can say with a fair degree of certainty that this longing—and the fountain of creative inspiration that so often accompanies it—are directly related to the process of spiritual transformation that so many of us are actively undergoing today. The idea that this longing to be creative is the voice of the Divine—in particular the divine feminine—calling out to us has also been shown to be a very valid one. All this, however, still leaves us with the question of exactly *why* the Divine calls us specifically to creativity.

In order to answer this question we need to look for a moment at the whole idea of the connection between creativity and spirituality. Although I have spent much of this book examining the relationship between these two phenomena, the connection between them is not on the surface an obvious one. In fact when I was younger and majoring in art at university, I saw creativity and spirituality as being at very opposite ends of the spectrum. Creative people were people like my friends in my art classes. We were rebels flaunting traditions, experimenting with drugs, pontificating that "God was dead", and mocking in every possible way the people we thought of as religious hypocrites—those who espoused Christian ideals in church on Sunday and spent the rest of the week gossiping, cheating people at work, polluting the environment, or at best giving little thought to the suffering of humanity.

Eventually, I came to see spirituality as something apart from organized religions, but even then I thought of spirituality in very obvious ways: spiritual people were the saints and mystics who had visions of the Divine, or they were those individuals who were called to the ministry or to dedicating their lives to God in service, or they were ordinary people who were drawn deeply and sincerely to practicing the tenets of their religious tradition. But even at that point I wasn't aware of any obvious connection between the creative and the spiritual. This big gap in my understanding remained even after I had been exposed for years to the idea that divinely inspired creativity was one of the ways the spiritual transformation triggered by kundalini-shakti manifested. To my mind *this* inspired creativity belonged to the world of saints and mystics; it had nothing to do with my world or the world of the people I knew who were musicians, artists, and writers—even though many of them were spiritual seekers. It certainly had nothing to do with me.

My realization that there was indeed a connection between kundalini-shakti and the creative inspiration ordinary people experienced grew slowly out of my own experience with inspiration. As I gave myself over to the voice that was urging me to give vent to my creative expression and allowed this force to flow through me, I became gradually aware that I was in some kind of holy space and that the act of writing itself became a sort of prayer. Often after I had been writing in this space, I would read what I had written and think, "Jeez, this is really good; who wrote it?"

Since those early days I have, of course, met countless creative people who have had—as you probably have yourself—this same experience. When I interviewed John Tavener for *The Fiery Muse* and asked him about the music that has made him one of the world's foremost modern classical composers, he described his experience in these words: "To work is to pray; to pray is to work. If I couldn't compose I would be cut off from the Holy Spirit."

By the time I finished *The Fiery Muse* and had begun leading more workshops and speaking at more conferences I became aware of just how widespread Tavener's attitude was and, even more importantly, how widespread the deep, passionate *yearning* to be in this holy creative space was becoming. It was about then that I had the realization I described in Chapter One that was triggered by Gopi Krishna describing the great spiritual longing that he had seen begin in the 1970s and continue to sweep through the world that included the upswing in new religions; the interest in Buddhism, Hinduism, and other Eastern traditions; the enthusiasm over yoga and tai chi; even the misdirected fascination with the occult. All of these—even those that lead temporarily down false paths—were evidence, he said, that humanity's longing to grasp the spiritual side of life was growing by leaps and bounds. This yearning, he said, was the evolutionary energy propelling us forward on our journey. The very moment that he chuckled and said in his deep, lyrical Indian accent, "That, *that*—is kundalini!" I finally realized that he meant what he was saying quite literally. The yearning *is* kundalini-shakti.

In a few places throughout the book, I have referred to this yearning as being the voice of Shakti—as Shakti calling to us. But in a certain sense it is more than this. It is not just Shakti calling to us: it is her very real presence in our bodies and the way we *feel* her as she goes about the work of transforming us—and pushing us into the very activities that will, in a cyclical way, help move the process along.

Even though this realization was a major one for me, I still didn't understand exactly *why* this great cosmic force was calling out to me and so many others to be *creative*. At some level I had become aware that the act of being creative had actually become a kind of spiritual practice for me and for many others. This was especially clear to me when I was in that holy space Tavener described in which creative work actually becomes a prayer. But I still wasn't completely sure why Shakti wouldn't just call us to prayer, to meditation, to the ministry, or to any of the more obvious spiritual practices that so many people were being called to.

Over time I've come to think there are many reasons for this. The most central relates, I believe, to the essential nature of the divine feminine. She is after all the creatrix of the cosmos, and as the Tantric scriptures tell us, each of us individually is a microcosmic reflection of this great cosmic process. Thus one of the ways we can express our own true nature is by expressing ourselves creatively. In this sense we—men and women alike—are mothers of our creative works just as Shakti is the mother of the universe, and we sense this at a very deep level. This is why we so often use images associated with pregnancy to describe the creative process: we say that writing a book is like giving birth, we talk about a painting having to go through a period of gestation, we describe ourselves as being pregnant with ideas, and we call our books, compositions, and pieces of art our babies and liken them to children.

As the great creatrix, Shakti not only gives birth to the universe and each one of us, she—like the good mother she is—continually urges us onward. This is Shakti as the evolutionary energy, the transformative energy, of the cosmos.

When we mimic her by becoming creators and creatrixes ourselves, we pour her out into the universe. If you have observed this process in yourself you will have perceived that the more you express her, the more she fills you up. The more she fills you up, the more she transforms you. The more you are transformed, the better able you are to pour her out into the world and in the process transform the world.

This is the essence of what Mahadevi was talking about in the beautiful poem she wrote about her experience of awakening kundalini that was described in Chapter Two. By the time she wrote this poem Mahadevi had fully embodied the divine feminine. She recognized herself as being in a state of divine union with Shiva. Reading between the lines we can feel her delight at having received this divine call to write about her experience, and there is a sweet poignancy to her words:

> My jasmine white lord
>   has filled me through
>   to overflowing,
> With the precious juice
>   of Grace,
> So I could write
>   the best I ever could.

The reason her Jasmine White Lord has given her this gift becomes clear in yet another beautiful verse:

> If you these triplets copy
>   and read with love,

Disease
  and the curse of rebirth
  you banish,
To Shiva's heart you go
  and to bliss.

Thus Mahadevi is telling us that the products of creative expression
—in this case the words of her poem—have the power to transform.
This puts a simple expression like "Express yourself!" in a whole new
light. The call to express yourself creatively is a call to express your
true nature, to become aware of yourself as divine. Wendi summarized
this idea poignantly at the end of Chapter Six when she said she had
reached a point where she realized that she carried the essence of the
creator within her as she moved about her life and that she was able
to see herself as divinely feminine.

Another woman whose life experience has allowed her to follow
the call to create and in doing so express this divine essence is a woman
who lives in India named Kavita. While Kavita's journey, at least outwardly, has been a far more adventurous one than most of us have an
opportunity to follow, her inner journey is one most of us can identify
with, particularly in terms of how she has been able to allow herself to
express her creativity over the years. If you read between the lines you
will see how Kavita has continually been following her inner voice and
how this voice has led her where she needed to go, filling her all the
while with the sweet juice of creativity. It will also become apparent
how, the more Kavita poured this out, the more she was filled with it
and the further she moved along her spiritual journey.

This journey began when Kavita was growing up in upper New
York state in the early sixties. In an article about her life that she wrote
many years later for the Australian Spiritual Emergence Network
newsletter she describes being aware—as many of us were who grew
up in small towns where like-minded souls seemed few and far between—that her view of life clearly differed from others. Reading this
article it is easy to speculate that Kavita was destined for a life on the
spiritual path from a very early age; for she describes how, from very
young, the "real" world seemed like a dream to her, and she was drawn
into a world that seemed to exist on another level —a boundless,
exhilarating world of timeless space and wonder. She says:

I felt irresistibly drawn to this realm of mystery that held out something truer to me than the world of appearances and forms, and I was often torn between their contradictory demands. I would retreat into writing poetry and walking in nature, where I could open up to this realm and lose myself in its elusive essence.

Kavita spent much of her time lost in this world, contemplating it and writing poetry in an attempt to capture its beauty. Fortunately for Kavita her parents were loving and supportive, as well as being encouraging of her curiosity and creativity. They also helped her understand when her extreme sensitivity and ability to perceive the spiritual depths of reality veered too far from the norm. "Better pull your antennae in," her mother would say, "you can't live in the world like that!" But pulling her "antennae" in wasn't always easy for Kavita. She felt an aching need to reconcile her two worlds for she realized she couldn't afford to deny the presence of either one. This was not just a practical dilemma but an existential and spiritual one that took her years to even begin to resolve.

Kavita did very well academically; she loved learning and the world of ideas. By the time she finished high school her exposure to the ideas of great thinkers had combined with her natural compassion to create in her a passionate idealism. Hoping to find more like-minded thinkers and many answers in the quest for Truth at a great university, Kavita applied to Princeton University. Even though few women were being accepted at the time she was successful and, full of anticipation, she headed off to college. Needless to say the rigid, male-dominated environment of Ivy-League academe did not live up to her expectations of finding a world full of Truth-seekers. Still the four years Kavita spent at Princeton were a crucial step in her spiritual growth. While there Kavita enrolled in the creative writing program and began writing poetry seriously. Without realizing it, this course and the work she was doing provided her with the framework for exploring her inner world and what was happening within it. Describing this process, she wrote:

> The words and images seemed to flow directly from inner energy move-
> ments I was experiencing in my head—I can remember especially a
> strong sensation of a vortex of energy in the center, behind my eyes,
> and of being pulled through it into another dimension of perception.
> This point was to become a "turning point", as the progression of the

poetry itself continued to lead me on a passage through the "eye" of the storm into an expanse of consciousness that was seemingly limitless. I didn't know anything about kundalini or do any spiritual practices at the time; what happened seemed to be a natural unfolding from within, and I was both tantalized and terrified by its mystery.

This was indeed a natural unfoldment; it was part of the process of transformation Kavita had been experiencing quite unconsciously much of her life. As the process progressed over the four years, Kavita collected the poems into a book called *The I-Opening*—a title that is extremely appropriate on a number of levels. The little micro-cosmic "I" known as Kavita was opening to the great macrocosmic "I" that is the cosmic divine. But this "unfolding" was only able to happen in this natural way because Kavita was open to the process. When she experienced these powerful energy movements, she didn't fight them, she allowed them to flow through her. In this way, Kavita's writing *The I-Opening* provides a perfect example of how she opened herself to the Divine, allowed it to fill her up, and allowed it to flow out of her so she could be filled again.

By the time she had graduated from Princeton, this divine force was ready to propel Kavita further down the spiritual path and, as before, she was open to it. Completely disillusioned by the materialistic, consumer culture she had grown up in, Kavita dreamed of a society where physical needs were met simply so that the main focus of life could be creative and spiritual.

This set her off on a seven-year, round-the-world quest that took her through Africa, Europe, and Asia. While in these places she lived and worked in traditional societies as well as alternative communities. In Tanzania, for example, she traveled through the country working as a freelance journalist, staying in tribal villages and writing articles about her experiences. Later, she got a job in that country working with a regional development project that allowed her to research the traditional healing techniques of the "witch doctors". Later she made her first trip to India, where she spent time in the South staying with pre-Dravidian hill tribes and exploring their use of music in healing. This interest in traditional healing practices also took her to Malaysia, where she interviewed shadow puppet healers and wrote about her observations. Eventually Kavita made her way to Australia and New Zealand where she worked on organic farms and lived in New Age Communities.

Throughout her travels Kavita continued to express herself creatively, not just writing the freelance articles, but also continuing to write poetry when inspiration came in that form. The energy seeking expression in her also wove itself through different forms, finding at different stages new and unexpected channels. She began to draw, make batik paintings, learn to play the harmonium and the flute, and compose music on these instruments.

Connecting all these adventures, both inner and outer, was one central theme. "It was," says Kavita, "my passion to find the meaning of consciousness, the meaning in fact of this Creation, and to keep myself in environments that allowed me, as much as possible, to explore this." Kavita began to sense the source of this creation as an all-embracing feminine essence, a divine mother, and she felt it reaching out to her in much the same way that Mechthild and Mahadevi had.

Kavita's first marked experience of this came in the late 1970s when the persistent, unrelenting passion that was guiding her led her to a small village on a Greek island. She ended up spending two years on the island, working first as a goatherd and then as a gardener:

> The goatherd job was part of a string of jobs offered to me by the kind-hearted villagers, who, I was told later, thought I was a little retarded (at least it was clear to them that my life pattern was not that of any normal young woman, not to mention how often I was caught staring off into space and then suddenly dropping everything to dive into a notebook I carried everywhere with me)—and wanted to help me out! I was embarrassingly bad at this job, as the goats seemed to be much cleverer and quicker than I was, though the spectacular scenery, rugged rocks over the sea, made up for the humiliation. It didn't take long for the villagers to find me a job they thought might suit me better, as an assistant gardener on the island estate of the publisher of a large newspaper in Athens, a paradise of endless ever-changing flowerbeds, every kind of Mediterranean and sub-tropical fruit tree, winding cobblestone paths and pagodas, young and old olive groves, and trails winding down through the forest, all over- looking the sea.

Part of her work in this garden allowed her many hours each day to contemplate nature. As she did she became increasingly conscious of the energy patterns moving within her that she had tried to describe in the poetry she wrote at Princeton. At the same time she became ever more aware of these patterns as they moved in the world around her. She also began to feel her consciousness expand and to perceive a unifying principle that connected everything in the universe. The first time she associated this interconnectedness with the divine feminine, Kavita was working in the garden and looking out across the sea to a mountain on another island that the villagers called the Sleeping Goddess:

> I used to love to gaze across at her and feel her peace and stillness. I would open myself to the sense of eternity she radiated, and even later, when I left the island, I took that sense with me as an essence of being, though the visible symbol of the mountain fell away.
>
> From another point on the island, I could also see the mountains on the mainland in the distance, overlapping each other in the sparkling light of sunset, like waves pouring into the sea. This also felt to me like the melting of time, of earth into water into pure light, and myself melting into their Oneness. Later on I found out that the island where I was living was on the fault line of the huge volcanic explosion and tidal wave that had once destroyed an advanced civilization on Crete and Santorini thought by archaeologists to have worshiped the Divine Feminine. I felt that this "wave" of the Divine Feminine had somehow ripped through time itself and broken into me.

This connection with the divine feminine unleashed a stream of insights, spontaneous meditative experiences, and creative energy. While this outpouring continued to manifest in her writing, it also expressed itself for a time in various forms of artwork—a phenomenon that had never occurred in Kavita's life before and has not since. This visual phase lasted about three years and began while Kavita was working in the garden. One of her jobs was to water eight huge, ancient olive trees. She had all day to do this job, placing the hose by each tree and then waiting for about forty minutes while the water slowly filled a moat around each tree. As she sat in the penetrating Mediterranean light, it seemed as if the organic forms surrounding her were sinking like waves into her consciousness, and she began scratching these images on rocks. She describes these images as organic forms enfolded in and emanating out of each other like waves within waves:

It was a strange kind of drawing, based on contoured "waves" reminiscent of organic forms—leaves, flowers, shells, wings, budding seeds, sea waves, and so on—rippling into and out of each other. These forms were created on different scales unfolding out of and transforming into each other. The outermost form that emerged was usually an ethereal female head—as if the whole span of creation were contained within her.

While this visual phase lasted Kavita continued with her drawings and then went on to make batik paintings—a skill she learned in Malaysia where she apprenticed herself to a batik artist. By the time her travels took her to New Zealand she began working in clay and got a job with a potter. Although Kavita loved the sensual feel of the clay, she laughingly admits the pots she made were not a success. But the medium gave her scope, once again, to express the energies moving within her, and the wave-like shapes and figurines that came to life from the clay in her hands continued to carry the flow from her inner world into outer form: "Waves, flow, balance, the transformation of opposites into one another, the hidden unity weaving through the myriad faces of creation, the turning point of unity into profusion and back again: these themes, as they worked their way through my consciousness, seemed to flow naturally into whatever medium came to hand."

In all this, the inspiration and expression of the feminine was of paramount importance. Kavita says of this time:

...I felt totally, unconditionally accepted by the Divine in the feminine form, and thus able to merge with her essence in a way I never had with the masculine form of God I'd grown up with. Sitting still and contemplating her essence sensitized me to the point where I could tune into different levels of consciousness, like tuning the channel to subtle dimensions I never knew before existed. I was writing a journal at this time, and mythic visions would sometimes come to me, of the whole of nature—indeed the whole of existence—as the Divine Mother... This presages a similar sense of vast and all-inclusive spaciousness I was to experience years later when I met my spiritual teacher, as if my consciousness were a space in which everything was connected. Even then I would often associate this space with the openness of the Divine Feminine, the all-embracing, unconditional love that had always felt so maternal to me in its essence. It felt both prior to and beyond the appearances and events of space and time; it constantly gave rise to and re-absorbed them all, in a shimmering, vibrant, all-powerful stillness.

The teacher Kavita mentions here was Sri H.W.L. Poonjaji, a disciple of Sri Ramana Maharshi, whom she met in Lucknow, India. That Kavita, with the keen individuality and independence of spirit displayed so far in her story, would ever become attached to a particular teacher might seem surprising. Indeed she had always had an aversion to groups and had intentionally avoided gurus, organizations, and spiritual movements for years—and her road to meeting Poonjaji in India was one that took several years. The first step along this journey, however, was a realization in the early 1980s that her experiences of this all-embracing divine power had increased to the point where she was getting out of her depth and needed some guidance. She turned first to Buddhism, which appealed to her because of its rationality, sobriety, and the way it detailed the different levels of psyche. By this time, she had made her way to Australia. While there her interest in Buddhism grew, and she attended a ten-day Vipassana meditation retreat. The form of meditation she practiced there, widely taught by a Buddhist teacher named S.N. Goenka, is based on self-observation and focuses on the profound interrelationship between the body and mind.

During the retreat Kavita had an extraordinary experience of energy and light, much like the one Anya described in the last chapter, in which she felt an intense stream of energy surge from the base of her spine to the point just behind her forehead. The current then ran up and down her spine in waves that she has described as "liquid electricity". A few days later several points along her spine seemed to burst into radiating balls of fireworks. When she explained what was happening to the teachers at the retreat they told her to ignore the phenomena and continue to observe—since all experiences were to be observed and let go of. Although this advice would have been helpful for most types of experiences, it did not provide Kavita the help or information she needed at the time.

She left the Australian retreat feeling as if she was "nine months pregnant and looking for a place to give birth". Fortunately, she found one: a yoga ashram where they recognized that she had had a kundalini experience and prescribed exactly what she needed, in particular a peaceful, balanced lifestyle, regular yogic practices, and a great deal of work in the garden. All this helped the energy balance itself within her body: slowly over a period of several years, Kavita re-experienced the original meteoric rise of energy in a gradual, balanced manner, and it became much more integrated into her daily life.

After about six years, however, Kavita's time in this ashram was to end. Improprieties involving not the spiritual teacher himself but the national director of the organization came to light and a scandal ensued. Many people, Kavita included, left the ashram at this time. Following a period of feeling lost without the serene and well-ordered home that had been hers for so long, Kavita found work teaching yoga and working with people with disabilities. Later on, however, her desire to find a spiritual master took her back to India. After traveling around the country for a time, she met Sri Poonja, who taught Advaita Vedanta in the line of Sri Ramana Maharshi. When Kavita first met Poonjaji, as he was affectionately called, he was not well known. During the time she was with him, however, his renown spread. Over the next few years he became quite famous and a large group gathered around him.

From the moment Kavita met Poonjaji, many elements from her long spiritual journey began to coalesce. Kavita explains that Poon-jaji's teaching was that of non-dualism: "The basic tenet being that everything that appears is a projection of the Supreme Consciousness, and we are That Itself, not the limited appearances we think ourselves to be." Poonjaji indicated to Kavita that her experiences revealed that she already had perceived this truth; and now his confirmation and clarification—along with what is referred to in yoga as "direct trans-mission"—supported its blossoming within her. She says: "Indeed, three luminous years followed, where my inner world flowed so per-fectly with the outer, that there seemed to be no division. I felt that I had found what I had always been looking for, both inwardly and outwardly; in fact, that there was no longer any difference."

While Kavita was able to remain in this state of utter openness and perfect balance where her body and mind were melting in divine love, a remarkable period of creativity ensued that was sustained for almost three years:

> Poems flowed, heard from a source beyond mind, and ended in the publication of a book, with the support of the community, called *Love Songs of the Undivided*.

The love affair expressed in the poems was that of Consciousness itself with its own creations; the merging of the small "me" into the Universal "I"; the Oneness of the Supreme with all its forms. During this time I experienced myself, not just as the body and mind, but the Consciousness itself in which they were arising, and sometimes (in meditation, satsang, or at the end of writing a poem) their forms would "lose their lines", dissolving into the boundlessness of that Consciousness Itself. Altogether this was a time of openness and transparency to the timeless, formless Divinity within all things.

The essence of what Kavita was experiencing during this time is expressed poignantly in the following poem from *Love Songs of the Undivided*:

My heart makes love
In secret silence
To all that is.

My womb gives birth
To the universe
And my breasts
Suckle the stars.
Who knows near or far
In this cave of silence
Whose earth is the sky
No one sits but all
Existence.

I am this
Which never dies
Which rocks the seas of being
In its dreams
And cradles all creation
In the infinite unseen.

It is interesting that Kavita's intensive three-year period of writing began when she met Poonjaji and joined a number of other like-minded seekers just as Mahadevi's need to express herself bubbled joyously out of her when she joined the community at Kalyana.

Kavita's time in Lucknow was just one step on a long journey that, as you will see later in the book, has led her to deeper states of realization.

But what is important to reflect on now is how her journey began when she heard the voice that was calling to her from the very depth of her being. She then not only listened to the voice and allowed it to guide her, but she, like Mahadevi, allowed it to fill her with the sweet "juice of Grace" so that she could pour it back out into the world. It is through this cyclical process of the sweetness pouring in and being poured back out again and again that we—especially those of us who are on a creative-spiritual path—are transformed.

We cannot let ourselves forget that hearing the call—allowing ourselves to hear it—just as Kavita did is the first step for all of us. This is true whether the voice comes as a commanding call like the one Hildegard heard, the irrepressible song that erupted out of Mahadevi, or the quiet yearning that Wendi felt. The next step is, of course, overcoming our tendency to muffle it, push it down, and silence it with our fears.

The Art of Playing

"…without this playing with fantasy no creative work has ever yet come to birth. The debt we owe to the play of imagination is incalculable."

C.G. Jung

Of the many beautiful images from Kavita's story that capture my imagination, one of the most captivating is how lovely her drawings with the intricate, swirling organic patterns must have been. In order to create art like that you have to sink totally into the moment, let go of expectations, and play with art materials like you did when you were a child. It was in just such a state that Kavita was able to hear the voice of the divine feminine and let it lead her on her way.

A wonderful way to reach this state is to experiment with making tissue paper collages. Decades ago, a Jungian analyst named Edith Wallace discovered this activity could be a powerful technique for opening the unconscious:

> Working with tissue paper, glue, and brush brought forth freer shapes, which seemed to emerge from a greater depth of the psyche: it acted as an opener and channel builder. Eventually, shapes would emerge that had great impact and meaning. But this could happen only if the work was done playfully, unselfconsciously, as a child would do it, without preconceived ideas or notions, without manipulation. It meant just very seriously enjoying the process of playing while enjoying the colors, sometimes taking pleasure in what emerged, sometimes being surprised, pleasantly or unpleasantly, but always eventually finding meaning in what emerged.*

To do this exercise you need several different colors of tissue paper to choose from, a wide (about one inch) artist's paint brush, poster board, and liquid gloss acrylic medium.** Wallace's directions included working in silence, not using any tools such as scissors, and simply allowing whatever emerged to spontaneously arise. While she warned against "thinking"—in the sense of planning or interpreting—she encouraged attention and self-observation during the process. (An art workshop I took on using the technique encouraged the use of free-form, spontaneous shapes but did allow the use of scissors.)

The technique itself involves simply placing pieces of tissue paper on the board one by one and then brushing the acrylic medium over them. The idea is to layer the different colors of paper, allowing the surprising shapes and colors that arise from the layering to emerge. You need to brush slowly and carefully so that the paper doesn't wrinkle or tear—although wrinkles and tears can add to the overall effect.

1. *To begin, have the materials for creating your collage ready, then visualize the white light and create your protective space.*
2. *Spend a little time surrounded and filled by light. Keeping in mind the idea that the flow of emotion is a key to creating art, spend a little extra time seeing the light pulsing around your heart.*
3. *When ready, focus again on the movement of the light, allowing it to flow out of you, through your hands and your brush, and into your collage.*
4. *Later, when your collage is dry, go back and spend time with it, observing the images, colors, and patterns and the associations that arise from them.*
5. *If you like, write down your observations and the meanings you have discovered.*

* *More about Wallace, who died in 2004, and tissue paper collages can be learned at the website of Karen Stefano, an art therapist who trained with Wallace for many years. Both the Jung and Wallace quotes come from her site; the Wallace quote is from "Healing Through the Visual Arts" in* Approaches to Art Therapy *by J.A. Rubin, ed. Stefano's website is www.tissuepapercollage.net. This site, like others on tissue paper collage, shows beautiful examples.*

** *Acrylic medium can be found in any art store or ordered easily online. Liquid starch or slightly watered down white glue will work in place of acrylic medium but not as well. You can use dollar store tissue paper or find a thinner, better quality in an art store. Tissue paper that "bleeds" is wonderful to use and mix with regular tissue paper as it adds another element of surprise; it can be ordered online or found in some art and/or crafts stores.*

CHAPTER TWELVE

Love Begin the Song, And Let Me Hear How Well You Sing

It is not surprising that fear is such an issue when it comes to answering the call to creativity. Even divinely inspired mystics like Hildegard and Mechthild were afraid. In fact when Hildegard first received the divine command to write about her visions her answer was, quite simply, no. And she remained steadfast in this refusal for quite some time—even though she believed she was hearing the voice of God. In the introduction to her first book she explains that this refusal was based not on stubbornness, but on humility and fear. She was worried, she told us, that people would doubt her, have evil opinions of her, or say things about her that were untrue.

Since most people in those days would have considered the idea of God speaking directly to a woman ridiculous or even blasphemous,

Hildegard would have had good reason to suppose people were going to doubt her and publicly criticize her. This criticism could have easily resulted in her being silenced, excommunicated, or even executed. Although the last was fairly unlikely—Hildegard did not live in a time or place where the burning of heretics or witches was particularly common—it would have made little difference. In Hildegard's eyes, excommunication would have been a fate worse than death for it would mean that her soul would roast eternally in the fires of hell.

When Hildegard mentioned that "humility" also kept her from obeying the command, she was referring in part to a true humbleness and humility of spirit. But she was also referring to her fear that she was simply not good enough to do the job that was being set before her. For Hildegard, this concern would have been somewhat different than it is for most of us today as the idea of having enough "talent" would probably not have entered into her thinking. She was afraid rather that her faults and shortcomings made her unworthy of the task. Still, she was also afraid her work would not meet high enough standards and be criticized for this. Repeatedly in her writings she referred to herself as being incapable of writing well enough to express herself. Hildegard was, in short, afraid she was "unworthy" of the task—a feeling a great many of us can identify with.

Mechthild too was beset with fears about her own unworthiness. These fears kept her from answering the call to begin writing for decades. If you think back to her story you'll recall that she didn't actually begin to write about her visions until her confessor Heinrich interpreted her horrific dream about the flying devil to mean that she *must*. Describing how she felt after this conversation with Hein-rich, she said his insistence that she begin writing, "...causes me to weep because my utter unworthiness is obvious to my eyes..."

Later, during a visionary experience, she discussed these fears with her divine lover. He repeatedly reassures her and says, "So have no doubts about yourself!" But she continues to denigrate herself in the worst way. At one point she says if he, her divine lover, had given this miraculous ability to write to a man everyone would believe it:

But how is one supposed to believe
That you have built a golden house on filthy ooze...

This description of herself as filthy ooze is enough to make us shudder, but it is really just an extreme version of what many of us feel at times about our abilities and our work. And Mechthild had to deal not only with these self-doubts but also with very real fears about the ever-mounting persecution against her religious group, the beguines. In describing this she said:

> I was warned against writing this book.
> People said:
> If one did not watch out,
> It could be burned.
>
> [Book II, 26]

During another vision several years later she literally begs her divine lover to keep her safe from "eyes of evil cunning". Reminding him pointedly that he was the one who commanded her to write in the first place, she described the public rage against her as being so powerful that it must have been born in the heart of Lucifer.

One reason Mechthild and Hildegard managed to overcome such potent fears was that they realized there would be a price to pay if they didn't. About her original refusal to listen to the voice that was calling to her, Hildegard wrote: "Although I saw and heard these things, I nevertheless refused to write them...until I became sick, pressed down by the scourge of God. I was sick for a long time. Eventually, with the testimony of a certain noble man and a young woman of good wishes I started to write...As soon as I did that, I became healthy with a received strength..."

Not long ago while I was leading an intensive writing weekend for women I told the story about how Hildegard had received a divine command to "say and write" what she saw and heard and how she had refused to do it. Before reading them the above quote, I asked the women what they thought happened to Hildegard when she refused. Immediately the group chorused, "She got sick!" They didn't even need to think about the answer. They knew it instantly— just as you probably did.

When we hear Hildegard's story we can see clearly that she was being called on by the Divine; we can see that she was being filled with a holy fire; we can see that she had a mission, a purpose, a raison d'être, and we have not even the slightest doubt that her refusal to answer this holy call would bring dire consequences down upon her. When she talks about her refusal to speak and write what she saw and heard in her visions, we want to call out to her, "Oh, no! Hildegard, don't you dare refuse! Listen to that voice! There will be terrible trouble if you don't!" And when we hear that she finally got the courage to do what she was so clearly meant to do, we breathe a great sigh of relief.

How ironic that we can see this so plainly when we look at another person and yet fail to recognize the same truth in terms of ourselves. And yet we must. As the yearning to express ourselves creatively grows, at some point we have to admit to ourselves that we must do or die—if we don't pour the sweet "juice of Grace" that is flowing into us back out into the universe some part of our soul will shrivel up and die. Unfortunately, in order to do this we are going to have to repeatedly face fear.

This is because those of us on the spiritual-creative journey are destined to have a distinctive relationship with this particular demon. For ours is one of the only, if not the only, spiritual calling where the *practice* itself is so consistently beset by fear. As we all know, when it comes to our creative expression the vast majority of us, even the critically acclaimed and financially successful, are haunted by fears— fears that we are not good enough or talented enough, that our work will fall short of our ideals, that it will be rejected or ridiculed by others, that we will never be able to support ourselves with our art... The list, as I hardly need mention, goes on and on.

This, of course, does not mean that other spiritual paths are not also beset and booby-trapped along the way by fear. Naturally they are. As Emmet Fox told us in Chapter Three, the conquering of fear —as the emotion that stands opposite love—is at the center of all spiritual progress. But it is rare that the actual *practice* that goes along with any particular calling conjures up fear in and of itself. Someone might be terrified about being called to the ministry or becoming a nun—but they wouldn't likely be terrified of praying, going to mass, or singing the liturgy. Another person might be scared to begin meditation or chanting because they sense on some deep inner level that the practice will inevitably lead to an awareness of their inner faults—but it is the fear of coming face to face with these faults, not the meditation or chanting itself, that they are afraid of. Someone called to be a missionary in a strange land might be frightened but he or she is probably afraid of encountering new or dangerous situations, not of the activities actually involved in their spiritual practice per se like prayer and Bible reading. One of the few fear-inspiring activities I can think of that might be considered part of an actual spiritual practice is the giving of sermons for those who are called to the ministry. A friend of mine who is a minister in a traditional Christian church was at first terrified about this aspect of his calling—but writing a sermon and then giving it in front of others is in many ways an exercise in creative expression so it hardly proves to be an exception.

Thus, those of us whose actual practice, or at least a significant part of it, requires us to draw, paint, write, compose, or dance and, in so doing, lay the innermost part of our soul out on a mat that others may well run rough-shod over, have to overcome fear just to do the practice itself. This is true even for those of us who create just for ourselves and never show our work to anyone else, especially for those of us whose main fear is that our work is not good enough. For even if no eyes but our own ever fall on it, by virtue of being created the work obtains a kind of permanence that remains burned into our psyches—even if we destroy the work itself. Although I suppose there must be creative people who have overcome all the fears related to their creative process, this isn't true for either myself or the vast majority of fellow travelers I've met on this path. What seems to happen instead is that as soon as you have overcome a particular set of fears and gotten comfortable at one level of creative expression you are forced to jump off a cliff and face a new one and the fear that goes with it.

Chapter Three expresses the idea that the fears associated with our creativity can be conquered by giving ourselves over to our yearning to create and holding the intensity of that yearning in our bodies until the force of it propels us forward. Although this idea might have seemed a little simplistic to you when it was first introduced, by now it should be abundantly clear that this yearning is the voice of Shakti, of Sophia, of Shekinah—the divine feminine, the great cosmic power of the universe. Our fears, on the other hand, are individual. No matter how universal or common they are in nature, they are rooted in the small individual self, the self that does not realize its oneness with the Divine. And, it can hardly be repeated enough, this union is ultimately what the yearning is calling us to.

To understand just how powerful this yearning is—and how critical it is that we follow where it leads—we can turn again to the story of Shiva and Sati. If you'll recall, when the gods and goddesses originally come up with the idea of finding a wife for Shiva in order to siphon off some of his potentially world-destroying pent-up energy, they decide no one other than Shakti, the cosmic divine feminine herself, could possibly win Shiva's heart. Once this decision is made, Brahma offers to go to Shakti and beg her to help. Brahma is, in fact, extremely eager to see Shiva married. Although the reason for this mentioned earlier is that Brahma is the great creator god and does not want to see creation destroyed, there is another, far more personal, reason for Brahma's desire to see Shiva seduced: not long before, Shiva had seen Brahma in a state of great sexual excitement. Seeing the all-powerful Brahma in such a state made Shiva laugh at him in front of the other gods. This moment of ridicule haunted Brahma and made him long for the sweet revenge that would come from seeing the pure, untouched Shiva fall prey to the same overwhelming sexual urges. This great humiliation of Brahma's had occurred, not coincidentally, on the same day that he created the god Kama—and in Sanskrit *kama* means desire.

On that particular day, Brahma begins his work by creating the god Daksa, who is to be the progenitor of the human race. Directly after this, ten young men and one beautiful young woman spring fully formed from Brahma's mind. This young woman, whom Brahma gives the name Sandhya, or twilight, is beautiful beyond all imagining—so beautiful, in fact, that every male creature in the universe gazes on her with wonder at the moment of her birth. She has long black hair that curls around her pale forehead, her eyes are the color of the blossoming blue lotus, and her golden face is shaped like the moon.

Entranced, Brahma stands to get a better look at her. Just as he does, yet another god springs unbidden from his mind. Because this new god is even more physically perfect than Sandhya and, in a sense, the epitome of all one could desire, Brahma gives him the name Kama. Clearly the forerunner of the Greek god Eros and, later, the Roman god Cupid, Kama has skin the color of gold dust. His face resembles the full moon, and his eyes are like lotuses. He is tall and his arms are thick with muscles. His shoulders are as strong as a rogue elephant's, and his thighs and buttocks are smooth and round. Kama exudes a fragrance as sweet as an intoxicating flower's and a powerful magnetism. A bow is slung over Kama's brawny shoulders and a quiver filled with flowery arrows rests on his back.

The instant he is born he bows down deeply to Brahma and asks what great service he might perform with his life. After some thought Brahma replies that Kama's mission will be to use his exceptional attractiveness and his flowery arrows to cause all the male and female creatures in the universe to be continually attracted to each other. To underscore his point Brahma lists many beings—the great serpents, the monsters, the minor gods, human beings, animals, insects, worms, all the creatures of the seas—and concludes by saying, "There shall be none who shall not fall a victim of thy arrows." Brahma explains that in this way Kama would be responsible for the ongoing continuation of creation. This was so important, Brahma adds, that no one, not the other gods and goddesses nor himself, will be immune from the sting of Kama's arrows and the resulting flood of desire. Brahma then creates a wife for Kama, a beautiful goddess named Rati, and a companion—a powerful god named Vasanta who is to be the Springtime.

After thanking Brahma profusely, Kama pauses for a moment to ponder this great gift. Kama can't quite believe that Brahma has actually given him such power over the gods themselves. Upon giving the matter some thought, he decides to do a little experiment right then and there that will put his powers to the test. He immediately whips out his bow and begins firing arrows at the gods, aiming one right at Brahma. Instantly all the gods begin to stare even more intensely at the alluring Sandhya and are soon overcome with desire for her. The very instant that Brahma is struck by the arrow, he gazes at Sandhya and completely forgets that she, having sprung from his own mind, is technically his own daughter. Within moments he has fallen victim to the same overwhelming lust the other gods were experiencing.

This is the very moment when Shiva arrives on the scene. Seeing the great god Brahma in such an obvious erotically aroused state, the monk-like Shiva can't help but laugh. He then becomes serious, however, and reprimands Brahma for forgetting that Sandhya is his own daughter. This transgression is especially inexcusable, Shiva points out, because it was Brahma himself who wrote the scriptures prohibiting incest. Having put Brahma in his place, Shiva mounts his great bull and flies away. Chastened and ashamed, Brahma lashes out at Kama and blames him for his lustful behavior. In his anger he places a horrible curse on Kama that will result in Kama having to live his whole life under the threat of being "burned to fiery ash" at a moment's notice.

Astonished at this injustice, Kama pleads for mercy saying he had only been doing what Brahma had commanded him to do. Realizing that Kama is right, Brahma relents and tells Kama the curse will be lifted from him the moment he manages to get Shiva to take a wife. Kama is satisfied with this judgment and full of confidence. His success is assured, he feels, not only because of his own skill but also because his beautiful wife, Rati, and his friend, the Springtime, will help him. Happily, Kama speeds off into the world firing his arrows at all and sundry. As time goes on, he remains constantly on the lookout for Shiva and pierces the great monk-like god with a cascade of arrows every time he has a chance. Eventually, as we know from the story of Shiva and Sati, Kama succeeds.

The idea that kama, desire, is a bad thing is pervasive in many organized religions and in some of Hindu tradition. This is often because it is equated with desire for sensual pleasures, physical comforts, and all the aspects of the material world that pull us away from the ultimate reality of the spirit. This powerful story of Kama's creation, however, is telling us that there is much more to the concept of desire than just this. This is one of those profoundly deep symbolic stories that functions on many levels and has lessons for us arising out of each one.

On the most basic level it is telling us that desire is indeed potentially destructive. Brahma's sudden sexual fixation on his own daughter at the very moment Kama springs into action is obviously telling us that desire can indeed lead to the worst possible spiritual transgressions and even to ruination. But in the story Brahma is also telling us that some forms of kama are so essential that *no one*, not even himself or the other gods, is allowed to be immune from them. In making this decree, Brahma has in effect given Kama power over himself and all the other gods. The great god Brahma would never have done this if he hadn't believed it was essential to do so. He makes this very clear in the *Kālikā Purāna* when he is giving Kama his instructions:

> With this exceedingly handsome figure of yours and by using these...
> flowery arrows [O Purusa] do enchant the entire males and females and

do engage yourself in eternal creation...there shall be none who shall not fall a victim of thy arrows.

Whether it is me or Vasudeva or Siva or Purusottama—all of us shall be completely under your influence, what to speak of other living beings. Always entering into the heart of all the living beings invisibly, being yourself the source of happiness in their mind, you do engage yourself in eternal creation...

The duty of yours for the creation of the stream of the world has been assigned by me.

By stressing that these powers are assigned by Brahma himself, he is underscoring their importance. Brahma is the great creator god. He is responsible not just for creation but the continual re-creation of the world. He understands that without kama the perpetual, never-ending process of creation would cease. Knowing this, he grants Kama tremendous powers. In doing this Brahma is telling us that this form of desire, the yearning of two halves to form a whole—the attraction of polarities one for the other—is a fundamental cosmic principle.

Once this is understood, the deeper levels of meaning in the story start to unfold. The first of these tells us that in one of its manifestations this evolutionary force is also sexual energy. Brahma obviously wants all the creatures of the universe, the gods included, to keep procreating. The sexual nature of this energy and how it relates to creativity is dealt with in detail in the next chapter, but for now it's significant to point out that it is when kama is misused and misdirected—for example when Brahma is lusting after his own daughter—that it becomes such a powerful negative force. When Brahma is under the sway of this lust his reason vanishes and he forgets the unforgettable, that Sandhya is his very own daughter. After Shiva leaves the scene Brahma makes the situation even worse by becoming enraged and trying to blame his bad behavior on Kama:

> Then Brahma, the lord of the universe, was highly enraged like the devastating fire which was about to burn.
>
> He then spoke to Shiva: Oh Hara, Kama attacked me in your presence with his flowery arrows, for this he shall have to face consequences!

Brahma then compounds his transgressions by putting the horrible curse on Kama. Brahma has clearly lost his sense of justice and his ability to reason. However, the very moment that he takes control of his lust, his sense of justice and his reason return. He has stopped misdirecting the energy; he is immediately able to accept responsibility for his own actions and to recognize the truth of Kama's testimony. Brahma then responds to this realization—and this is a very significant point—by sending Kama off to use his power to unite Shiva with a partner.

This part of the story reminds us that sexual energy, directed in the right way, is absolutely necessary for the perpetual procreation of all living species. But what is even more important, especially from the great creator god's perspective, is not just that species keep replicating themselves but that they *evolve*. This is what Brahma means in the lines above when he talks about the "creation of the stream of the world". This is the key to yet another level of meaning in the story. Brahma wants us to know that kama creates the great river of life—the stream that is continually changing, perpetually transforming, moving the universe, and all of us in it, on its great journey forward.

To make sure we get the idea that this evolutionary process concerns both the macrocosm of the universe and the microcosm of the individual, Brahma tells Kama not only that his arrows will be stronger than the weapons of the gods, his abode—his sphere of influence—will be everywhere:

The power of the weapons of Vishnu, Rudra and Brahma shall not be equal to the power of your arrows.

The heaven, the mortal world, the nether world, and the eternal world of the Creator [brahmalok], all these places are the abode of yours because you are omnipresent. What should we say more, in fact, there is none equal to you.

Wherever there are living beings, grasses or trees everywhere up to the assembly of Brahma shall be your abode.

All this confirms that Kama's power, the attraction between polarities, is necessary for evolution. And, as mentioned throughout the book, the Tantras and many other Hindu texts tell us this evolution is leading us to Oneness. In terms of the macrocosm, the polarities are Shakti and Shiva who evolve out of the divine One at the beginning of time and cause the universe to spring into being. In this scenario Shakti is the evolutionary force that is propelling the created universe through history and, ultimately, towards the point in time when she and Shiva will reunite and, along with the entire universe, be absorbed back into the

One. In terms of the microcosm this refers to kundalini-shakti who is lying coiled at the base of the spine, waiting patiently until she is awakened and can begin her journey to her beloved Shiva who waits for her at the crown chakra. In this case kundalini-shakti propels the individual's evolution towards the realization of Oneness with the Divine.

On the highest level then our yearning, our desire, our kama, is nothing less than the voice of the most powerful force in the cosmos— the force that is leading us on the journey that is the purpose of creation, our journey back to the One. This, in turn is the force that our fears are up against. Our fears, ultimately, do not stand a chance. To bring this home to us there is another extremely significant scene in the story of Brahma and Kama. When Brahma hurls his horrible curse at Kama, Kama is terrified by Brahma's wrath and throws away his arrows. But he doesn't run away, instead he faces Brahma: "Though he was speaking the truth his voice was soaked with emotion and fear; because it is fear which affects all the virtues."

In spite of this fear Kama challenges the great god Brahma and confronts him about the injustice of what he has done. Kama manages to proclaim his innocence with great eloquence. By the end of his speech the text tells us that he has regained control of himself. He has, in other words, conquered his fear. At this very moment Brahma realizes the injustice of what he has done and tells Kama how the curse can be removed. This is, of course, by working to bring about the union of Shiva and Shakti when she appears in the form of Sati.

Pared down to a basic symbolic level this vignette is saying: yearning faces fear; yearning conquers fear; yearning is able to move forward towards the ultimate goal, the union of masculine and feminine principles in the universe and in ourselves.

By turning to your yearning, focusing on it, and doing whatever you need to do to hold it in your body—you are accessing a great cosmic force. When your yearning is aimed, like Kama's arrows, in the right direction, you are, by your intention, turning towards the light, allowing yourself to be pulled willingly towards it—towards what, in Christian terms, Teilhard de Chardin, called the Omega-point.

The "stream of creation" will not be denied. All blockages, even our greatest fears, will eventually be overcome by this force. This stream is carrying us along, moving us forward whether we know it or not, whether we want it or not. All that remains for us is to *choose* to flow with it, to choose with our deepest intention to move with it instead of against it. Like most spiritual principles this is so simple it is hard to believe it's true. But as is said about so many spiritual principles, "It is simple, but it's not easy." Virtually all the stories about individuals in this book have told us this. Christine's story from Chapter Three is a very typical example: her longing "to know herself" has led her through literally years of tough psychological and spiritual work in which she had to look deeply into herself, face her faults, and take on the painful task of examining the source of her wounding.

No one can escape the difficulties and challenges inherent in this journey towards wholeness and, ultimately, Oneness. But after learning from the story of Brahma and Kama, you can take heart and find great succor in the knowledge that you have this great cosmic force on your side. All you have to do is to stop struggling against the current and let yourself be borne along by this great cosmic river.

Mechthild's story provides us with another way of looking at this. In much the same way that the creator-god Brahma longs for us to be active participants in the on-going stream of creation, Mechthild's divine lover indicates that both he and God, the creator of the universe, long for *her* to create too. Thus, when her Lover tells her she must write, his commands are never harsh. They are cloaked rather in an almost unbearable sweetness; he cajoles, encourages, and pleads with her. In one of the most tender examples of this he calls out to her, saying, "Beloved, begin the song and let me hear how well you sing."

Mechthild responds by saying that she hasn't been able to sing because her throat has been hoarse, and it's clear that fear is the cause of this affliction. But her Lover's gentle pleading and his obvious longing to hear her sing gives her the encouragement she needs to overcome her fear. Once this has occurred, she says:

...the sugar of your sweet kindness
Has let my voice resound, so that I can now sing...

This is very similar to the experience Mahadevi described earlier when she said her Jasmine White Lord had filled her to overflowing with the "precious juice of Grace" so that she could write the best she ever could. With these phrases Mechthild and Mahadevi paint an image of a divine being who is almost aching to hear us sing out and express ourselves. This image has been a powerful one for me in terms of my own struggle to write and express myself. Even though I had sensed for years that my yearning to write was part of my own spiritual transformation, and I eventually realized this was the voice of the divine feminine calling out to me, I never moved on to the logical conclusion that this must also mean that Shakti *wanted* me to write. Now, however, I am absolutely convinced this is true. The Divine longs to hear our passionate expressions just as fiercely as we long to express ourselves. In one of the simplest, yet most profound passages in Mechthild's book, God says to her:

> Downward I reach,
> Widely I roam,
> Upward I yearn,
> Long I wait.
> [Book III, 5]

Somehow I find this image of a divine force that reaches out, searches tirelessly, and longs passionately and patiently for me to express myself and move forward on my journey extraordinarily comforting. No matter how afraid I have been, as soon as I have been able to dig deep down beneath these fears I have found this bedrock, this certainty that, ultimately, the fear is going to be conquered and that eventually, one way or another, the force that wants to move me along is going to move me.

Although I may have first learned great truths like this from saints like Mahadevi and holy women like Mechthild, they have been made real to me over the years by the simple everyday stories of people like Britta. This has been especially true because so many of these daily stories deal not with the big blazing dreads like the threat of persecution, but the little, quiet, insidious apprehensions like the thought that our work will never, ever be quite good enough. From Britta I not only learned that this fear can be overcome, but also that it is never too late to grasp your work and fling it out into the universe with joy.

Several years elapsed between the first time Britta contacted me and the time when I was finishing up the first draft of this book. Britta had by then reached the age of ninety-one. And although I knew she had heart problems, she always seemed so vibrant and vigorous I fully expected her to live to one hundred. But quite suddenly, just a few months before I began this chapter, Britta's son contacted me from

Denmark to tell me that she had unexpectedly passed away. On the one hand, I was stricken by her loss; on the other, I couldn't help but think this was a person whose passing no one should regret. She had lived an amazingly full life and—most importantly—remained true to herself. She never faltered in her belief that she had had a true experience of the Holy Spirit or that this experience had transformed her, enriched the creative gifts she already had, and given her new ones.

This did not mean Britta wasn't afraid. She was sometimes terrified, and she had to battle fears and feelings of inadequacy, particularly in terms of her writing for, if you'll recall, Britta was an artist and had had no ability to write before her experience. These feelings of inadequacy were especially strong in her early years of writing poetry. She was afraid the poems weren't any good or that they would be laughed at or misunderstood.

· For a long while after she began writing her poems these fears and insecurities kept Britta from showing them to anyone. After about two years, however, she got up the courage to show them to a friend. This woman was very impressed with the poems and suggested Britta put them into a book that could be shared with others. Britta was extremely hesitant but eventually her friend prevailed. In 1961, Britta collected the poems together and published them herself in the form of a small book. When she wrote to me about the book she seemed to remember the experience as if it had happened yesterday:

> I called the book *Kaerlighedens Budskab*. This is Danish for *The Message of Love*. I had 200 copies printed and they were soon gone...I belonged at that time to a ladies club. They loved the book, and they bought them all. The money went to a children's fund. Later I even got letters thanking me for all the good it did! The letters showed that some very sick people had been helped by the poems—and some very troubled people had found a way out of their troubles...

Over the years, however, Britta lost touch with the joy and confidence she had right after her poetry had been made public. The deep-down insecurities and fear that they weren't really quite "good enough" crept back up. She left Denmark not long after this, and when she later mastered English she struggled to translate some of the poems. But she failed at this effort and the poems lay hidden in a drawer for more than thirty years.

However, when Britta started writing about her experience in the letters she was sending to me, she started to think about the poems again and began to recapture the joy and confidence she had had when her book first came out and she had received so much praise. In one letter to me she wrote: "All these years later I have just now realized that the poems in that book reveal a great deal about what we have to do to have a happy life. In most verses is the word 'Love'!"

Once again Britta tried to translate a few of the poems into English. This time she succeeded and sent a few to me. But other than this, the poems remained hidden away until one day when Britta received an astonishing surprise. Without letting Britta know, her daughter and granddaughter in Denmark had been painstakingly working for two years to translate about a hundred of Britta's poems into English. When they were finally finished with the project they sent a printed copy to Britta. When Britta called me to tell me about the poems, she was overcome with emotion. She was profoundly moved by what her daughter and granddaughter had done and the translation had come at an auspicious moment in her life.

The time Britta had spent over the previous couple of years revisiting her experience, writing about it, showing it to someone, and committing herself to the idea that her story would be made public had changed something in Britta. She had come to a new level of understanding about her life-long yearning for the Holy Spirit. She had turned toward it, grasped it, acknowledged it, and was moving forward with a new strength of purpose. Britta had, in short, *owned* this experience and her longing in a way she never had before.

Britta's earlier fears about the inadequacy of the poems vanished; she was filled with joy at their beauty. And while she never failed to mention that they were "inspired" and that she couldn't fully take credit for them, she also realized that she had had an indispensable role in their creation and that she could take joy and pride in what she had done.

Soon after the call to tell me about the translation, she called again to say that she had decided—at ninety-one years of age—to begin looking for a publisher. She also said if she couldn't find one she was determined to self-publish them and begin taking them to bookstores herself! After this we had a number of conversations about how she should go about looking for a publisher and, failing that, how she could have the poems self-published and still have a beautiful book.

Although Britta's death came before she realized this final dream, it seems to me that what matters most is how her total commitment to her experience and the "message of love" she had received in the poetry affected her. She was radiant and filled with joy and enthusiasm about her work right up until the end of her life.

In looking back through her poems I found one that reminds us that we can overcome the fears and doubts that assail and, more over, why Britta at least believed we need to:

Why do I get these thoughts?
    There must be a reason.
Keeping them with me
    they must die with me—
But when passing them on
maybe someone
    in them will find
    a small seed
which may grow and flower
    to throw off new seeds.

Walkabout with Wonder

It doesn't seem to matter how many times I read Mechthild's description of her divine lover urging her to begin to write by saying "Love, begin the song, and let me hear how well you sing", tears sting my eyes every time. This image of the Divine reaching out to us, longing to hear the creative expression of our souls, and then, surely, delighting in what we have expressed is as comforting as it is moving.

Looking at your creative efforts—and your fears about them—from this perspective is like flipping a great switch that completely alters the way you see your efforts to make art and to express yourself. Your creative work isn't something that you, struggling and all alone, are forcing onto an uncaring world. It is something that is being urged out of you by the Divine—a Divine who longs to hear what you have to express as much, or even more, than you long to express it.

The following exercise is a simple one and not one that should be done only once. It involves nothing more than taking a walk, as you probably often do, in as natural a setting as possible, with the intention of seeing every living thing around you as an expression of divine creativity, being aware of yourself as not only another creation of the Divine, but as a divine creator yourself.

As you walk, listen to and sense the divine creation that is all around you. Tune into the thought that the trees and plants around you have been called into being and into gradual growth and transformation by the Divine. All this has been implanted and encoded into the tiniest seed, just as your own longing to create and grow has been encoded into the seed that is your soul. You, too, are imprinted to create and grow—just as surely as a rosebush is to burst forth with the brilliance of the flower, the peach tree the sweetness of the fruit, and the lilac the scent of its blossoms.

Be sure to bring any materials you might like to have such as a notebook or sketchpad with you.

1. Go to the place where you are going to begin your walk and find a place to sit. Take a few moments to breathe in the radiant white light and create your protective space as you did in the first two exercises.

2. *Sit for a moment in the light that surrounds you allowing it to intensify around your heart and move upwards, filling your mind with light.*

3. *Once you and your protective space are filled with light move your consciousness back to the area of your heart and sense the light intensifying.*

4. *Feel the light pulsing with the rhythm of your heart and feel your heart opening.*

5. *In this state of openness—but remembering that you are still surrounded by your protective space—begin your walk.*

6. *As you walk, listen for the voice of the Divine, calling out to you to begin the song so that this great cosmic presence can hear how well you sing.*

7. *If you stop to write, sketch, or express yourself in some way—or do so later—pause before you begin to visualize the light that pulses around your heart flowing upward and outward and into your creative work.*

CHAPTER THIRTEEN

Tantra and the Transmutation of Desire

When we think about Shakti's journey towards Shiva and cosmic union it may seem like an extremely abstract concept. The same can also be true of kundalini-shakti's journey up the spine and her goal of bringing us to the realization of Oneness. I know there are many times in my own life when I couldn't care less about Self-Realization or cosmic union. All I care about is how I can get the words that are banging around my head down onto a piece of paper. I imagine you feel the same way at times— the ultimate goal of the spiritual journey doesn't seem nearly so important as the immediate need to get the image in your mind's eye onto a canvas or turn the faint melody that is haunting you into notes you can sing. And none of these seem as important at times as just getting through your day with your soul intact.

And this is all as it should be. These are the immediate concerns of our daily lives. These are the concerns of the here and now. And virtually every great spiritual teacher has told us that living in the *now* is the key to peace, joy, and spiritual fulfillment. Since this is so, it would be surprising if the symbology of Shiva and Shakti's yearning for each other didn't also have very practical implications for both our creative expression and the living of our daily lives, and this is indeed the case.

As we travel the path that Kama's shooting arrows have set for us, we discover that the great power of our longing is not just about overcoming our fears but is also about bringing balance into our lives. Most of us today live terribly out of balance lives. Being out of balance brings disharmony, and disharmony is the condition that blocks and destroys our creativity more than anything but fear. This is particularly true when a lack of balance exists between the aspects of the divine masculine and feminine contained within ourselves. Just as Shakti yearns for Shiva, our inner feminine cries out to be recognized, honored and brought into balance with our inner masculine.

Before looking in more detail at how this plays out in terms of our creativity, we need to delve a bit deeper into the nature of kama and the attraction of polarities, especially those we see as masculine and feminine. One of the great keys to understanding the importance of this attraction lies in acknowledging the fact that spiritual energy is, in its most fundamental form, also sexual energy.

The idea that a relationship exists between sexual energy and spiritual attainment is an idea as ancient as Hinduism itself and references to it can be found throughout both Hindu scriptures and yogic texts. This is reflected in the belief that abstinence from sexual intercourse—known as *brahmacarya*, or brahmic conduct—has always been considered an important step on the road to realization. Although people frequently assume this edict was originally made because there is something inherently immoral or "unspiritual" about sexual activity, this is not the case. Rather, as Georg Feuerstein succinctly explains in *The Encyclopedic Dictionary of Yoga*, the spiritual aspirant was encouraged to practice brahmacarya in order "to preserve and cultivate the great power in semen". Feuerstein goes on to give an indication just how great this power might be by explaining that one of the most common names for semen is *bindu* and that bindu is also the term used to "represent the inaudible, transcendental 'sound' of the Absolute". This is nothing less than the elemental cosmic vibration that is believed to be held in the sacred word *om*. Many hatha yoga and Tantric texts speak of this inextricable relationship between spiritual and sexual energy. These texts state clearly that when Shakti, the cosmic creative force and spiritual energy of the universe, is rooted in the body at the lowest chakra in the form of kundalini-shakti she manifests as the sexual energy and the sexual drive. This does not mean, however, that there is necessarily anything low or base about sexual energy.

Quite the contrary, this great force is the life energy—no matter what form it takes in the human body. In fact, the very first time I heard the word kundalini, it was described to me in this way. The speaker, a man who was trying to find a very simple way to describe this indescribable force, said that when kundalini stirred and moved outward in the procreative act she created new life in the womb; when she stirred and moved upward along the spine she created new life in the brain and consequently the mind. Although I now know this description to be rather simplistic, it is still fundamentally correct.

Many advanced hatha yoga asanas are based on this principal, which is summed up in the yogic term *ūrdhva retas*. In Sanskrit "ūrdhva" means upward and "retas" is another term for semen. Ūrdhva retas refers to a technique the ancient yogis tried to master that would allow them to reverse the flow of the seminal fluid so that it would move up the spine rather than outward as it would normally during sexual intercourse. Now that we have a better understanding of human physiology it is more widely held that it is not actually the semen but the life essence held in the semen that flows upward. An example of one of these hatha yoga techniques is known as the *yoni-mudhrā*. (Mudhrā means "lock" or "seal"; in general, mudhrās are hatha yoga practices that are related to asanas.) In yoni-mudhrā the yogi concentrates on the root chakra and, while inhaling, contracts the perineum, the area of the body that lies between the anus and the scrotum in men or the vulva in women. For male yogis, one of the purposes of this technique was to develop the ability to stop the outward flow of semen during climax.

The idea behind this practice is that semen contains the highest concentration in the body of *ojas*. According to Georg Feuerstein in *Tantra: The Path of Ecstasy*, ojas is the quintessential vital principle and is the subtle life force that nourishes the human body. In women, this vital principle is known as *rasa* and the vaginal secretions that correspond to retas are frequently referred to as *rajas*. Yoga tradition has long held that this vital essence is needed to nourish the brain, especially in the case of the yogi who has reached a state of samādhi. Feuerstein pointed out that these beliefs about ojas are the reason so many yogic traditions consider sexual abstinence or at least severely restricted sexual activity necessary for obtaining success in yoga.

Another example of a hatha yoga and Tantric practice related to ūrdhva retas is *vajrolī mudhrā*. In this mudhrā the yogi strives to master the ability to draw his ejaculate back up into the penis. The idea behind this practice is that, if it can be done during intercourse, the yogi will draw not only the ojas from his own semen but also the rasa from the female into his body and will in this way absorb a perfect balance of masculine and feminine energies. In *The Encyclopedic Dictionary of Yoga* Feuerstein quoted the section of the *Hatha-Yoga-Pradīpikā* that suggests anyone who masters this technique would have no need of following any other discipline or practice.

This interrelationship of sexual energy and spiritual energy forms the basis of Tantric practice. In mainstream Tantra, known as the right-hand path, the purpose of virtually all the rites and practices is the transmutation of sexual desire into desire for spiritual attainment and transmutation of the actual sexual secretions into ojas or rasa. Historically, in the right-hand path the rites and disciplines used to attain spiritual enlightenment were based on the symbolic union of male and female. In any rites that actually involved male and female participants, the rituals were highly structured, disciplined, and constrained. While some rites with male and female participants may have been designed to increase sexual stimulation, the purpose of these practices was to increase the amount of ojas and rasa available for spiritual transmutation. These precious substances were not to be released or squandered in sexual release. Unfortunately, as Feuerstein points out in *Tantra* this essential fact is almost totally ignored by contemporary Western Tantric practitioners who "take their lead from the *Kama-Sutra* rather than the Tantric heritage". (For a brief description of left-hand path Tantra see the Notes for this chapter; for a more complete understanding of Tantra in general Dr Feuerstein's book is essential reading.)

Other traditions also recognize the inextricable bond between sexual and spiritual forces. In Taoism, for example, a system sometimes known as Taoist yoga exists in which the relationship between sexuality and spirituality can easily be seen. Unfortunately this system is far too complex to be described in detail here. In general, however, Taoist yoga is a practice designed to bring about a transformation that ultimately leads to long life on the physical plane and enlightenment on the spiritual. The transformative force that forms the foundation of this process is called *ching*. In its most base physical manifestation, ching is semen. In a more subtle form, it is sexual energy. On the most subtle level, it is an essence of the cosmic life force. Taoist texts, like their Tantric and hatha yoga counterparts, describe semen as being "precious" and say that one must guard against squandering it. In *Tao: The Chinese Philosophy of Time and Change* authors Laszio Legeza and Philip Rawson described Taoist yoga practices that begin with the stimulation of the sexual organs and then move the energy that is created upwards. This transformation occurs in stages in the fiery heat of three centers or "furnaces" that are believed to be located in the pelvis, abdomen, and chest. During this process, the fire transforms the base ching into a more subtle form and then combines it first with the vital energy known as chi and then with *shen*, a term often translated as "luminous personal spirit".

According to many authorities, including Legeza and Rawson, rituals in some branches of Taoist yoga have involved sexual intercourse. This was believed to be necessary so that masculine or *yang* energy could combine with the female or *yin* energy much as they are said to do in vajrolī mudhrā. In Taoism, a balance between both energies was believed to be essential for enlightenment.

The relationship between sexual energy and spiritual energy has even been recognized in the Judeo-Christian tradition. Many references to it can be found in Kabbalah and in some other strains of Jewish mysticism. The concept of the union of masculine and feminine energies in a sacred marriage is, in fact, at the very heart of Kabbalah. In *On the Mystical Shape of the Godhead* Gershom Scholem gave many examples of the sexual imagery used to express this marriage. In Chapter Four, Section VI of this book, Scholem described passages in the sacred Kabbalistic text the *Zohar* in which the union of Yesod—the ninth Sefirah and the one that corresponds to the phallus—and Shekinah is seen as the "supernal archetype of earthly sexual union and is uninhibitedly depicted in such terms".

Scholem added to this in *Major Trends in Jewish Mysticism*, where he described ritualistic sexual practices among other Jewish mystical sects that are meant to replicate this divine union. In one, ritualized sexual intercourse between a man and his wife is to take place every Shabbat as close to midnight as possible. During this mystical coupling the man symbolically represents the Godhead and the woman, Shekinah. This reenactment of the divine marriage on the physical plane is believed to draw Shekinah and the Godhead ever closer together on the cosmic plane so that they may one day unite and end the fragmentation that has been the cause of all human suffering.

If the link between sexual and spiritual energy that these practices point to really does exist, allusions to it should also be found in works of the great mystics. They are, after all, the individuals who have had the most direct experiences of the spiritual. And this is indeed the case. Mystics throughout history and across traditions have used sexual imagery to describe their experiences. Mahadevi's works have already given us wonderful examples of this. She uses the imagery of tossing on her bed, mad with longing, throughout the night and of dressing as a bride, rubbing her body with alluring scents, and then "gasping" and "crying" when her Lover does not come to her.

The same is true of Mechthild. It goes without saying that many of the examples of her writing used so far have literally pulsed with sexual tension. One of the best examples of this is the verse in which she describes lying down on a bed with her divine lover while he bids her to remove all her clothes. Another wonderful example of this is found in a verse from Book II that hasn't yet been quoted. In it Mechthild says she longs for the day when she can take her Lover in her arms, eat him, drink, and have her way with him. Once she does this, she says, her Lover will never be so far away that she cannot entwine her limbs with his. Then, she adds, she will never cool off.

She then goes on to describe a wedding celebration that becomes increasingly extravagant and passionate. Speaking of herself in the third person, she writes:

The narrower the bed of love becomes, the more intense are their embraces.

The sweeter the kisses on the mouth become, the more lovingly they
gaze at each other...
The more ardent she remains, the sooner she bursts into flame.

[Book I, 22]

In another verse she describes how her Lover kisses her passionately
with his divine mouth and "caresses her, as well he can, on a bed of
love". She then goes on to describe the "exquisite pain" she feels when
she becomes "truly intimate" with him.

Writings like these by saints and mystics have left Westerners
baffled; they have long wondered why such spiritual people would use
such "unspiritual" imagery, especially given the fact that so many of
these individuals were virgins and celibates. The yogic understanding
of the link between spiritual energy and sexual energy is a key that un-
locks mysteries such as these. Even more importantly, however, understanding this relationship provides critically important information
about how some of us are going to experience this energy in our daily
lives. Although this is relevant to all of us, it has some more immediate
implications for those of you who, like Anya and Kavita for example,
are experiencing transformation in an accelerated or erratic vein rather
than a steady and gradual, and therefore less perceptible, process like
the one Wendi is experiencing. For it is my experience that people
undergoing the more erratic types of transformation frequently report
having energetic experiences that are at times overwhelmingly sexual
in nature. This can be extremely disconcerting. In spite all the sexual
liberation that has supposedly been going on for the last three decades
many women still harbor deep down feelings that there is something
dirty about sex or still believe that really "good" girls don't have strong
sexual desires. Even if you are no longer plagued by these ideas, you
may have been led to believe that the reason abstinence is encouraged
or insisted upon in so many Eastern religions is because sexuality is
somehow the opposite of spirituality. Imagine then the consternation
you might feel if you suddenly find yourself overcome by feelings of
extreme sexual arousal in the middle of a meditation or while concentrating deeply on a sacred text.

In *Tantra* Feuerstein credited Gopi Krishna with substantially
broadening kundalini awareness in the West. As Feuerstein explained, Gopi Krishna was motivated to do this after experiencing a

spontaneous awakening of kundalini and discovering how little explicit information was available to help him even in India when, in the early stages, his process went awry. Over the decades Gopi Krishna's main focus came to be encouraging Western science and medicine to research the ideas put forth in the ancient texts on kundalini so that they could discover more about how it transformed the body and mind of the person experiencing it. He felt this information was critically needed at this particular time because an ever-increasing number of people would be experiencing this transformation. Although he believed this information was important for everyone, he knew from his own experience that those individuals who were undergoing the more rapid and/or erratic processes would benefit from it even more.

In dedicating his life to this Gopi Krishna also greatly increased the understanding of the exact relationship between the spiritual and sexual energies and, even more importantly, of how we might experience this intricate relationship in our physical bodies. He was able to do this not only because he searched out the sacred texts that explained what occurred during the awakening of kundalini but also because he spent decades observing the process in his own body with extraordinary mindfulness.

True yogis throughout the ages have been able to describe these processes because they have reached a state of awareness in which they have actually been able to observe the energy moving through their own bodies. This is not as unusual as it may sound. It is exactly what Anya was describing when she talked about seeing particles of energy running through her body like a "river of fire" during her profound mystical experience. Kavita was talking about the same phenomenon when she described the radiating balls of fireworks that burst along her spine and the current she saw running up and down it that she called "liquid electricity". Even in my own limited mystical experiences I have often been able to see with my mind's eye energy currents moving through my body and, especially, my brain. If ordinary people like Anya, Kavita, and I have been able to observe the movements of this energy, you can imagine how clearly great yogis were able to see it.

Because Gopi Krishna made these observations in his own process, he was able to explain the information found in the yogic texts in ways that were easier to understand. One of his most important contributions was to explain that this awakening was a two-poled process that involved, at one end, activity in the genital area at the base of the spine and, at the other, in the dormant center in the brain known as the brahma-randhra. In Sanskrit this term means the brahmic opening; brahmic here refers to brahman, the Absolute or the Divine that is beyond all knowing, not to the god Brahma. In this sense, the brahma-randhra is the point through which we are able to perceive —to whatever degree we can—the Divine. The brahma- randhra is generally held to be located somewhere in the brain above the sushumnā, the central channel or nadi that the awakened kundalini travels along. This center remains dormant or, symbolically, unopened, until kundalini-shakti finally manages to reach it. Once this has occurred the brahma-randhra springs into activity. This begins the process of transformation in the brain—the organ of perception—that allows the mystic to *perceive* levels of reality that were once hidden. Once this center is activated, the brain, or at least the center itself, is believed to need more "nourishment" than it would normally. As already described ojas is the nutrient that fulfills this need. In addition, the brain also needs what might be thought of as more psychic "fuel". Based on his study and his observations, Gopi Krishna described this fuel as a very pure and potent form of prana, or prana-shakti. In *Living with Kundalini* he explained how after his spontaneous awakening he could see this potent prana being drawn from literally every organ in his body and pulled up his spine. At the same time he was aware of an extraordinary level of activity occurring in his reproductive organs. Given the hatha yoga and Taoist views on ojas and ching already discussed, this occurrence is not at all surprising. In both his writings and lectures Gopi Krishna stated frankly that there were times when his genitals were not only swollen but also pulsing and vibrating as if this area of his body was some type of overcharged electrical generator. As he observed this process in his body, it became clear that these organs were producing ojas and were at the same time the richest source of potent prana.

It might be reassuring at this point to interject a brief description of Gopi Krishna's kundalini experience and stress that it was an extraordinarily rare type of awakening. One of the factors that made it so unusual was the spontaneity with which it occurred. As we've seen in stories like Kavita's and Anya's spontaneous awakenings do occur; however, these types of experiences can best be described using the expression "kundalini risings" explained in Chapter Five. In other words, the ordinary women, myself included, whose stories have been told throughout the book have all been experiencing some type of as yet incomplete kundalini process. None of us are anywhere near having a true kundalini awakening.

This is, however, indeed what happened to Gopi Krishna. Kundalini not only awakened, it also traveled all the way up his spine and activated the brahma-randhra. Prior to this experience Gopi Krishna had been meditating for three hours every morning before dawn without fail—including the morning after his wedding night—for seventeen years. This intensive, long-term meditation was a key factor in triggering the awakening. It occurred on a cold Christmas morning in Northern India in 1937 when he was thirty-four years old. As he sat meditating, he became aware of a powerful, pleasurable sensation at the base of his spine. As he continued to meditate, the sensation began to spread and extend upwards. It continued to expand until he heard, quite without warning, a roar like that of a waterfall and felt a stream of liquid light enter his brain. In *Kundalini: the evolutionary energy in man* he described what happened after this exquisitely beautiful light began to suffuse his consciousness:

> The illumination grew brighter and brighter, the roaring louder, I experienced a rocking sensation and then felt myself slipping out of my body, entirely enveloped in a halo of light...I felt the point of consciousness that was myself growing wider, surrounded by waves of light...I was now all consciousness, without any outline, without any idea of a corporeal appendage, without any feeling or sensation coming from the senses, immersed in a sea of light simultaneously conscious and aware of every point, spread out, as it were, in all directions without any barrier or material obstruction...bathed in light and in a state of exaltation and happiness impossible to describe.

This initial experience triggered a transformative process that lasted for twelve years. During this time, the sensations of light, splendor, and joy alternated with, and were sometimes completely overshadowed by, sensations of fire, unbearable heat, and bleak depression. Immersing himself in the ancient teachings on the subject, Gopi Krishna found that much of it was in symbolic and cryptic language. He discovered one reason for this was that the Tantric yogis had not wanted the knowledge to fall into the hands of those who were not prepared or who did not have a teacher to guide them as it was held that premature or incorrect awakening of kundalini could cause exactly the kinds of distressing symptoms he was having at times. Fortunately, he eventually also discovered a number of simple practices (see Chapter Fifteen) that helped him begin the process of bringing the energy back into balance. In *Living with Kundalini* he described one of his first tastes of this more integrated experience:

> [The state] assumed such an awe-inspiring, all-mighty, all-knowing, blissful, and at the same time absolutely motionless, intangible, and formless character that the invisible line demarcating the material world and the boundless, all-conscious Reality ceased to exist, the two fusing into one; the mighty ocean sucked up by the drop, the enormous three-dimensional universe swallowed by a grain of sand, the entire creation, the knower and the known, the seer and the seen, reduced to an inexpressible sizeless void which no ordinary mind could conceive nor any language describe.

Eventually Gopi Krishna came to live in a state of integrated awakening in which his entire consciousness and the world around him was bathed in what he described as "liquid light". He experienced a virtually constant state of bliss. He also received phenomenal amounts of creative inspiration. Between the age of forty-six and his death at eighty-one, he wrote seventeen books on kundalini and higher consciousness. Three of these books were entirely in verse. One of them, *The Shape of Events to Come*, a volume of some two hundred pages, provides an excellent example of how creative inspiration came to him: it was composed in three weeks while he sat on the living room floor amidst the hubbub of a tiny four-room house in New Delhi where he lived with his wife, son, daughter-in-law, and their two small children.

Although what happened to Gopi Krishna was very rare, his frank talk about both the positive and negative aspects of his experience has proved invaluable to ordinary spiritual seekers. Even though any "symptom" we might encounter is generally going to be far milder and vastly less intense than anything he experienced, his discussions have provided us with a framework that helps us understand what is going on in our bodies. Before going on to discuss this framework in more detail, it is important to stress that at this point in time no one can be absolutely certain exactly what happens in any type of kundalini awakening or activity. There is huge disagreement among contemporary yoga and Tantric teachers on virtually every aspect of this process. The whole concept of the chakras provides a perfect example of this: some teachers believe they look exactly like they are drawn complete with complex images, symbols, and colors; others believe they are simply whirling vortices of energy; still others believe that they are nothing more than a symbolic representation of nerve plexuses found in the nervous system. Some teachers believe they are several inches in diameter; others say they are microscopically small and reside inside the sushumnā. Some say they exist in the physical body; others that they exist only in the subtle body (an "energetic" body that exists in conjunction with the physical body). Some traditions say there are seven chakras; others that there are ten or more. Some believe the crown chakra sits well above the head; others that it resides right at the crown, and still others that it is, in fact, the pineal gland.

The fact that this level of disparity exists on everything from the nature of the nadis to what constitutes ojas was one reason Gopi Krishna's main thrust in life was to encourage scientific and medical research on the kundalini process. However, until the time in the future when this research is done there is no way to be unequivocally certain about any of it. In the meantime, the best we can do is to examine the differing references in the yogic texts—keeping in mind they were often written in cryptic and symbolic language—and use our common sense. Perhaps most importantly, we also need to observe what is happening in our bodies. Gopi Krishna often said his body was a "laboratory" for his observations. He emphatically encouraged each one of us to observe our bodies in the same way and share our perceptions so that we could add to the growing level of knowledge.

Nowhere is this more relevant than in the area of the relationship between sexual and spiritual energy. As mentioned above, people can be extremely disconcerted by having what they perceived to be sexual sensations during spiritual experiences. In fact, in my many years of speaking with people about spirituality, I have met scores of people who have had to deal with this issue. For example, a friend of mine who had a profoundly mystical near-death experience during an operation had spontaneous orgasms that often occurred while she was driving to work on the freeway. Another woman I met told me that every time she entered a state of intense spiritual awareness—where she was filled with a sense of bliss and at-oneness and nature seemed to glow with light—parts of her vaginal area would become so swollen she could hardly walk. A man I've communicated with for years has described getting erections and almost overwhelming sexual urges when he reads spiritual texts. My own experiences, as I've described in detail elsewhere, were replete with sexual sensations. In *The Fiery Muse* I described how, right after an experience I had many years ago on an ocean beach, powerful sexual sensations originated in my genital area, moved in waves up my body, and seemed to burst in orgasms near my heart. Often these bursts would be accompanied by poems or stories that would flood so rapidly into my mind I could hardly scrawl the words onto paper before they disappeared.

In each of these cases, the realization that these patently sexual sensations were simply the result of the brain's need for more potent prana and ojas was sanity saving! However, before I could come to this level of understanding I had first to be able to accept the fact that what I was experiencing really was related to kundalini. Certainly in my early days of studying the subject I would never have believed this was possible. Kundalini awakening, as I understood it, was something that happened to extremely advanced yogis and great spiritual masters. While this is true of what I've referred to as "full" kundalini awakening, Gopi Krishna made it clear that partial and incomplete awakenings were part of a whole continuum of experiences related to kundalini. He also explained that the term full awakening—even when it referred to great spiritual masters such as Buddha—was, in a certain sense, a misnomer because no one alive today really knows what lies at the far end of this continuum.

Inherent in this notion of partial awakenings, is the idea that the brahma-randhra and possibly other important centers in the brain can spring into some degree of action long before kundalini was "fully" awakened or even successfully rising to any degree. Gopi Krishna noted that this could occur not just in people who were active spiritual seekers but in other individuals as well, particularly those who spent great amounts of time in the focused concentration that is so much a part of our Western lifestyle. He pointed out that this type of riveted concentration actually mimics one of the limbs of classical yoga, the eight-limb path set out in the *Yoga-Sūtras* of Patanjali. The name of this step is *dhāranā*, a Sanskrit term that means literally "concentration" and is often described as continuous, focused attention. The *Yoga-Sūtras* [III.1] refer to it as binding one's consciousness to a fixed point. In order to practice dhāranā, spiritual seekers throughout the ages have been encouraged to focus their single-pointed attention on a powerful, uplifting image such as a lotus or the face of a great spiritual master. One purpose of fixating the mind in this is to keep it from leaping from object to object and attaching itself to each one in turn.

If you look at Patanjali's eight-limbed path as a model you will see that dhāranā is the sixth limb or step in the system. This single-pointed focus leads to the seventh limb, *dhyāna*, which is meditation. In this process, dhāranā is meant, through practice, to deepen naturally into dhyāna. As one continues to practice dhyāna, concentration deepens ever further until all the fluctuations of normal consciousness cease and the eighth limb, the mystical state known as samādhi, is reached.

While one of the purposes of this ever-deepening concentration is the withdrawal of the mind and the senses from the outer world, it also has the effect of stimulating the brahma-randhra. Once the brahma-randhra is stimulated it begins to call out, as it were, for the potent prana and ojas it needs. In this sense kundalini is not so much a separate substance as a combination of these two manifestations of the life energy. Symbolically, this can be visualized as Shiva, who is said to reside just above the crown of the head, calling out for Shakti, who lies coiled at the base of the spine waiting and longing for his call.

The great advantage of looking at the continuum of kundalini experiences as having these two poles is that it helps you understand the factors necessary for it to proceed smoothly and in the healthiest manner possible. The first of these factors is that the ojas and/or potent prana—assuming that a combination of these two substances is what is indeed rising in kundalini awakenings—have to be able reach the brahma-randhra or, in partial awakenings, flow smoothly upward in varying degrees. Exactly how far it goes is yet another area of disagreement among both texts and teachers.

Probably the most common suggestion is that kundalini flows upward only as far as it can go, then stops and flows back to the root chakra. There it remains until it makes another attempt to reach the crown chakra. Once this chakra is reached, kundalini activates the brahma-randhra and permanently resides at the crown instead of returning back to the root chakra.

The main problem with this theory as I see it is that it doesn't explain how or why the brain/mind of the person is transformed when kundalini is only partially awakened. And, as we have seen in the stories throughout this book, *something* has clearly been transformed in the brains/minds of the women who have experienced partial awakenings. Gopi Krishna postulated—and hoped it could some day be tested—that while kundalini might rise and fall in some cases, it was also possible that some degree of potent prana and possibly even ojas might flow all the way to the brain. There the prana and/or ojas might enrich certain areas other than the actual brahma-randhra. These other areas, sometimes referred to as "chambers" in yogic texts, are held to be related to other types of mental functioning, for instance, creativity. Gopi Krishna and others have postulated that this rising of limited amounts of potent prana and/or ojas would explain why people so often developed new and surprising talents even after kundalini experiences that were clearly far from true awakenings. A good example of this is the way Britta's artwork came alive after her experience and how she spontaneously developed the ability to write poetry.

Regardless of exactly what is flowing upward or how far it goes, it is almost universally agreed that this process can be impeded by certain types of blockages. Although such universal agreement doesn't exist on exactly what the different blockages are or how they impede the flow of kundalini, many of the suggestions make a good deal of sense. The most obvious are actual physical blocks. Depending on the school of thought, these might include breaks or cracks in the spine, misaligned vertebrae, muscle spasms, scar tissue, and so on. Other schools also believe that psychological trauma can be held in the body as a sort of physiological memory and that this phenomenon can create blockages that are as real as the physical ones. Christine gave an example of this earlier in the book when she suggested the energy flow had been blocked in her body by the trauma of early sexual abuse.

Contemporary yoga teachers and body workers often refer to these blockages as *samskarās*, particularly if they are psychological in nature. Since this term is being used so frequently, it's important to take a closer look at it. Technically, according to Feuerstein, the word samskarā means "activator". In yoga philosophy, it is believed that everything we do or experience, either consciously or unconsciously, leaves an indelible imprint on our inner being. As "activators", these imprints have a dynamic force of their own and are believed to propel the individual consciousness into action. Since the purpose of yoga is to still this level of consciousness, samskarās can be thought of as agents that block our progress. Some schools also believe they may block the flow of prana throughout the body and/or the flow of potent prana and ojas up the sushumnā.

Regardless of what these blockages are caused by, some traditions also hold that they keep kundalini from rising up the sushumnā and cause it to rise instead up one of the other two central nadis. As described earlier, these two nadis are known as the idā and the pingalā. The idā, symbolically represented by the moon, runs along the left of the sushumnā; it is held to be responsible for cooling the body. Represented by the sun, the pingalā is located to the right and is thought to heat the body. As can be imagined, risings through these channels can be problematic. This is, in fact, what happened in Gopi Krishna's case: kundalini rose mainly through the pingalā and caused him at times during the first years of his awakening to experience heat and images of fire instead of those of blissful, radiant light that were present once the process was corrected and the upward flow moved to the sushumnā.

According to a number of sources, the quality of prana and ojas is just as important as the quantity available. These sources hold that the purity of the life energy taken in and circulating in the body is influenced by a number of factors that include the wholesomeness and freshness of food, the amount of pollution in the air, and the degree of impurities the body is exposed to in general.

The possible effects of wayward risings and impure or insufficient amounts of prana/ojas reaching the brahma-randhra can be gleaned from the ancient texts as well as from the experiences of many contemporary people. They range from mood swings and a general sense of disorientation to depression and to conditions that might masquerade as mental illness or, in some cases, might actually be related to some forms of mental illness. Fortunately, a good deal of work is currently being done in this area. One of the most solid sources of information on all this is Joan Harrigan, Ph.D., a clinical psychologist whose center, Patanjali Yoga Care, is located in Tennessee. With the guidance of her teacher from India, Swami Chandrasekharanand Saraswati—a yogi whose lineage traces all the way back to the great eighth-century Hindu saint Shankaracharya, Dr Harrigan has written an outstanding book called *Kundalini Vidya* which pulls together an extraordinary amount of information and is an invaluable reference. (For more information on Dr Harrigan, her website and how to order her book, as well as information on other sources, see this chapter's Notes.)

While focusing as I have done in the last few pages on what can go awry with the kundalini process might cause some apprehension, it really shouldn't. For when you look at this information from a positive perspective, you see that it reveals the basic factors needed to ensure that this process moves along in the smoothest and healthiest manner possible. Simply said, sufficient amounts of prana and/or ojas need to be available; they need to flow as smoothly as they can; and they need to be as pure and unadulterated as possible.

Based on the observations of his own process and what he gleaned from studying the yoga and Tantric traditions, Gopi Krishna firmly believed that lifestyle was the most important issue influencing these factors. Moderation and regularity were his guiding principles in this regard. Within this framework, simple things like sleep and diet are of paramount importance. In order to produce enough prana, for instance, the body needs sufficient amounts of sleep; regularity in sleep patterns also helps so that the body does not continually have to waste energy in readjusting. In terms of ojas, it seems patently clear that not "squandering" it is the key to having enough available. The purity of the prana and ojas available are affected by factors that range from how fresh and chemical free our food is to how free we are from negative emotions like anger and aggression. As is discussed in more detail in Chapter Fifteen, issues like these also effect how freely prana and/or ojas can flow. It seems probable that negative emotions could create potent samskaras, and it's common knowledge they can turn our muscles into rock hard lumps. On the positive side we know that body work and working on psychological issues can release them.

It is no coincidence that the type of lifestyle that promotes creative inspiration can be summed up with the word "balanced". The concept of balance is central to creativity of all sorts—especially when it comes to the balance of the masculine and feminine within. When Kavita sat in the penetrating Mediterranean light and created the organic drawings of the ethereal female heads, her creativity was directly connected to the divine feminine. However, she says:

> The times when I have been most creative since then have often been fueled by a passionate longing for the feminine and masculine within me to merge, a kind of inner marriage of Shakti and Shiva...Maybe I needed first to open to and merge with the Divine Feminine within me, as a counterbalance to, and liberation from, the intimidating judgment of the masculine God—and my own judgmental, critical mind. Then, later, I needed to reconcile and re-unify the Feminine with a beloved, rather than feared, Masculine...I felt like the feminine side was opening up more and more for a long time as an intrinsic part of my spiritual evolution, and at a certain point the need to reconcile it once again with the masculine came into play. But so far this last phase has not resolved itself, and there is a great deal of tension and disorientation as the two aspects struggle with each other, trying to find a new and hopefully greater synthesis...I feel this dichotomy between the feminine and masculine within me has been my biggest challenge in life in general...

Kavita speaks here with tremendous insight about a dichotomy that we will see, in the next chapter, is central not just to her but to all of us. It takes us right back to the beginning of this chapter and Shakti and Shiva's yearning for each other. This is the yearning for balance—a state in which our inner masculine and feminine natures work together to create, just as the eternal dance of Shakti and Shiva creates and recreates the cosmos.

Clay—Connecting with Mother Earth

This exercise in working with clay is one in connecting to Mother Earth and to our bodies in a very visceral way. This exercise will produce a simple clay bowl that can be used for things that are dry—not water or food. Unless you are someone who has experience working with clay, your first pot will probably be quite basic and a bit imperfect. Although lovely works of art can be made with this technique, this exercise is meant to be more meditation than art project; the joy is in the process more than in the end result.

Pinch pots are some of the oldest archeological artifacts found; this means human beings have been making pinch pots since they first discovered clay. Making this type of pot is an extremely simple exercise that is meant to connect you with your basic, primal nature. Working with clay is in itself a visceral experience. It comes from the earth. It is earth. As you make your pinch pot focus on this connection to the earth, and through it, to your root chakra. As your pot takes shape and comes into being, focus on this chakra —the seat of kundalini-shakti and of your most basic desires. If you are doing this exercise in conjunction with the one from Chapter Seven, be particularly aware of your pelvis as the container that holds kundalini-shakti in your body.

Allow yourself to sink into the sensual experience of working the clay, and as you do, tune into these basic desires, keeping in mind that it is only society's false values that have made us think that sexuality is the opposite of spirituality and remembering that Tantra tells us that the transmutation of sexual energy is, in fact, the source of spiritual energy—the energy of transformation.

You will need some self-hardening clay—about a pound (it should be moist and very easy to manipulate).

1. *Have your materials ready and enter your light-filled, protected, meditative space.*
2. *During this exercise, stay aware of the clay and the visceral experience of working with it; focus on your pelvis and your root chakra. Enjoy the sensations that flow through your body as you sink into the sensuality of the experience.*
3. *Begin with a lump of the self-hardening clay—a portion about the size of a tennis ball will make a small bowl.*

4. Shape the lump into a ball with your hands. As you do, begin to focus on your breathing making sure it is deep and regular. When the lump of clay is almost round, place it on a flat surface and use the palm of your hand to roll it into the most perfectly round sphere you can. As you roll, be conscious of the rhythm of your breathing.

5. Be aware of the clay, and how the simple circular motion of your palm transfers itself into the creation of a nearly perfect sphere. Once you have your sphere, gently push your thumbs into the center to make a hole. Begin pinching up the walls, rotating the clay as you pinch. Stay in a meditative state as you do this. The more rhythmic and regulated your movements are, the more uniform the thickness of your pot will be.

6. As you rotate and pinch, the shape of your bowl emerges. Keep the thickness of the sides of the pot as even as possible. Occasionally push your thumbs deeper so that any excess clay on the bottom is squeezed up to the sides of the bowl. Continue to breathe and stay aware of your breath! See how the rhythm of your breathing and the rhythm of the rotating and pinching fall into a pattern.

7. Whenever you have the beginnings of a nice bowl shape, you can set the clay on a flat surface and push it down a little to form a flat bottom for your bowl. Then begin rotating and pinching again. At some point you may want to set the bowl on the surface again and leave it there while you move your hands to pinch around the bowl.

8. Because of differences in clay and skill, there is no set thickness for the sides of your bowl. The trick is to stop just before the clay gets wobbly and begins to loose its shape. Since there is no way to know this the first time you work with the clay, just stop whenever you want. If you go too far, just squish the clay into a ball and begin again—or wrap it in plastic wrap and store it in the refrigerator until you'd like to try again.

9. When the consistency of your bowl is about the same as hard leather (usually after about 24 hours), you can "burnish" the bowl—i.e. smooth out the imperfections—by rubbing and smoothing it with the back of a spoon.

10. Once your bowl is completely dry—usually in a few days—you can paint it using acrylics. You can also experiment with different finishes. If you have burnished your bowl, you can coat it with floor wax or even different colors of paste shoe polish—just rub on the polish, let it dry a bit, and then buff it.

* *Searching "pinch pots" on the internet will show you many examples of the beautiful bowls and vases that can be made with this technique. Many sites also provide instructions for making other interesting objects, like whistles and little animals.*

Shiva, Shakti, and the Balance of Power

If we look again to the story of Shiva and Sati as it is told in the *Kālikā Purāna* we find it is a wonderful source of information about the balance between the divine masculine and feminine. In fact, the story begins with a warning about the dire consequences that arise when these two forces are out of balance: Brahma, Vishnu, and the other gods and goddesses are in a state of panic. Shiva, the celibate, ascetic god is amassing so much psychic energy in his meditation that the very fabric of the cosmos is in danger of being blown apart. When the gods and goddesses come together to discuss the situation it immediately becomes obvious to them that the root of the problem is Shiva's unbalanced state; his masculine force is running rampant and, unless it is tempered and brought into balance by the feminine, it will destroy creation. Brahma quickly explains that the only solution to the predicament is to get Shiva to take a wife. However, this in itself creates another problem that the *Kālikā Purāna* stresses a good deal: the gods and goddesses realize right away that this woman must be Shiva's equal. Despairing of finding such a paragon among themselves, they bewail the certain demise of the cosmos. When Brahma comes up with the suggestion of asking Shakti, the divine mother herself, to help them, the other gods and goddesses praise him highly—Brahma has comprehended the essence of the problem and come up with a solution.

The meaning behind this scenario is clearly that it isn't enough for the divine feminine simply to be present, she must be equal to the masculine presence. A weak feminine will not do. A true state of balance is possible only between equals. The urgency of this message about the need for balance is underscored a little further along in the story when Brahma is struck by Kama's arrows and begins to lust after Sandhya. His sexual energy, which is of course also the spiritual energy kundalini-shakti, is misdirected and sent outward instead of upward. The masculine is once again without the feminine. In this state of imbalance Brahma becomes a destructive force; he loses touch with the feminine qualities of justice and mercy and tries to destroy Kama, even though Kama is innocent of wrongdoing. Fortunately, Brahma quickly regains control of the misdirected energy. As soon as he does, he recovers his spiritual balance and comes to his senses. He is able to listen to Kama's plea for mercy and spare him. Then, just in case we have missed the point that this story is about the absolute necessity of balance between the masculine and feminine, Brahma sends Kama off on the vital mission of getting Shiva to marry Sati, who is of course Shakti in disguise, so that Shiva's unbalanced energies do not destroy the world. In short, Brahma has regained his own equilibrium and then sends Kama out to bring equilibrium back to the world. In the end, Brahma's strategies are successful: Shiva takes Sati to be his wife, and when he does his energies come into balance. Harmony is restored to the universe.

This lesson about the balance of the masculine and feminine polarities is so important, the *Kālikā Purāna* comes back to it yet again and renders it in even more dramatic imagery when, after eons of blissful marital union, Sati dies in a burst of flame. The moment

Shiva loses his beloved, cosmic balance and harmony are once again destroyed. As first described in Chapter Seven, Shiva begins to circle the earth in rage and despair with Sati's dead body in his arms. As he does, his unfettered energy shakes the cosmos and throws the world back into turmoil. In the heat of his burning grief, boiling tears flow from his eyes and he scalds and floods the earth below. Realizing the cosmos is about to be destroyed, the other gods and goddesses swing immediately into action and send Brahma, this time with Vishnu to help him, to calm Shiva.

Brahma knows the only way to accomplish this is to convince Shiva that Shakti will come again in the future as the goddess Parvati. When she does, Brahma assures Shiva, she will marry him and that the two will even have a child. Once Shiva is persuaded all this will be so, the destruction stops. But even then true equilibrium and harmony are not restored. This occurs only when Shiva comes to earth near the place where Sati's yoni has fallen. Resting there, Shiva takes the form of a linga and waits patiently for Parvati to manifest. This scene, of the phallic linga rising up out of the earth and the vaginal yoni embedded deep within creates a potent and powerful image of the masculine and feminine, the transcendental spirit and the embodied spirit, and the ultimate overriding need for the balance between polarities. Since the *Kālikā Purāna* contains so much Tantric material, we know the writers wanted us to understand that this need for balance of masculine and feminine polarities is as essential within each one of us individually as it is to the universe.

Another one of the serendipitous discoveries that have characterized the writing of this book occurred when I was looking for stories from other traditions that would illustrate this need for masculine-feminine balance. From the very early stages of writing the book I'd been pestered by the insistent notion that I needed to find a Greek myth to express this point. Although I knew I wouldn't need this material until one of the final chapters, the thought kept nagging me, and so, quite early on I took a detour into Greek mythology. While there, it seemed I'd found the answer to my problem in the story of Hermaphroditus, the offspring of the great god and goddess, Hermes and Aphrodite. Hermaphroditus, who was half man and half woman, seemed to represent the notion of balance perfectly. Even better, I thought, was the fact that he was a "combination" of the very masculine, intellectual Hermes and the very essence of femininity, the goddess of love Aphrodite. Assuming this would all fit perfectly I went back to writing the book.

Unfortunately, when the time came to gather more information on Hermaphroditus I couldn't find much material—no fascinating stories, no great adventures, nothing that would show how he illustrated perfect balance. Because Greek mythology really isn't my field, I could imagine myself doing weeks of fruitless research, and I became extremely frustrated. Little did I know, the answer to my problem had been handed to me way back when I had first read about the creation of Kama in the story of Shiva and Sati. Kama, as has been mentioned, is almost indisputably the forerunner of the Greek god Eros, known also by his Roman name, Cupid. The many similarities between the two support the idea that Cupid has descended from Kama: for example, both are exceedingly beautiful, both have bows and quivers full of arrows slung over their shoulders, and both have the power to draw men and women together. One passage in the *Kālikā Purāna* even describes Kama as having a beautifully rounded bottom—a feature that still characterizes the Cupid we know today.

Once I noticed these similarities, I began to suspect I just might find the story I needed if I looked more closely at Cupid. Those of you who know Greek mythology have probably already guessed that I found just what was needed in the heart-rending story of Cupid and Psyche.

Although much earlier versions of this story must have existed, the first one still known today was written in the second century CE by the Roman satirist Apuleius. Since then the powerful and important message behind the tale has been reworked over the centuries by great thinkers that range from Origen, one of the early Christian church fathers, to Chaucer.

Apuleius' version of the tale appears as a story within a story in his famous work *Metamorphoses*, which is better known as *The Golden Ass*. The story begins long ago in ancient Greece with the birth of Psyche, whose name means "the soul". The third daughter of a king and queen, Psyche is graced from the moment of her birth with such extraordinary beauty that people adore her. As she grows older, her beauty increases and, as it does, this adoration turns into veneration. Soon, the people who have been worshiping the goddess Venus—

known to the Greeks as Aphrodite—begin to worship Psyche's beauty instead. Psyche, however, has not asked for any of this. She sees her great beauty as a curse. It has placed her so far above the crowd that no one, not even the handsomest young prince, will attempt to ask for her hand in marriage, and she languishes alone even though legions come to pay her homage.

Over time the adoration of Psyche spreads and the altars once dedicated to Venus fall into disrepair and the offerings to her dwindle away until Venus becomes incensed. Furious that anyone could adore a mere mortal more than her, she plots her revenge. She finds her son Cupid, the god of love, and begs him to shoot Psyche with an arrow that will cause her to wed the most despicable creature that can be found. Cupid flies off to do her bidding.

Soon a decree comes down from the heavens that Psyche must be dressed as a bride and left on the highest sacrificial rock. There she will be wed to the cruelest of all serpents who, her family assumes, is death itself. Psyche's parents weep and wail as they take her to the rock, but Psyche goes willingly to what she thinks is her death.

Once her parents and the mourning crowds have left her to her fate, Psyche lies down upon the rock and falls asleep. When she awakens she finds herself in a beautiful palace garden where her every desire is instantly fulfilled. When night comes she finds a bed in the palace and falls asleep. During the night she is visited by a man who makes her his wife. Night after night her husband comes to her but he always leaves before dawn and she never sees his face. He even tells Psyche that she must never, ever look upon him. Because of this, Psyche assumes she is quite literally married to a hideous monster. Unbeknownst to Psyche her husband is in fact Cupid, and he is hiding from Psyche because his beauty is so great no mere mortal can bear to look upon it.

Even though Psyche believes she is married to a monster, she comes to cherish her husband. Still, she is tormented by the fact that she cannot see him. She is also miserable when he flies off every morning and leaves her alone. Eventually, she begs him to let her two sisters come to visit and provide her with some company. Cupid, aware that these sisters were always consumed with jealousy over Psyche's beauty, warns her against the idea. But Psyche continues to plead and Cupid cannot resist her entreaties—especially once she tells him she is pregnant.

As soon as the sisters arrive for their first visit and see the magical, wish-fulfilling garden, they realize what Psyche has not: she must be married to a god. Eventually, they even deduce that it must be Cupid himself to whom she is married. Now completely riddled with jealousy, they tell Psyche her husband is a vile monster who is planning to eat her and the unborn child and convince her that she must stab him to death.

Determined to look on this monster before she kills him, Psyche sneaks a lamp into their bedchamber. When her husband falls asleep, she lights the lamp. As she gazes on Cupid's beautiful face, she realizes the gravity of her error and tries to stab herself. But the knife leaps from her shaking hands and a drop of burning oil falls from the lamp. The oil lands on Cupid's shoulder and grievously wounds him. When the pain jolts him awake, he discovers what Psyche has done and is forced to flee back to his mother Venus' home.

Venus now discovers that her son has not only defied her orders, he has gone so far as to defame her illustrious name by marrying a lowly mortal. Venus flies into a terrible rage and, blaming Psyche for this state of affairs, sets out to destroy her. In the meantime Psyche, consumed with love and longing for Cupid, is searching heaven and earth for him, hoping to find him and beg his forgiveness. She prays for protection from the raging Venus, but no one is able to help her. Finally, she concedes defeat and gives herself up to Venus. But before Venus can manage to kill her, Cupid recovers from his wound, discovers that his beloved is in peril, and flies off to beg his father, who is the great god Jupiter, for help.

Jupiter decides to intervene on his son's behalf. He realizes the solution to the problem is a simple one: all he has to do is make Psyche Cupid's equal. To this end he calls all the gods and goddesses to a great celebration and gives Psyche a draught that turns her into an immortal goddess. Now, Cupid and Psyche can enjoy eternal love; Venus can take motherly pride in her daughter-in-law's great beauty and is no longer shamed by her son marrying beneath himself. A great wedding ceremony ensues, and Cupid and Psyche are married as equals before all the gods and goddesses.

Clearly the story of Cupid and Psyche, like that of Shiva and Sati, tells us that the divine feminine not only needs to be present, she needs to be recognized as equal. Just as obvious is the fact that we live in a period in history when the masculine is still more honored than the feminine at every level. This is true whether it refers to the way women are still treated in most parts of the world or the way our society honors "masculine" traits more than "feminine" ones. As you are probably well aware, the cumulative effect of this imbalance on a worldwide level is posing an ever-increasing threat. Almost thirty years ago in India I heard Gopi Krishna make the point that the main cause of the proliferation of war and the thoughtless destruction of the environment was that traits associated with the masculine side of our natures like intellect and reason had been allowed to run amok without being tempered by the traits from the feminine side like emotion and intuition.

The underlying message of the stories like those of Shiva and Sati and Cupid and Psyche is that, ultimately, this cosmic equilibrium can come increasingly into being only as more and more of us as individuals achieve it collectively within ourselves. This doesn't mean we don't continue to work for balance in the outer world—including everything from political efforts to improve the lot of women and children everywhere to our eco-feminist battles to save Mother Earth. It does mean, however, we must remain first and foremost extremely vigilant about the state of the divine masculine-feminine balance within our own souls.

Some of the most important work on how to achieve this balance has been done in the last few decades by the Jungians. Chief among them is Marion Woodman who has become known internationally for her work in this area. Marion's first ground-breaking contributions to Jungian analysis came in the field of eating disorders where she made great strides in helping women come to terms with living fully in their bodies. Two of her widely influential books on this subject are *The Owl Was a Baker's Daughter* and *Addicted to Perfection: The Still Unravished Bride*. Over the years her work with women on body imagery has grown in a very natural way to include work on the embodiment of the divine feminine.

When I had the honor of interviewing Marion for this book a strange synchronicity occurred. No matter what I wanted to ask her, Marion wanted to talk about a movie she'd seen the night before. This was not the direction I wanted the conversation to take! I knew I only had a limited amount of time before Marion, who was recovering from a major illness, became exhausted, and I was afraid we would never get to the areas I wanted her to discuss. Years of conducting interviews have made me fairly adept at getting people onto the topic I want to hear about, but every time I asked another question to redirect her, Marion went back to the movie. When she launched into a detailed plot outline, I groaned inwardly, gave up, and listened. But even then it wasn't until months later when I rented a copy of the movie for myself that I realized Marion had been giving me exactly the information I needed, for on a deep symbolic level this particular film is about nothing other than the balance between the inner masculine and feminine.

Entitled *Chocolat*, the film made a huge impact when it first came out and was nominated for several Academy Awards in 2000. Although it has faded from the public eye since then, I suspect it will remain lodged deeply in the collective unconscious and be hailed as a classic in years to come. The story the movie tells takes place during Lent in a devoutly Catholic village in France not long after World War II. The village is ruled like a fiefdom by the mayor, a count whose ancestors reigned over the village for generations. The count, himself ruled by his intellect, is devoid of love and compassion and is completely emotionally repressed. His wife has left him, but he has refused for months to admit this to either himself or the villagers. Totally obsessed with rules and regulations, particularly those of the Church, he rams a hateful, puritanical morality down the throats of the townspeople. He edits and rewrites the sermons of the young village priest until they reflect his own belief in a God of judgment and punishment. There is no room for mercy in the count's religion. The letter of the law of the Church means everything. The body is to be denied, pleasure is a transgression, and sensuality is a sin. Setting himself as an example before the villagers he tortures himself with self-deprivation. In one telling scene, his housekeeper, who is afraid he is starving himself during Lent, brings him a plate of freshly baked bread, glistening with butter and ruby-red jam. When he refuses it, she starts to take it away, but he makes her leave it. He sets it on his desk close to his hand where the sight and smell torture him as he works long into the night.

Into this village on a cold wind-swept day comes a mysterious, voluptuous woman with her young daughter in tow. Named Vianne, the woman has come to rent an old, dilapidated patisserie. She scrubs, paints, and repairs and then, in blatant defiance of the fact that most of the villagers will have given up sweets for Lent, opens her shop: a chocolaterie. But this is no ordinary chocolate shop. Vianne is follow-ing in the footsteps of her mother, a Mayan her father had fallen in love with while searching for medicinal remedies in the jungles of Central America. Although the tribal shaman warned that this woman was of a special breed who were fated to wander from village to village bringing the mystical healing properties of cocoa and magical herbs to people in need, Vianne's father ignored him and brought her home. She tried to settle down, but she could not and soon she was wandering from village to village through France. She passed this fateful trait onto Vianne.

As soon as the chocolaterie is opened, it is filled with seductive, sensual delights that restore lost libidos, empower the powerless, and bring long-unrequited lovers together—even those in their golden years. To entice the villagers into the shop, Vianne drapes the shop window with red satin and decorates it with tantalizing chocolate confections. In the middle of this display she sets an enor-mous, naked chocolate goddess. The braver villagers are enticed into the shop by the display and word of the mysterious powers of the chocolate spreads. Before long more and more of the villagers are seen, in spite of their sacred Lenten vows, slipping through the doors of the chocolaterie. Angered at what he sees as wanton sinfulness, the count begins to persecute Vianne. At the same time he steps up his own self-torture, nearly starving himself.

The count's attempts to run Vianne out of business fail, and she continues to revel in her sensuality, express her passionate love of life, and display her deep humanity. As he becomes increasingly enraged, the count creates a campaign to "boycott immorality" and uses every power in his means to get Vianne run out of town.

When his attempts fail, he eventually goes berserk. Taking up a dagger, he breaks into the shop, crawls into the window, and begins to destroy the display. He chops off the goddess's head, hacks off her arms, and stabs her through the heart. As he does, a bit of chocolate flies into his mouth. As the morsel melts on his tongue, his rigid control too begins to melt away. He puts another piece of chocolate into his mouth and almost swoons. He clutches the goddess's head and shoves it in his mouth. At that moment he is completely undone.

With both hands he grabs at the confections that lay scattered about the window and begins to crush them into his mouth. He eats and eats until, with chocolate smeared on his face, he falls to his knees and finally collapses. Having finally allowed himself physical release from so much deprivation, his repressed emotions are able to break through. He sobs out his grief over the loss of his wife until he falls asleep, sprawled across the chocolate and the silky red satin cloth.

Marion's description of the film and this moving scene was first triggered by a question I asked her about a Jungian archetype known as the Black Madonna. The Black Madonna is a black-skinned image of Mary that has surfaced in Christian art and statuary for centuries. Examples range from statues found in tiny chapels in the Swiss Alps to gold-leaf icons in Byzantine style. In Jungian terms it is a powerful archetypal image because it paradoxically combines darkness with the image of light, goodness, and female perfection associated with Mary. In her most recent book, *Bone: Dying into Life*, Marion referred to this image often and said:

> The Black Madonna is pushing through from the unconscious in dreams. She is bringing the living feminine into everyday planetary life; no longer can she be frozen into a goddess on a pedestal or a goddess in bed. She utterly rejects patriarchal projections that chain her in stereotypes—naive victim, stupid, melodramatic, histrionic, hysterical—all those words that have imprisoned her, reduced her to silence. She will no longer be silent. There is no turning back. She strides into dreams rich and juicy, full of fun and vibrant sexuality and intense spirituality—all One.

Although Marion made this observation in the context of healing and her own battle with cancer, which is the focus of *Bone*, it seemed to me that the image might also be important in terms of creativity. I was a bit hesitant to ask Marion if she thought this might be so because I worried that she might think I was trivializing the concept. After all, the issue of creative expression might be thought to pale beside the life and death struggle with cancer Marion was describing in *Bone*. But she did not see this as a trivial issue at all. She agreed with my observation immediately and used the story of *Chocolat* to illustrate her point. For her, the dark chocolate goddess was a Black Madonna who, like Vianne, represented the embodied divine feminine—sensual, sexual, and compassionately spiritual. In contrast to this, the count symbolized not the divine masculine but the patriarchy, in other words, the masculine nature run amok, unbridled, and unmitigated by the feminine. In *Chocolat* one of the ways the patriarchy manifests is in the count's obsession with the dogma of the Church—the rigid rules, regulations, and restrictions that stand in counterpoint to the love and humanity of the basic Christian message and represented in the film by the earthy, compassionate, caring Vianne. In Marion's view, adhering to dogma, whether it is in the Church or society at large, is one sure way to annihilate the creative spirit:

> ...this is what I see in terms of creativity: if you try to follow dogma in your life and you try to worship the Divine separated off from the body, from humanity, you end up so unbalanced that you lose your creativity. This is because you are not living with the inner fire. And when those energies that are repressed start to come up they crash into anything that has to do with dogma or with any of the cultural standards that don't allow the living spirit to live.

When Marion said this I asked her if this might not be another way of talking about the divine marriage—the union of the masculine and feminine—in the sense that the creative energies were feminine energies and that the dogma was a kind of perverted masculinity, in other words, the masculinity we are referring to when we talk about the "patriarchy". She agreed, saying:

> I see it that way because the more anyone worships dogma, the more fierce the instincts in the basement of the psyche become. [And they will erupt] one day—or you will sink into depression. That can happen. As long as we are merely trying to obey the rules of society, doing what we are supposed to be doing and thinking what we are supposed to be thinking, we are not going to be creative because the creativity comes out of the living body.

In this simple phrase "the living body" Marion sums up much of what this book has been about. For me, the living body is one that embodies the divine feminine but also gives the divine masculine the place of honor and respect it deserves in the creative process. Once this is clear, it becomes possible to really absorb the many practical implications this balance has for our creative expression. In my own writing life, the most basic way this balance expresses itself is in what I think of as the interplay between intuition and editing.

I see the first step in the creative process as a feminine, intuitive, emotional one. Like many writers and artists I begin by putting myself in the most open, receptive inner space I can; then I simply let whatever is ready to flow stream on out. Although some people might think of the receptive state as being the feminine aspect of this process, I don't. The receptive state is merely the preparatory state; it is the flow itself that is feminine; it is Shakti, Sophia, Shekinah; it is the creative force of the universe, manifesting. Once this flow has exhausted itself for the time being, the masculine inner voice comes into play, looking over what has been expressed, cutting this section, moving that one, spotting errors, inconsistencies, and oversights and coming up with ways to fix them.

This is no great secret; it is simply the way many successful creative people work—balancing the feminine and masculine in the creative process in a very basic way. But in my many years of teaching workshops on creativity, it has been amazing to me how many people assume you can have true creativity without the heart and the head working together and playing their respective roles. In our masculine-dominated society it is often the heart that is forgotten. This is one reason the whole issue of being able to feel, experience, and hold emotions was tackled so early in the book. Without emotion there is no power, no propulsion, no movement forward. Even our word emotion has the word "motion" as its root.

But even in our masculine-dominated society the head is sometimes forgotten too. Many individuals assume that as long as the creative spirit has been given full rein, nothing else is important, no editing is necessary. This is rarely the case. In fact, when a first draft, or first attempt at any creative work, flows out in an essentially finished form, my experience is that the masculine "editor" side has been working all along—but functioning so smoothly and unobtrusively that its presence passes completely unnoticed.

Technique is another aspect of the masculine side of the creative process that has an essential role. In writing, for instance, a knowledge of the rules of grammar and the foundations of the structure of the language are essential. I am often stunned at how frequently people who want to be writers assume they learned everything they need to know about their language in grade school. No one ever thinks they can start playing Chopin *Études* without taking piano lessons or practicing—but people assume they will be able to write great novels without a similar amount of effort. Similar assumptions are also sometimes made about art.

Some extremely significant comments about the role of technique in the creative process can be found in Arthur Abell's book *Talks with Great Composers* that was quoted briefly in Chapter Four. I first read this book in the 1970s and it has had a major influence on my ideas about creativity and inspiration ever since. Abell, an American who often wrote music reviews, lived in Europe between 1890 and 1918. One of his main desires in traveling to Europe was to interview the great composers who were living then. This included such august company as Johannes Brahms, Richard Strauss, and Giacomo Puccini. He also interviewed Engelbert Humperdinck, best known for composing the opera *Hansel and Gretel*, about what he had learned over the years from his friend Richard Wagner. Although much of the book was written during Abell's years in Europe, it wasn't published until 1954. The reason for this delay was that, Brahms—after giving what, in my opinion, is one of the most significant and revealing interviews ever done with a creative genius—made Abell promise that he wouldn't publish the material for at least fifty years as it would be that long, Brahms felt, before his music would be widely understood and appreciated. Abell kept his promise, but we can be thankful that he never let go of his dream of publishing the book for it contains an extraordinary amount of insight into inspiration.

All of these men believed they received the inspiration for their compositions from a higher power. But they also believed that this in-spiration could not be fully utilized unless the proper technical training was first in place. Abell quoted Brahms, who put this succinctly: "But don't make the mistake, my young friend, of thinking that because I attach such importance to inspiration from above, that that is all there is to it, by no means. Structure is just as consequential, for without crafts-manship, inspiration is a 'mere reed shaken in the wind' or 'sounding brass or tinkling cymbals'..."

When Abell asked Strauss about whether it was necessary to have "knowledge and technical skill of a high order", Strauss answered: "Of course, that is self-understood. God does not do for man what he can do for himself...He must acquire by laborious study and application the technical mastery of his craft; but he will never write anything of lasting value unless he has Divine aid also..."

When Abell questioned the composers on technique, each one indicated that technique is not only necessary, it must also become so ingrained that it is second nature. When both masculine and feminine aspects of creativity are given there due in this way, a time comes when they work together seamlessly. The creative material flows upward and outward from our depths while the editor or technician gently replaces a word, adds a daub of color there, or changes a sharp to a flat without ever interrupting the creative flow.

Unfortunately, in both my personal experience and in what I have seen leading workshops what most of us hear instead of the positive, supportive voice of this masculine technician/editor is the harsh inner voice of criticism. Interestingly enough, almost everyone who has worked with this harsh inner voice over the years in my workshops described it as a masculine one. This has generally been true even when it turns out that it was a mother who was the most critical or a female teacher who had the most lasting negative influence. This supports the idea that the role of internal critic is a manifestation of the inner masculine and provides us with an important clue about how to deal with it: silencing this voice isn't the answer—the voice of the inner masculine voice is essential to the creative process—the answer lies in transforming it.

The first step in this process is to go inside and sit with this voice, just as you have learned to sit with your powerful emotions. Once you do this you will most likely discover that this voice sounds very much like someone who frequently criticized you or like a kind of conglomeration of all the voices who ever have. For many of us this is focused in one person, usually a parent, who told us we weren't good enough or talented enough or harangued us about the foolishness of our interest in the arts. This negative sound is then often augmented and solidified by the voices of negative teachers, relatives, or so-called friends over the years.

The next step is getting past this negativity and facing these demons. This, as you probably already know, often involves a great deal of inner psychological work. The purpose of this book is not to discuss this kind of psychological/spiritual work in detail, especially since many of you may well have already been involved in it for years. However, it's worth noting that a breakthrough in this process often comes, as it certainly did in my own case, when you realize that the people denigrating your artistic endeavors did it not because they really thought you had no ability but because they were themselves afraid. Sometimes these fears were for you; they might have been afraid you would fail or be hurt psychologically or left financially destitute. Sometimes these fears were for themselves; they might have been afraid of the power your creativity represented or of facing the fact that they themselves may have misspent their own lives by not following their dreams.

Since facing down these demons is often a life-long process, you can take heart in the fact that just sitting with this voice, listening to it, and recognizing where it originated is a powerful tool in many ways. This makes you conscious of the voice; it brings it out of the dark recesses of your mind where it was able to surreptitiously eat away at your confidence and joy in your work and allows you to face it. This, in turn, provides you with an opportunity to ferret through the destructive nonsense it's spewing and find the gems of constructive criticism. For example a message like "Rip this painting up! It is a piece of crap; that yellow looks like vomit." can become something like "That yellow really has too much green in it; I need to lighten it up."

In my own creative life I have found over the years that the more I have allowed myself to have a dialogue with this voice—and, in other words, stopped trying to slam the door on it—the more clearly I have been able to hear the voice of the editor, the technician, and the constructive critic over the destructive shrieking of everyone who ever tried to tear me down. How much of this has been the result of the inner work I have done and how much has simply been allowing my inner masculine to speak, I honestly can't say. But I suspect the two have gone together hand in hand and neither would have been accomplished without the other.

Marion's comments in *Bone* added another dimension to my view of the inner masculine by describing it as a "spiritual warrior", a sort of crusader with sword held high, whose duty is to protect the inner feminine. Marion calls this the "new masculine". This is a masculine nature that rejects the rigid, dogmatic, and especially the misogynist attitudes of the patriarchy and instead honors the feminine. She adds, "For me, the new masculine loves the feminine, loves what she values, who she is...this I AM that is the soul. The masculine will honor that soul, try to protect her, try to strengthen her..."

Offering an example from a typical writer's life she described the situation in which an author becomes so caught up in her obligations to promote her work that she is not able to take time for her writing. This is when we need, she said:

> ...a warrior with a sword who says 'I will protect you. I will protect the spontaneity, the love of life...the passion that comes from the depths of who you are.' That masculine will make time, will make sure that you're not too tired, too exhausted to live that creative side of your life—to see with your inner eye, to hear with your inner ear. His sword loves the feminine so much that it will protect her against outer forces or inner forces that would destroy her.

This image resonated with me in another way and helped me look at one of the conditions I think is essential to creative inspiration. For years I've been writing and speaking about the importance of creating a space in which your particular creative endeavor can occur. By this I don't mean just a physical space but a mental space as well. When I first thought about Marion's protective inner masculine I had first visualized him as a sort of knight who put his lady on a pedestal and then valiantly fought off all foes. But then I realized a more appropriate image was one of a warrior who used his sword to hack down green, leafy branches and build her a shelter. This shelter is the "space" needed for creative work.

One of the richest sources for my understanding of the elements necessary in creating this space has come from *Talks with Great Composers*. As I studied the book over the years I came to realize individual elements could be separated out from what each of these great composers said about their working environment and organized into a set of guidelines that create an environment that inspiration can flow through. Although each of these composers knew they could not control inspiration or force her to come, they understood that they could build a fountain into which she was likely to stream.

The first step in this process is of course creating the physical space for your work, even if it is only a sectioned-off space of a room.

The second step involves setting aside time. The attitude can't be that you will do it when you "get time". You must set aside the time, and the more regular you can make it, the better. This is, of course, extremely difficult for those of us who have families and jobs. Still, there's no way around it; it must be done. Even if it is just a short space of time. This is one reason the concept of "morning pages", which have been used to good effect by authors such as Julia Cameron, is such a powerful tool: it sets aside a regular amount of time that becomes virtually sacrosanct.

When you are in your physical space at the appointed time, you can easily begin to create your mental space. Abell's composers tell us that the first two essential elements in this process are an ardent desire and an intense resolve. Strauss said, "I can tell you, from my own experience, that an ardent desire and fixed purpose combined with an intense resolve bring results." And in Puccini's words, "I feel the burning desire and the intense resolve to create something worthwhile."

The next element in this process, virtually all the composers agree, is focused concentration. Strauss explained the reason for this, saying, "Determined concentrated thought is a tremendous force and this Divine Power is responsive to it." Each of Abell's composers described moving from this state of focused concentration into what they referred to as a trance-like state. Wagner went so far as to call this state the "prerequisite of all creative endeavor" and Brahms said:

> I have to be in a semi-trance condition to get such results—a condition when the conscious mind is in temporary abeyance and the subconscious mind is in control, for it is through the subconscious mind, which is part of Omnipotence, that inspiration comes. I have to be careful, however, not to lo lose consciousness, otherwise the ideas fade away.

Instead of using the word "trance" as they did in the nineteenth century most of us would now think of this as a meditative state. And it is almost certainly no coincidence that the two mental conditions these composers refer to, focused concentration and meditation, follow each other in Patanjali's eight-limb path where they are known as dhāranā and dhyāna.

When most of Abell's composers discussed the various elements in their creative process—the physical space, ardent desire, strong sense of purpose, fixed concentration, and a meditative state—they spoke of them in a way that indicated they were incorporated into a repetitive set of behaviors that were virtually ritualistic. Brahms, for instance, always sat down at his piano, assumed a prayerful attitude, and contemplated the words of Jesus "I and my Father are one" and "...he who believes in me will also do the works that I do; and greater works than these will he do." For Brahms these words confirmed that we are all one with the Creator. Contemplating this thought would help trigger the trance-like state that would result in the "thrilling vibrations" that he referred to as "the Spirit illuminating the soul-power within". Then, and only then, would he begin to compose.

Constructing a ritual like this is another job of the inner masculine. It builds the structure and then the vibrating, illuminating creative spirit can begin to flow. It is also the masculine that keeps us on track and reminds us that we need to follow these rituals regularly and without fail. In other words, we must do them religiously.

Underlying and forming the foundation for this structure are, according to Abell's composers, two fundamental principles. The first is the belief that a divine source of creative inspiration does indeed exist. In Strauss' words: "A firm belief in this Power must precede the ability to draw on it purposefully and intelligently. That much I know." Going hand in hand with this is the absolute conviction that we can in fact access this source. Both Brahms and Puccini use the term "appropriate" when describing this: "The great secret of all creative geniuses is that they possess the power to appropriate the beauty, the wealth, the grandeur, and the sublimity contained within their own souls, which are parts of Omnipotence, and to communicate those riches to others. The conscious, purposeful appropriation of one's own soul forces is the supreme secret." The other great secret—what Puccini called the "soul force" and Brahms the "soul-power within"—is nothing other than the manifestation of the divine feminine within the human body.

Each of the stories referred to in this chapter, Kama's creation, Shiva's marriage to Sati, Cupid and Psyche, the count's reconnection with the feminine, along with countless other myths and legends, cry out, compelling us to realize the critical importance of the balance between the masculine and feminine sides in our own inner natures and, ultimately, the realization of the union of our individual souls with the Divine. As the Tantras would have it, we are all Shaktis making our way to Shiva, our Beloved.

Making an Invocation

In ancient Greece, plays would often begin by the actors singing an invocation to the gods, asking to receive inspiration, in other words to be filled with the spirit. For Brahms one of the great secrets to "appropriating" the inspiration of the "soul-power within" was to invoke the Divine in much the same way. When discussing this idea with Abell, Brahms asked him why he thought Milton opened Paradise Lost *with the words "Sing heavenly Muse" and followed them with an invocation for her to aid him in the creation of his "adventurous song". When Abell replied that he really didn't think it too important, Brahms blasted him, saying that this showed his "profound ignorance of the law of suggestion". Brahms went on to explain that Milton's invocation revealed a psychological truth that creative geniuses such as Homer and Virgil were fully cognizant of. They, said Brahms, "were well aware of it; they felt the need of aid from a higher source, a source outside themselves...In other words, they sought inspiration from above just as I do when I compose and just as Beethoven did."*

When Brahms prepared himself each day to begin what he clearly saw as the sacred art of composition, he included an invocation to the Divine, asking that the Divine be with him in his efforts and allow him to create something that would benefit humanity and be of lasting value. In this exercise you will create an invocation that you can use every time you begin your creative work.

Having an invocation like this and using it every time I begin to write has been the most powerful and helpful aid I have had in all my years of writing. I cannot recommend it strenuously enough. The purpose of the exercise below is to write out whatever ideas come to you for your invocation. After this you might need to edit them, paring them down so that your invocation is short and to the point—something that can easily be repeated each time you begin to do your creative work.

Whenever you say your invocation your attitude should be a positive one; assume you will receive the divine assistance and inspiration you are asking for. As Wagner said, anyone who could feel the "universal currents of divine energy vibrating the ether" could be inspired. Based on what can be learned from Abell's composers and how innovations have been used over the ages, your invocation—in addition to whatever else you would like to have in it—should:

+ Clearly address the Divine
+ Ask for the Divine's assistance in the work you are about to do
+ Ask for your work to be of value and of benefit
+ Have a positive tone—assuming you will receive the assistance you need, rather than begging for it

1. Settle yourself in the place you are going to do your creative work—at best, a space you have set aside especially for this purpose. Have writing materials ready.

2. Create the mental space you need by filling yourself with white light and creating a protected space as you did in the exercise for Chapter Two—being aware that this is the meditative state Wagner called the "the prerequisite of all true creative effort".

3. When you are filled with white light, allow yourself to feel the "thrilling vibrations" that Brahms said illuminated the "soul-power within".

4. Focus for a moment on the idea that you are about to create an invocation, then bring your awareness back to the radiant light.

5. Allow the light to flow upward, and outward into your pen and paper. Write out the ideas that come to you for your invocation.

6. Later, if needed, take some time to polish it and edit it down to a few simple sentences that you can say each time you begin your creative work.

CHAPTER FIFTEEN

The Precious Juice of Grace

The concept of balance and all it entails is one that seems to keep resurfacing in my life and that, I suspect, re-emerges in one form or another in the lives of all those who are dedicated to spiritual growth. The first time I encountered it was in the 1970s when I was just getting out of university and programs like EST and Silva Mind Control were in their heyday. At that time I enrolled in one of those positive thinking/power of the mind type courses. Although, ironically, it did not turn out to be a totally positive experience (a subject for another book!), some of the lessons I learned proved to be invaluable. Several of these were concepts that the course material called "universal laws".

One of these was the phrase "balance is the key to power". On one level, this referred to the idea that balance—in this sense, moderation—in all things was a key to healthy living and a successful life. On another level, it referred to polarities—all the "yins" and "yangs" of the universe—and the essential need for balance between the poles of each particular pair. On yet another level, and this was the one most stressed, the phrase was related to bringing our physical, mental, emotional, and spiritual natures into balance.

At the time when this course was being taught, this was an extremely innovative concept. The phrase mind/body/spirit was just beginning to come into use and the term "holistic" was one hardly anyone had heard. What's more, the people who developed the course had found a very inventive way of illustrating the concept—using the biblical story of the Four Horsemen of Apocalypse as a metaphor for our physical, intellectual, emotional, and spiritual natures. The story of the Four Horsemen appears in Revelation 6 when the first four of the legendary Seven Seals are broken open. Out of the first seal comes a powerful, positive figure; he rides a white horse; he carries a bow, is given a crown, and goes forth to conquer. The riders breaking out of the next three seals are much darker symbols. They burst forth riding a red horse, a black horse, and a pale horse. The red horse rider carries a sword and "takes peace from the earth"; the black horse rider carries a scale and brings the famine that inevitably follows war; and the pale horse rider brings pestilence and death.

According to the way these symbols were analyzed in the course, each of the riders represented one of three aspects of our being and the destruction that is reaped when any one aspect is out of balance and dominates the others. Red horse riders are ruled by emotions that run rampant. They crash through life rarely reasoning things out or thinking about the consequences of their actions, often causing pandemonium and chaos. Black horse riders—by far the most prevalent in our society—are governed completely by their intellects. Out of touch with their intuition and emotions, they reason their way through life, thinking when they should be feeling and experiencing a famine in their emotional life. Pale horse riders are controlled by their bodily desires and physical needs. Focused on the material world, they tend to be motivated by their fear of death, being alone, or losing their security.

Each of these three riders also has positive traits. Red horse riders have powerful emotions that can motivate others and move mountains. Black horse riders have organized minds, excellent reasoning skills, and the ability to plan and accomplish goals. Pale horse riders tend to be much more comfortable with their emotions than black horse riders; they relate well to others and can be highly motivated people who are in tune with their bodies. According to the course, the secret to accessing these positive traits and having them available for use in your life is to keep the "horses" in balance. In short, the less you are controlled by your predominate nature, the better off you will be. And, even more importantly, if you could manage to get all three natures into perfect balance, you could become a white horse rider. In the generally accepted interpretations of Revelation, this white horse rider is held to represent Christ. In the one used in the course, he was believed to represent the Christ—or the Divine—within. In other words, once all three natures are in perfect balance the possibility of becoming truly spiritual emerges. While I don't believe—as the course suggested—that getting these three natures into balance would automatically bring about some type of spiritual awakening, I have definitely come to believe over the years that having all three in harmony is a key factor in experiencing spiritual awakening and the transformation of consciousness that goes hand in hand with it.

If you take a careful look at Revelation 6 and the chronicle of the Seven Seals, you will see that the individual who came up with this interpretation took a tremendous amount of license. Still, the imagery is powerful, and I don't know of anyone who was exposed to it who was not better able to understand the different aspects of their being better and see how much richer—and ultimately more spiritual—life can be when all sides of our selves are in balance.

One of the most important things about this conceptualization of the Four Horsemen was that it, like the early holistic or "mind/body/spirit" movement, reminded us of the importance of the body in the equation for spiritual and psychological growth. For me, this early exposure to the importance of our physical nature was one of the reasons I eventually became so drawn to the philosophy behind Tantra and hatha yoga and the idea that Shakti was held in the body. This, in turn, led me to explore the possibility that Sophia and Shekinah were also the Divine-with-us in the same very physical, rooted way.

If you were to take only one idea from this book, I think the most important would be that this process of transformation that we—whether we know it or not, whether we believe it or not—are all undergoing is rooted in the physical body. This does not, as some people think, make the process less spiritual or less holy. Indeed, when you look at it from the other side of the coin, it means that our bodies are more spiritual, more holy. It makes the whole process of living life as a physical being a holy one.

In his writings Gopi Krishna repeatedly emphasized how kundalini-shakti worked through the body and literally transformed the brain —the organ of perception—so that the mystic could perceive the divine, cosmic force which forms the very essence of our being and the entire world around us. Not surprisingly, his thoughts in this regard were yet another way the concept of balance came into my life, for Gopi Krishna continually stressed the importance of living a balanced, moderate life. The guidance he gave to anyone who might be experiencing kundalini awakening—indeed anyone on the spiritual path—always emphasized taking care of the body. This guidance was based on a combination of what he gleaned from ancient yogic texts and what he learned during his own premature and dramatic awakening.

One of his first guidelines was to stress the importance of regularity, especially in sleeping and eating. It was essential, he said, that the body was replenished each night with adequate sleep. It was also important to eat the healthiest, most natural, and freshest food possible. He also recommended having a diet high in protein and eating several small meals at regular times throughout the day rather than having three large ones a day. In fact, he believed his life was saved at one point by advice from an early yoga text that said the yogi who was experiencing kundalini should never fill the stomach too full and, more importantly, never under any circumstance let the stomach become completely empty. Gopi Krishna also felt that work needed to be balanced with recreation and rest. He made it clear that our society's workaholic, stress-filled culture was the opposite of the one needed to foster the healthy awakening of kundalini-shakti and urged those on the spiritual path to avoid overburdening themselves with work and to create the most stress-free, peaceful life possible for themselves.

He also urged those on the spiritual path to avoid excessive amounts of concentration—for instance, prolonged focus on a computer screen—for it mimics dhāranā, or focused concentration, the sixth step in the eight-limb path of yoga set down by Patanjali. As mentioned in Chapter Thirteen, dhāranā stimulates the brahma-randhra and triggers a call for more potent prana and ojas to rise up from the base of the spine—a call that the body might not, for many reasons, be able to answer; one of these being that the body's supply of prana and ojas has been depleted through excessive sexual activity. Another potential problem caused by the excessive stimulation of the brahma-randhra can arise when the reproductive organs begin to generate the needed ojas and prana, only to have their upward journey obstructed by blockages—a situation that can result in a tremendous amount of pent-up sexual energy. Of course, concentrating on computer screens isn't the only mental activity that mimics dhāranā. Focused concentration of any type can have the same effect. Intense, prolonged reading is a good example, especially—according to the many people I have interviewed over the years—when the reading materials are of a spiritual nature.

Given all this, it is not surprising that Gopi Krishna recommended that those on the spiritual path, and especially anyone experiencing any type of kundalini activity, have the type of balanced lifestyle that avoided extremes of all types—whether they related to overindulgence in sexual activity or spending excessive amounts of time focused on deeply spiritual books. He even advocated moderation in meditation and intense prayer as these might trigger more stimulation of the brahma-randhra than the body was ready to support. And when a hectic lifestyle demanded more focus and concentration than might be good, he urged that it be balanced out with time spent in the most natural setting possible or in an activity like gardening—an ideal pastime because it combines physical labor with a hands-on experience of nature.

A good example of how excellent this advice is can be found in how much Kavita was helped after her profound, unexpected spiritual awakening—the one that left her "feeling nine months pregnant and looking for a place to give birth"—in the ashram she found in Australia. There she began to live an orderly, low-stress life, going to bed, rising, and eating at fairly regular times, and working in the garden instead of staring at a computer screen all day or stressing her mind with too much mental effort. In this environment—much like ones in the olden times when seekers practiced hatha yoga in ashrams and, under the guidance of their teachers, sought to unlock the secrets of kundalini—Kavita thrived and brought the process she was experiencing into balance.

While this type of balanced life—or as close an approximation as we can get to it—prepares the body so that it can support a spiritual awakening, it is, of course, only part of the process. Once when Gopi Krishna was asked how one could reach higher consciousness, he said the first thing would be to act on a daily basis as if you had already achieved the state. The first step in doing this, he said, would be to be continually aware that you were one with every other human being you came in contact with. Although you would act quite normally in these everyday encounters, you would have the thought at the back of your mind that no division, no boundary, no essential difference exists between you and the other individual and that the same divine essence that moves through you, moves through him or her.

Out of this awareness of your Oneness with others—indeed with all living creatures and with all of nature—another characteristic of the enlightened saints and mystics that you should emulate would naturally arise: the desire to be of selfless service, the ache to end suffering and injustice, the passionate commitment to make the world a better place.

In his writings Gopi Krishna stated that by voluntarily cultivating characteristics of higher consciousness such as these—and the others described throughout this book—you would be helping Shakti, the evolutionary energy, in her goal of transforming both yourself and the human race as a whole. Shakti is, of course, working on this from the other direction; she is calling to you from the depths of your being, asking you to help her in this process of transformation, crying out, making you yearn to take part in the very activities that will move you along the path she has set for you. In the stories of women told throughout this book—whether they be great mystics or ordinary women like you and me—we have seen many wonderful examples of how Shakti has been busily working through us in this way.

Seeing this in the great mystics like Mahadevi, Hildegard, and Mechthild is one thing, but seeing it in the lives of ordinary women is another. As mentioned earlier, the very fact that the mystics were saints or visionaries makes them seem so far beyond us that we think we can't possibly be like them. However, when we see the same characteristics expressed, albeit at the near end of the continuum, in the lives of ordinary, everyday women we can begin to understand that the profound spiritual transformation experienced by the saint-like women of yesteryear is indeed happening in us. Looking back on these ordinary women's stories, it is interesting to see that while each of them exhibited most, or all, of the characteristics of the individual on the road to enlightenment, one of these traits tended to rise to the fore in each one of the women. Britta longed to be a better person by being as ethical and morally upright as she possibly could and following what she called the "Jesus way" to the best of her ability. Christine's clearly stated goal was to know her true self and, in this way, come to know the God she believed existed deep within her very own being. In the gentle feminine hills of the Greek Islands and the swirling, organic patterns she found in nature, Kavita had glimpses of divine union. She longed to bring the divine masculine and feminine within into perfect balance and one day make the realization of divine Oneness a permanent part of her consciousness. Wendi and Anya both longed to change the world —to bring balance, right wrongs, end suffering: Wendi—subtly, surreptitiously, and joyously—by bringing concepts associated with the divine feminine to an unsuspecting corporate world; Anya, from her early humanitarian efforts to help Viet-namese boat people to her later commitment to saving Mother Earth, by working tirelessly to end the suffering and devastation she saw around her.

And, of course, each of these women, like Mahadevi, Hildegard, and Mechthild, and so many of the great saints and mystics, expressed themselves creatively. They received creative inspiration and they allowed this expression of the divine feminine to flow back out of them. At the very beginning of this book we looked at the idea that this type of yearning to be creative was fueled by the same cosmic force that was propelling us along the evolutionary path. Thinking back on the stories told, I think we can safely say this is the case.

Gopi Krishna once wrote "[Shakti, the evolutionary energy,] has conferred unmatched creative powers on the more advanced recipients of the favor and fashioned them into vessels to enlighten humanity." Mahadevi, Hildegard, and Mechthild are wonderful examples of the "more advanced recipients"; but Britta, Christine, Wendi, Kavita, Anya, and you and I are all equally wonderful examples of recipients of some degree of this great cosmic favor. As such, we are all vessels, and although we may be quite far from being able to bring enlightenment to humanity, we are nonetheless being called on to bring whatever degree of light we can to our troubled world.

This is a sacred calling and it is what makes our creativity and our creative expression a spiritual practice. All it takes is for us to be consciously aware that in doing so we are, as Gopi Krishna advised, acting as if we had already achieved enlightenment.

We are even acting like Shakti, the mighty, powerful creatrix of the universe; we are mimicking Sophia, the "master workman" who was at God's side in the creation of the heavens, the earth, and the life upon it; and we are emulating the upper Shekinah, who is the "full expression of ceaseless creative power...in which what is concealed within God is externalized".

As vessels occupied in this holy act of creative expression we are bringing the active power of divine love into the universe. We are vessels being filled, as Mahadevi says, with the "precious juice of Grace", so that we can empty ourselves and pour this soothing grace over Mother Earth and all the beings who inhabit her. And we must never forget that in its most basic, physical form, this vessel is the body. In 1 Corinthians 6:19 Paul called the body a "temple" that houses the Holy Spirit. This saying from Paul has been repeated so often and in so many contexts that it has become commonplace, but it is, in fact, one of the deepest and most profound messages in the Bible. It tells us unequivocally that the Holy Spirit—the active power of the Divine, regardless of the name we give her—is within us. She is as close as the next breath. Her power is our power. All we have to do is recognize her for who she is, learn to hold her within our bodies—even when she is at her most active—with patience and courage, and listen to her so that she can guide us through the process of evolution and transformation that leads, ultimately, to Oneness.

Notes

Chapter One

1. In the strictest Judeo-Christian theological tradition—and especially the Jewish rabbinic tradition—the word "divine" is used only to refer directly to God or an actual attribute of God. In this book, the term is used—as has become quite common—to refer to a great deal that is loosely related to God or what we might think of as the highest spiritual realms.

2. Throughout the book I capitalize the term "Divine" when it is a direct substitution for the term God—Allah, Jehovah, Brahman, the Void, the Goddess or any other name you choose to give the cosmic Absolute. When "divine" is used in any other way, for instance as an adjective in "divine feminine", I don't capitalize it. This is done simply because I don't think of the divine feminine as equaling the cosmic Absolute. Rather, I see the divine feminine and divine masculine as inseparable manifestations of the way we know and experience the Divine. For the same reason, I don't generally capitalize the word "goddess". As you read through the book and see what a deep love and veneration I have for the divine feminine, you will understand that I mean no disrespect by this. It is simply that I want to make a distinction between references to the Divine —the Absolute that is beyond gender—and the way the Divine manifests in our lives.

3. In recent times, a tremendous amount had been written and said about the chakras and what they represent and/or are associated with. Some of this seems to have little basis in ancient scripture. One of the best sources for a description of the chakras and what was traditionally believed about them remains Arthur Avalon's book *The Serpent Power*, which contains a translation and interpretation of the Tantric text the *Sat-cakra-nirūpana*.

4. The principle that the human being is a microcosmic representation of the macrocosm is essential to Tantra. A more detailed description of this concept can be found in Georg Feuerstein's *Tantra: The Path of Ecstasy* and the more difficult to find *Man as Microcosm in Tantric Hinduism* by Grace E. Cairns.

5. Although the characteristics of higher consciousness as delineated by individuals like Richard Maurice Bucke and Gopi Krishna are mentioned

throughout the book, it is worthwhile to list them here. The characteristics of the mystical experience that often triggers the beginning of transformation of consciousness and the characteristics of one whose consciousness is being transformed are often lumped together, but I have found it helpful to divide them into these two categories—keeping in mind always that these experiences and characteristics occur on a continuum and that the whole process of spiritual transformation is one in which we grow into them. (More detailed descriptions of the physical sensations associated with this process can be found in Joan Harrigan's books or on her website as listed in the Bibliography and Suggested Reading section.)

The characteristics of the mystical experience itself include:
+ A vision of brilliant light, flames, or fire
+ An experience of cosmic sound—sometimes described as the "music of the spheres"
+ An experience of profound love and/or bliss
+ An awareness of Oneness with the Divine and/or an awareness of the Oneness of all
+ Sensations of light, "energy", or heat in the lower back or moving up the spine

The characteristics of higher consciousness include:
+ An awareness of the Oneness of all beings and all things
+ A loss of fear of death
+ A strong ethical and moral nature
+ A deep compassion for others
+ A passionate desire to right wrongs, end suffering, and make the world a better place
+ Experiences of the extra-ordinary known as siddhis, iddhis, or charisms
+ Experiences of divine inspiration—ranging from true revelation to inspired creativity

Chapter Two

1. Mahadevi Akka is also known as Mahadeviakka and Akka Mahadevi. In Sanskrit "maha" means great and "devi" means goddess; Akka is a term of endearment that is used to refer to a beloved elder sister or, sometimes, an aunt. Any other name she may have been known by in childhood has been lost in time.

2. Verses like Mahadevi's are known as *vacanas*. Although the term simply means "saying" or "thing that is said", vacanas are generally spiritual in nature. Mahadevi's were first spoken in her native Kannada, a Dravidian language that it still spoken today by millions of people in Southern India.

3. Dr Siddhayya Puranik, a scholar and poet in his own right, is the author of *Mahādēvi*, a study of Mahadevi's life and vacanas that was commissioned by the Institute of Kannada Studies.

4. The poems beginning *Four parts of the day, O Mother you must be crazy,* and *Not seeing you* are translations done by A.K. Ramanujan in his wonderful book *Speaking of Shiva*, which includes brief biographies and the poetry of the Virashaiva saints, Basavanna, Devara Dasimayya, and Allama Prabhu, as well as Mahadevi.

5. The poems beginning *He paralyzed my will* and *I've bathed in turmeric* are from an extraordinary and difficult to find book, *Vacanas of Akka Mahādēvi*, which was put together by Manohar Appasaheb Adke in India in 1973 to honor his beloved mother, Shrimati, who was a dedicated devotee of Mahadevi's teachings. The vacanas in the book are in both English and Kannada.

6. Virashaivism, or Veerashaivism, is still a popular Shaivite religion in Southern India. More on Basavanna, Allama Prabu, and the origins of the Virashaivas can be found in *Speaking of Shiva*.

7. Allama Prabu is held to be one of the great saints of India, and there are extensive records of his life—including a detailed description of his interrogation of Mahadevi when she first sought to join Basavanna's community. It can be found in Puranik's *Mahādēvi*.

Chapter Three

1. The Association for Research and Enlightenment was founded by Edgar Cayce in 1931. Cayce lived from 1877 to 1945 and is held to be the most well-documented psychic of the twentieth century. Focused on helping others, he gave thousands of "readings" to people diagnosing illnesses and pointing to pathways for better health. Today the A.R.E.'s goal is to help people live better by using the information found in the Edgar Cayce material. The A.R.E. offers

courses and study programs on topics that range from holistic health and personal spirituality to dream interpretation and reincarnation. It is located in Virginia Beach, Virginia.

2. New Thought is a spiritual movement that began in England and developed in the United States during the late 1800s. It grew out of the teachings of a number of different individuals, and their slightly divergent ideas founded several different strains of the movement. In general they all have in common the idea that God is omnipresent, divine thought is a force for good, and prayer and positive thinking have great, indeed ultimately unlimited, power. Unity Church, founded by Charles and Myrtle Fillmore, is one of the many spiritual movements that comes out of New Thought. Religious Science and Divine Science churches are other examples. *As a Man Thinketh* by James Allen is a good example of New Thought and shows where ideas popular today, like the Law of Attraction, have their origins.

3. Emmet Fox was one of the most influential promoters of the ideas associated with New Thought. During the 1930s he often gave Sunday sermons to crowds of more than 5,000. More than 3,000,000 of his books and pamphlets have been printed over the years, and many of his books are still in print. Two of the most popular, *The Sermon on the Mount* and *The Ten Commandments*, offer new interpretations of these sections of the Bible, emphasizing the power of divine love and the inherent divinity of each human being. People who have read these works and who are familiar with the teachings of Alcoholics Anonymous will notice similarities that are probably not coincidental: the mother of Bill W.—the famed founder of AA—was Emmet Fox's secretary for many years, and *The Sermon on the Mount* was popular reading among early AA members.

Chapter Four

1. When referring to prana as the life force that infuses all creation, it's important to note that not all Hindu philosophies see spirit and matter as one. Most, however, do and are known as *Advaita*, or non-dualistic, traditions. The primary dualistic, or *Dvaita*, Hindu tradition is known as *Samkyha*. This doctrine sees a distinct difference between matter and spirit. For the Samkyha, spirit is identified with the transcendental Self and known as *purusha*. All else is known as nature, or *prakriti*. The goal of the practitioner is to renounce

everything that is not pure spirit. This stands in direct opposition to Vedanta and other Hindu philosophies that see everything as a manifestation of the One. But it stands in particular opposition to Tantra and all the other Shakti traditions that see nature not just as a manifestation of the One, but as an expression of the cosmic divine feminine herself that is to be embraced. Interestingly enough, Classical yoga—as it is described by Patanjali in his famed *Yoga-Sūtras*—is a Dvaita tradition. Earlier and later yoga traditions— sometimes referred to as Pre-Classical and Post-Classical yoga—are all firmly based in Vedanta philosophy and in the Advaita tradition. The origins of hatha yoga are, thus, definitely Advaita.

2. Arthur Abell's book *Talks with Great Composers* is an extraordinary book that provides a great deal of insight into the relationship between creativity and inspiration. It has been in and out of print for the last fifty years. The 1998 version published by Citadel appears to be available on Amazon. If this is not the case copies can be obtained from other online sources for rare and used books such as www.abebooks.com. It can also be found in some libraries.

3. Teilhard's references to the "crimson glow of matter" and "the divine radiating from the blazing depths of matter" can be found in *The Heart of Matter*. His essay "The Eternal Feminine" can be found in *Writings in the Time of War*. A good overview of his life is in Ursula King's biography, *Spirit of Fire: the life and vision of Teilhard de Chardin*.

4. Barbara Newman's *Sister of Wisdom* is a superb scholarly examination of the "feminine" in Hildegard's work; Sabina Flanagan's *Hildegard of Bingen: A Visionary Life* provides an interesting and well-researched view of her life. Lovely copies of her illustrations can be found in Matthew Fox's *The Illuminations of Hildegard of Bingen*.

5. Wisdom and the Wisdom books of the Bible: The books Proverbs, Job, and Ecclesiastes are found in both the Catholic and Protestant Bibles. The Book of Wisdom (also known as the Wisdom of Solomon) and Ecclesiasticus (also known as the Wisdom of Jesus Son of Sirach) are found in the Catholic Bible, but only included in the Apocrypha of the Protestant Bible. In the Jewish tradition, all of these books are part of the Septuagint, but only the first three are included in the Tenach.

THE DIVINE FEMININE FIRE

6. Hildegard's first description of Sophia can be found in Newman's book on page 47.

7. The biblical quotes on Wisdom/Sophia are taken from Thomas Schipflinger's *Sophia-Maria: A Holistic Vision of Creation*, which uses *The Revised English Bible* as its source.

8. Information on how the Logos and Wisdom came to be associated with Christ can also be found in the writings of the early Church Fathers such as Origen.

9. Hildegard's description of Caritas is Newman's translation from *De operatione dei* (*The Book of Divine Works*) and can be found in *Sister of Wisdom* on page 69.

Chapter Five

1. Although I use the term "full" awakening here, many spiritual teachers believe that even what I am describing as such is not really a full or complete awakening in any sense. They say that levels of awakening may exist that go far beyond anything that we are aware of today.

2. It is not known whether the text known as *Panchastavi* was the name of its author or simply the name he or she gave it. An exceptional translation and exposition of the original text can be found in *Secrets of Kundalini in Panchastavi* by Gopi Krishna. It contains both the Sanskrit text and its English translation and a thorough description of the transformative process triggered by kundalini-shakti.

3. While the actual *Kulārnava Tantra* text cited in the Bibliography and Suggested Reading section might not be too easy to locate, some interesting selections from it can be found in David Gordon White's *Tantra in Practice*.

4. The quote from *Rasarnava* can be found in *Panchastavi* on page 175. Rasayana was a school of alchemy in India that sought to change mercury (*rasa*) into gold on the most basic level, but on a higher spiritual level was, like Western alchemy, about spiritual transformation. This is particularly clear in Rasayana because rasa mean "essence" in Sanskrit and stands for the "nectar of immortality"

294

also known as *amrita* that is believed to flow when kundalini-shakti is fully awakened. More on this can be found in David Gordon White's *The Alchemical Body: Siddha Traditions in Medieval India.*

Chapter Six

1. The quote from *Rasarnava* can be found on page 175 of *Secrets of Kundalini in Panchastavi* by Gopi Krishna.

2. Sir John Woodroffe, whose pen name was Arthur Avalon, made a tremendous contribution to Western understanding of Tantra, kundalini-shakti, and the worship of Shakti with his book *The Serpent Power.* More information can be found in the many books written by him that are listed in the Bibliography and Suggested Reading section.

3. These translations of the biblical quotes concerning Wisdom can be found in *The Revised English Bible* that includes the Apocrypha.

4. The full text of Hildegard's "O fire of the Spirit" (*O ignis spiritus*), which is far more lengthy than what is quoted here, can be found in both English and Latin in Barbara Newman's *Voice of the Living Light: Hildegard of Bingen and her World.*

Chapter Seven

1. Because of the wide divergence in opinions about Kabbalah even among Kabbalists and scholars, I have relied on Scholem's seminal scholarship for much of the information, particularly his books *On the Mystical Shape of the Godhead, On the Kabbalah and its Symbolism,* and *Major Trends in Jewish Mysticism.* Other books on the subject, including those by authors more current than Scholem, are those by Neil Asher Silberman and Leo Schaya that are listed in the Bibliography and Suggested Reading section.

2. According to Scholem, Saadiah Gaon's statement regarding the "created light" was that it had been created by God so "that this light would give his prophet the assurance of the authenticity of what has been revealed to him". He added, "...it is a more sublime form than that of the angels, more enormous in its creation, bearing splendor and light, and is called 'the Kavod of God' (in the Bible) and Shekhinah in rabbinic tradition".

THE DIVINE FEMININE FIRE

3. In *Major Trends in Jewish Mysticism* Scholem quoted Saadiah who refers to the Kavod (The Glory) as "the great radiance called the Shekinah" and goes on to say that it is "identical with the ruah ha-kodesh, the 'holy spirit', out of whom there speaks the word of God". E.R. Wolfson, in *Through a Speculum That Shines*, said these views come from Judah ben Barzillai, and translated it: "[God] created the Shekinah, which is pure and holy spirit...this spirit, which is called the Shekinah of his glory, is the Holy Spirit...from which the prophets heard the voice..."

4. Regarding Shekinah as the created light, Scholem quoted similar references from two other great medieval Jewish philosophers. Judah Halevi called Shekinah a "fine substance that follows the will of God, assuming any form God wishes to show the prophet" and Maimonides called it the "created light, that God caused to descend in a particular place in order to confer honor upon it in a miraculous way". Moses ha-Darshan, the Rabbi of Narbonne, developed this imagery even further by saying that the angels were created from the radiance of Shekinah and, in this way, conceptualizing it as the "primal matter of creation".

5. Although these simplified descriptions of the Sefiroth might give the impression the divine energy flows in one direction, this is not so. The forces of the Sefiroth interact in complex patterns on one another. And the divine energy flows both downwards and upwards.

6. The Sefiroth are given different names and interpretations in different systems: *Keter* (Crown), *Chokhmah* (Wisdom), and *Binah* (Insight or Discernment), *Hesed* or *Gedullah* (Grace or Love), *Din* or *Gevurah* (Judgment or Severity), and *Tif'ereth* (Mercy or Glory), *Netsah* (Endurance), *Hod* (Splendor or Majesty), and *Yesod* (Foundation). This ninth Sefirah, Yesod, is also frequently known as *Tsaddik*, which means "the righteous one". (The "H" in "Hesed" and "Netsah" is more properly rendered "Ch" as in Chokmah.)

7. Concerning Scholem on Shakti, it is important to point out that, after making his comparison between Shakti and Binah of the "upper Shekinah", he went on to discuss the differences between Shakti and the lower Shekinah. One extremely important one is that when Shekinah flows out into creation, she does not *become* the world the way Shakti does; the spark of the Shekinah "operates in everything and animates everything" but still remains separate.

He also pointed out that none of the masculine Sefiroth can be identified with Shiva as none are passive and are all seen as "active and flowing".

Chapter Eight

1. When I use Holy Spirit I am referring not just to this specific phrase but to all the uses of spirit (ruah, etc.) throughout the Old and New Testaments that clearly refer to a divine spirit—some of the phrases used are God's spirit, the Spirit of God, the spirit the Lord sent down, etc.

2. Ecclesiasticus is part of the Catholic Bible; however, in the Protestant Bible it is part of the Apocrypha. In Judaism it is not part of the Torah but does belong to the holy books of the Jewish-Alexandrian tradition contained in the Septuagint.

3. The biblical quote that begins "I am the word" is the translation found in *The New English Bible* and the one that begins "There I grew" in *The Revised English Bible*. The translation of Paul's quote on the spirit dwelling within comes from *The Revised Standard Edition*, as does the version of Ezekiel's story.

4. Gelpi's *The Divine Mother: a trinitarian theology of the Holy Spirit* is an extraordinary contribution to our understanding of the feminine in Christianity. Although it may be a bit difficult to find, it is highly recommended for anyone who is seriously studying this topic.

5. More information on feminine imagery in the Bible can be found in *Created in Her Image* by Eleanor Rae and Bernice Marie-Daly, and more on symbolism in the early Syrian Church can be found in *Symbols of Church and Kingdom* by Robert Murray.

6. More information on ruah, on the Holy Spirit as God's active force, and on the relationship between Sophia and the Holy Spirit can be found in Yves Congar's *I Believe in the Holy Spirit*.

7. In *The New International Version* of the Bible, Genesis 1:2 is rendered: *Now the earth was formless and empty, darkness was over the surface of the deep, and the Spirit of God was hovering over the waters*. In this passage the Holy Spirit has often been interpreted as hovering like a mother dove because the Hebrew

word for "hovering", ruhhapa (or "moved across" as it is translated in *The Revised Standard Version*) also means "brooding" and carries the connotation of a mother bird hovering/brooding over her nest.

8. The translation of gifts of the spirit from I Corinthians 12 is from *The New English Bible* and from I Corinthians 14 from *The Revised Standard Edition*.

9. The translation of the quote beginning "The Lord said to Moses" in from the *Revised Standard Edition*.

10. For an extraordinarily well-researched and comprehensive overview of the history of the divine feminine see Rosemary Radford Ruether's *Goddesses and the Divine Feminine: A Western Religious History*.

Chapter Nine

1. Although the seven separate books that make up *The Flowing Light of the Godhead* have been arranged as they are in today's versions of the book as long as copies of it have existed, no one is absolutely sure this is the order Mechthild wrote them in.

2. Not all of the Church's objections to the beguines were based on the fact that they were women. The Council of Vienne in 1312 ordered all beguine communities be dissolved or join established orders, but it also ordered an investigation into the beghards, who were their male counterparts.

3. It is essential to point out that Mechthild's thoughts and feelings about her body were extremely complex and at times conflicted. She was after all a product of a period in history that stressed body/spirit duality: the spirit was believed to be good and the body was held to be weak at best and evil at worst. There are passages in *The Flowing Light of the Godhead*, for instance, in which she indicated that she saw her body as her enemy. In Book IV, 2 she even described how she, as was common among the religious in those days, would scourge her body with fasting and beatings. In the same passage, however, she talked about the exquisite feelings of passion and love she experienced, and it is clear that the framework of seeing herself as the Lover and Christ as the Beloved provided her a way out of this, a way she could live in her body, experience her bodily sensations and understand that they were not sinful. In fact, it seems her attempts at

self-punishment were meant not to drive lustful feelings from her body, but to increase the likelihood of her divine lover visiting her again sooner.

4. One of the reasons Mechthild's work is only now receiving public attention is that really accurate translations have only recently been done. Part of the problem has been that no copies have ever been found of her original manuscript, which was written in Middle Low German, the common speech of her day in what is now Northern Germany. However, copies of the manuscript that had been translated into Middle High German and Latin (at least Books I-VI) have helped modern German scholars Hans Neumann and Gisela Vollmann-Profe bring out a very accurate critical edition, which was completed in 1993. Frank Tobin was then able to use this edition to make his excellent translation into English, which has been used as a main reference for this book. Tobin's translation was published by the Paulist Press in 1998.

Chapter Ten

1. Anya's use of the phrase the "fire within" is highly significant as it is an image found in both Tantra and Taoism and has been used by many mystics in addition to the ones in this book. In *Spirit of Fire: the life and vision of Teilhard de Chardin*, Ursula King wrote, "His vision consumed his heart with a fire from within." She indicated that he saw this fire as existing not just within himself, but also as being the "stuff of the universe". She added, "He spoke of the fire as a spark, a glow, a blaze, as flames that illuminate, set alight, and consume. Nowhere is this vision more radiant and empowering than in his descriptions of his mystical experiences."

2. Although it is not particularly common to have the intense kinds of experiences described in this chapter, anyone interested in a more thorough description of them, the physical sensations associated with them, and their relationship to kundalini-shakti can find a great deal of information in Joan Harrigan's book *Kundalini Vidya: The Science of Spiritual Transformation* or on her website: www.kundalinicare.com.

Chapter Eleven

1. Hildegard's description of the voice that commanded her to begin writing about her visions is described in her introduction to her book *Scivias*, which

has been translated by Bruce Hozeski and is listed in the Bibliography and Suggested Reading section under the title *Hildegard von Bingen's Mystical Visions*.

2. Mechthild's dream of the devil and more about her doubts about herself and her ability to write are found in Sections 1 and 2 of Book IV of *The Flowing Light of the Godhead*. Section 2 ends with Mechthild repeating how her confessor, Heinrich, interpreted the dream and the visions that followed it:

> He said I should boldly go forward with a light heart; God, who had been leading me, would certainly preserve me. Then he gave me a command that often makes me ashamed and causes me to weep because my utter unworthiness is obvious to my eyes; that is, he commanded me, a frail woman, to write this book out of God's heart and mouth. And so this book has come lovingly from God and does not have its origins in human thought.

3. Mechthild's use of the phrase "a frail woman" to refer to herself in the context of writing down God's word was a clever formulaic device used by a number of medieval women mystics which proclaimed their humility and, at the same time, stressed that it must indeed have been God who put the words in their mouths as such exalted utterances could not possibly have come from them. (For further information on this device and its use by Hildegard, see the Notes for Chapter Twelve.)

4. The quote from Mahadevi that begins "I must sing, dance" and the poem that refers to the "precious juice of Grace" are found in Adke's *Vacanas of Akka Mahādēvi*.

5. The idea that different forms of creative expression can be a spiritual practice has been around for a while, and a number of books have been written on how you can turn your writing, painting, journaling into one. That the act of being creative in and of itself is a spiritual practice is not quite so widespread. Julia Cameron explored this idea in the introduction to *The Complete Artist's Way: Creativity as a Spiritual Practice*, a compendium volume that includes *The Artist's Way* and two of her other works.

6. What Kavita refers to as "direct transmission" is known in yoga as *shakti-*

pāta which means literally "descent of power". It is based on the belief that a truly realized guru can awaken kundalini-skakti in a disciple simply by touching him or her. Some contemporary gurus even claim to bring this about by glancing at their students or being in the same room with them. While shakti-pāta, or shakti-pāt as it is more commonly known, has a long tradition in yoga, how frequently those who call themselves gurus today actually bring about a true awakening of kundalini-shakti simply by touching a student is a matter of debate.

Chapter Twelve

1. Hildegard often referred to herself as unworthy of the task at hand. She repeatedly pointed out that she was "only poorly educated" and referred to herself as a "poor little figure of a woman". Some scholars suggest that these references are at least in part a formulaic device she, like Mechthild and other medieval women, used to accentuate the idea that she was incapable of doing these writings and they *must* therefore be coming from God. But to what degree this is so is open to speculation. It's my opinion that while she may have been using these comments to stress the fact that she was receiving divine intervention, she did this because she believed it was so and that she, with all her faults and shortcomings, could not have possibly accomplished what she did without the grace of God flowing through her.

2. Towards the end of her life Mechthild joined a Cistercian convent in the town of Helfta and took her vows. The Church had been encouraging beguines to make this move for quite some time, and it is almost certain that Mechthild did so to escape persecution.

3. The three quotes from the *Kālikā Purāna* can be found, respectively, in Chapter One, Verses 54-61; Chapter Three, Verses 1-2; and Chapter 2, Verse 8.

Chapter Thirteen

1. Hatha yoga was developed as a systematic, organized, well-thought out system to encourage the rapid, even forceful, awakening of kundalini. In fact, the word "hatha" means force. One reason so many yoga teachers today are completely unaware of this is that the ancient yogis couched the references to kundalini in cryptic language that could not be understood by the uninitiated,

in other words, anyone who did not have an enlightened guru to guide them through the process. The ancient yogis believed this would prevent people from trying to awaken kundalini without being properly prepared and would ensure that they were ready for each succeeding step before they took it. This is one reason the idea of lineage is so important—each teacher passed his expertise carefully onto the next person in the succession. For more information on Tantric lineages see David Gordon White's book on Tantra listed in the Bibliography and Suggested Reading section.

2. Orthodox Tantric practices are generally referred to as right-hand path traditions. Over time some Tantric practices developed that came to be referred to as left-hand path traditions. In these the symbolic rites were turned into actual sexual intercourse and even sexual orgies. The left-hand path also became more concerned with the development of the psychic powers known as siddhis and magic. Some of these left-hand path rites also focused on developing dark arts such as fostering siddhis for the power they could bring over others. The books by White and Feuerstein on Tantra listed in the Bibliography and Suggested Reading section both have excellent information on the distinction between these customs.

3. Gopi Krishna's life story is told in *Kundalini: the evolutionary energy in man* and, in much more detail, in *Living with Kundalini*, both published by Shambhala.

4. Joan Harrigan's website, www.kundalinicare.com, also lists classic signs and symptoms of kundalini awakening which are described in more detail in her book. Joan is a clinical psychologist who has a deep understanding of the issues that sometimes challenge those who experience what she calls a "kundalini rising" in a very intense or rapid form.

5. Many other contemporary writings on the relation of challenges and psychological issues at times related to the kundalini processes can be found in the books by Yvonne Kason, M.D., Bonnie Greenwell, Ph.D., and Christina and Stanislov Grof, Ph.D. Information is also available from the websites of the Spiritual Emergence Network and the Kundalini Research Network.

Chapter Fourteen

1. The story of Shiva, Sati, and Kama referred to here is told in Chapters One, Two, and Three of the *Kālikā Purāna*.

2. A recent version of the tale of Cupid and Psyche can be found in the translation of *Metamorphoses*, Books IV, 28-35, V and VI, 1-24, published by Egbert Forsten.

3. Gopi Krishna wrote extensively on current world conditions that he felt were created by the state of imbalance in the world. His books can be ordered from Amazon or directly from the Institute for Consciousness Research, www.icrcanada.org.

4. An interesting exploration of the Black Madonna can be found in China Galland's book *Longing for Darkness: Tara and the Black Madonna*.

Chapter Fifteen

1. The term "holistic" really came into its own when, in 1978, the American Holistic Medical Association was founded by Norm Shealy, M.D., and a number of other practioners.

2. To the best of my knowledge the use of the Four Horsemen of the Apocalypse as a metaphor for the four aspects—body, mind, emotions, spirit—of our being was originated by Thomas and Jane Wilhite in the 1970s. Although courses that teach this concept are still in existence, my use of it here is not meant to be an endorsement of them.

3. All the quotes from Gopi Krishna in this chapter are found in his book *Higher Consciousness*.

4. The description of the upper Shekinah as the "full expression of ceaseless creative power..." is from Chapter Seven of Scholem's *On the Mystical Shape of the Godhead*.

Bibliography and Suggested Reading

Creativity and Inspiration

Abell, Arthur. *Talks with Great Composers*. New York: Citadel Press, 1994.

Cameron, Julia. *The Complete Artist's Way: Creativity as a Spiritual Practice*. New York: Tarcher/Penguin, 2007.

Cornell, Judith. *Drawing the Light from Within: keys to awaken your creative power*. New York: Prentice Hall Press, 1990.

— *Mandala: Luminous Symbols for Healing*. Wheaton, IL: Quest Books, 1994.

Degler, Teri. *The Fiery Muse: Creativity and the Spiritual Quest*. Toronto: Random House of Canada, 1996.

Fincher, Susanne F. *Creating Mandalas: For Insight, Healing, and Self-Expression*. Boston: Shambhala, 1991.

Kavita. *Love Songs of the Undivided*. Pondicherry: All India Press, 1994.

Goddess Traditions and Feminist Spirituality

Cady, Susan, Marian Ronan, and Hal Taussig. *Sophia: The Future of Feminist Spirituality*. San Francisco: Harper & Row, c. 1986.

Christ, Carol P. *Rebirth of the Goddess: Finding Meaning in Feminist Spirituality*. New York: Routledge, 1997.

Coburn, Thomas B. *Encountering the Goddess: A Translation of the Devī-Māhātmya and A Study of Its Interpretation*. Albany, NY: State University of New York Press, 1991.

Eller, Cynthia. *Living in the Lap of the Goddess: The Feminist Spirituality Movement in America*. New York: Crossroad, 1993.

Frymer-Kensky, Tikva Simone. *In the Wake of the Goddess: Women, Culture, and the Biblical Transformation of Pagan Myth*. New York: Free Press, 1992.

Galland, China. *Longing for Darkness: Tara and the Black Madonna*. New York: Penguin/Compass, 1990.

Kinsley, David. *Hindu Goddesses: Visions of the Divine Feminine in the Hindu Religious Tradition*. Berkeley: University of California Press, 1988.

Patai, Raphael. *The Hebrew Goddess*. Detroit: Wayne State University Press, 1990.

Ruether, Rosemary Radford. *Goddesses and the Divine Feminine: A Western Religious History.* Berkeley: University of California Press, 2005.

Stuckey, Johanna H. *Feminist Spirituality: An Introduction to Feminist Theology in Judaism, Christianity, Islam, and Feminist Goddess Worship.* Toronto: Centre for Feminist Research, York University, 1998.

Hildegard von Bingen

Baird, Joseph L. and Radd K. Ehrman, trans. *The Letters of Hildegard of Bingen, Volume 1.* New York: Oxford University Press, 1994.

Dronke, Peter. *Women Writers of the Middle Ages: A Critical Study of Texts from Perpetua (d. 203) to Marguerite Porete (d. 1310).* Cambridge: Cambridge University Press, 1984.

Feiss, Hugh, trans. *The Life of Hildegard von Bingen by Gottfried of Disibodenberg.* Toronto: Peregrina Publishing Company, 1996.

Flanagan, Sabina. *Hildegard of Bingen: A Visionary Life.* London and New York: Routledge, 1989.

— ed. and trans. *Secrets of God: Writings of Hildegard of Bingen.* Boston: Shambala Publications, 1996.

Fox, Matthew, ed. *Hildegard of Bingen's Book of Divine Works.* Santa Fe, NM: Bear & Company, 1987.

— *The Illuminations of Hildegard of Bingen.* Santa Fe, NM: Bear & Company, 1985.

Grössman, Elizabeth. *Hildegard of Bingen: Four Papers.* Toronto: Peregrina Publishing Company, 1998.

Hozeski, Bruce, trans. *Hildegard von Bingen's Mystical Visions: Translated from Hildegard's Scivias.* Santa Fe, NM: Bear & Company, 1986.

Newman, Barbara. *Sister of Wisdom: St. Hildegard's Theology of the Feminine.* Berkeley: University of California Press, 1989.

— ed. *Voice of the Living Light: Hildegard of Bingen and her World.* Berkeley: University of California Press, 1998.

Mahadevi Akka

Adke, Manohar Appasaheb, ed. and Armando Menezes and S.M. Angradi, trans. *Vacanas of Akka Mahādēvi.* Dharwar, India: Manohar A. Adke, 1973.

Alphonso-Karkala, John B. *An Anthology of Indian Literature.* New Delhi: Indian Council for Cultural Relations, 1987.

Hirshfield, Jane, ed. *Women in Praise of the Sacred: 43 Centuries of Spiritual Poetry by Women*. New York: HarperPerennial, 1994.

Puranik, Siddhayya. *Mahādēvi*. Dharwad: Institute of Kannada Studies, 1986.

Ramanujan, A.K., ed. and trans. *Speaking of Shiva*. London: Penguin Books, 1973.

Tharu, Susie and K. Lalita. *Women Writing in India: 600 B.C. to the Present, Vol. 1*. New York: The Feminist Press, 1991.

Mechthild of Magdeburg

Anderson, Elizabeth A. *The Voice of Mechthild of Magdeburg*. Oxford: Lang, 2000.

Bowie, Fiona, ed. and Davies, Oliver, trans. *Beguine spirituality: mystical writings of Mechthild of Magdeburg, Beatrice of Nazareth, and Hadewijch of Brabant*. New York: Crossroad, 1990.

Brackert, Helmut, *et al*. *Liebe als Literatur: Aufsätze zur erotischen Dichtung in Deutschland*. München: C.H. Beck, 1983.

Flinders, Carol Lee. *Enduring Grace: Living Portraits of Seven Women Mystics*. San Francisco: HarperSanFrancisco, c. 1993.

Franklin, James C. *Mystical Transformations: the imagery of liquids in the works of Mechthild von Magdeburg*. Rutherford, NJ: Fairleigh Dickinson University Press, 1978.

Hollywood, Amy. *The Soul as Virgin Wife: Mechthild of Magdeburg, Marguerite Porete, and Meister Eckhart*. Notre Dame, IN: University of Notre Dame Press, 1995.

Murk-Jansen, Saskia. *Brides in the Desert: The Spirituality of the Beguines*. Maryknoll, NY: Orbis Books, 1998.

Pintchman, Tracy, ed. *Seeking Mahadevi: Constructing the Identities of the Hindu Great Goddess*. Albany, NY: State University of New York Press, 2001.

Tobin, Frank. *Mechthild of Magdeburg: A Medieval Mystic in Modern Eyes*. Columbia, SC: Camden House, 1995.

— trans. *Mechthild of Magdeburg: The Flowing Light of the Godhead*. New York: Paulist Press, 1998.

Wiethaus, Ulrike. *Ecstatic Transformation: Transpersonal Psychology in the Work of Mechthild of Magdeburg*. Syracuse, NY: Syracuse University Press, 1996.

Sacred Texts and Myths

Rao, S.K. Ramachandra. *Śrī-sūkta: text with translation and explanation/Vedas. English & Sanskrit. Rgveda.* Bangalore: Kalpatharu Research Academy, 1985.

Shastri, B.N., trans. *The Kālikāpurāna (Part I & Part II).* Delhi: Nag Publishers, 1991.

Tapasyananda, Swami, trans. and commentary. *The Saundarya-lahari of Sri Sankaracarya:* Madras, Sri Ramakrishna Math, 1987.

Taylor, Thomas, trans. *Apuleius' Golden ass, or, The metamorphosis: and other philosophical writings viz. On the God of Socrates & On the philosophy of Plato.* Somerset, UK: Prometheus Trust, 1997.

The Oxford Annotated Bible: Revised Standard Version. New York: Oxford University Press, 1962.

The Revised English Bible: With the Apocrypha. New Rochelle, NY: Oxford University Press, 1989.

Wright, Constance S. and Julia Bolton Holloway. *Tales within Tales: Apuleius through Time.* New York: AMS Press, 2000.

Zimmerman, M. et al., text, intro., and commentary. *Metamorphoses Books IV, 28-35, V and VI, 1-24: the tale of Cupid and Psyche/Apuleius Madaurensis.* Groningen: Egbert Forsten, 2004.

Self-help and Psychology

Bragdon, Emma, Ph.D. *A Sourcebook for Helping People with Spiritual Problems.* Los Altos, CA: Lightening Up Press, 2006.

Greenwell, Bonnie, Ph.D. *Energies of Transformation: A Guide to the Kundalini Process.* Cupertino, CA: Shakti River Press, 1990.

Harrigan, Joan Shivarpita. *Kundalini Vidya: The Science of Spiritual Transformation.* Knoxville, TN: Patanjali Yoga Care (www.kundalinicare.com), 2002.

Woodman, Marion. *Addicted to Perfection: The Still Unravished Bride.* Toronto: Inner City Books, 1982.

— *Bone: Dying into Life.* New York: Viking Compass, 2000.

— *The Owl Was a Baker's Daughter: Obesity, Anorexia Nervosa, and the Repressed Feminine.* Toronto: Inner City Books, 1980.

Woodman, Marion and Elinor Dickson. *Dancing in the Flames: The Dark Goddess in the Transformation of Consciousness.* Boston: Shambhala, 1996.

Shakti and Kundalini-Shakti

Avalon, Arthur (Sir John Woodroffe). S'akti and S'akta. Madras: Ganesh & Co. Private, Ltd, 1969.

Avalon, Arthur and Ellen Avalon (Sir John Woodroffe and Lady Ellen Elizabeth Grimson Woodroffe). Hymns to the Goddess: Translated from the Sanskrit by Arthur and Ellen Avalon. Madras: Ganesh & Co. Private, Ltd, 1964.

Brown, Cheever Mackenzie. The Song of the Goddess: The Devī Gītā: A Spiritual Counsel of the Great Goddess. Albany, NY: University of New York, 2002.

Kieffer, Gene, ed. Kundalini: Empowering Human Evolution: Selected Writings of Gopi Krishna. New York: Paragon House, 1995.

Krishna, Gopi. Higher Consciousness: The Evolutionary Thrust of Kundalini. New York: The Julian Press, 1974.

— Living with Kundalini. Rev. by Leslie Shepard. Boulder, CO: Shambhala, 1991.

— Secrets of Kundalini in Panchastavi. New Delhi: Kundalini Research and Publication Trust, 1978.

Kinsely, David. Tantric Visions of the Divine Feminine: The Ten Mahāvidyās. Berkeley: University of California Press, 1997.

Kumar, Pushpendra. The Principle of Śakti. New Delhi: Eastern Book Linkers, 1986.

Silburn, Lillian. Kundalini: Energy of the Depths. Albany, NY: State University of New York Press, 1988.

Sovatsky, Stuart. Words from the Soul: Time. Albany, NY: State University of New York Press, 1998.

Walters, Dorothy. Unmasking the Rose: A Record of Kundalini Initiation. Charlottesville, VA: Hampton Roads, 2002.

Shekinah and Jewish Mysticism

Samuel, Gabriella. The Kabbalah Handbook. New York: Jeremy Tarcher, 2007.

Schaya, Leo. Pearson, Nancy, trans. The Universal Meaning of the Kabbalah. London: George Allen & Unwin, Ltd, 1971.

Scholem, Gershom. Major Trends in Jewish Mysticism. New York: Schocken Books, 1995.

— On the Kabbalah and its Symbolism. New York: Schocken Books, 1996.

— On the Mystical Shape of the Godhead: Basic Concepts in the Kabbalah. New York: Schocken Books, 1991.

Silberman, Neil Asher. Heavenly Powers: Unraveling the Secret History of the

Kabbalah. New York: Grosset/Putnam, 1998.

Wilken, Robert L., ed. *Aspects of Christianity in Judaism and Early Christianity.* Notre Dame, IN: University of Notre Dame Press, 1975.

Wolfson, Elliot R. *Circle in the Square: Studies in the Use of Gender in Kabbalistic Symbolism.* Albany, NY: State University of New York Press, 1995.

— *Through a Speculum That Shines.* Princeton, NJ: Princeton University Press, 1994.

Sophia, Wisdom, and the Holy Spirit

Bloch, Ariel and Chana Bloch. *The Song of Songs: A New Translation with Introduction and Commentary.* New York: Random House, 1995.

Camp, Claudia V. *Wisdom and the Feminine in the Book of Proverbs.* Decatur, GA: Almond Press, 1985.

Cole, Susan, Marian Ronan and Hal Taussig. *Wisdom's Feast: Sophia in study and celebration.* San Francisco: Harper & Row, 1989.

Congar, Yves. *I Believe in the Holy Spirit.* New York: Crossroads, 1997.

Fiene, Donald M. "What is the Appearance of the Divine Sophia?" in *Slavic Review,* Fall, 1989, pp. 450-476.

Gelpi, Donald. *The Divine Mother: a trinitarian theology of the Holy Spirit.* Lanham, MD: University Press of America, 1984.

Jonas, Hans. *The Gnostic Religion: the message of the alien God and the beginnings of Christianity.* Boston: Beacon Press, 1958.

King, Karen L. *Images of the Feminine in Gnosticism.* Philadelphia: Fortress Press, 1988.

Lang, Bernhard. *Wisdom and the Book of Proverbs: A Hebrew Goddess Redefined.* New York: Pilgrim Press, 1986.

Meehan, Brenda. "Wisdom/Sophia, Russian Identity, and Western Feminist Theology" in *Cross Currents,* Summer, 1996, pp. 149-167.

Mollenkott, Virginia R. *The Divine Feminine: The Biblical Imagery of God as Female.* New York: Crossroads, 1987.

Montague, George T. *The Holy Spirit: Growth of Biblical Tradition.* New York: Paulist Press, 1976.

Murray, Robert. *Symbols of Church and Kingdom.* Cambridge: Cambridge University Press, 1975.

O'Connor, Kathleen. *The Wisdom Literature.* Wilmington, DE: M. Glazier, 1988.

Pope, Marvin H., trans. *The Song of Songs: A New Translation with Introduction and Commentary.* New York: Doubleday, 1977.

Rae, Eleanor and Bernice Marie-Daly. *Created in Her Image: Models of the Feminine Divine*. New York: Crossroads, 1990.

Rogers, Rick. *Theophilus of Antioch: the life and thought of a second-century bishop*. Lanham, MD: Lexington Books, c. 2000.

Schipflinger, Thomas. *Sophia-Maria: A Holistic Vision of Creation*. York Beach, ME: Samuel Weiser, Inc., 1998.

Sheeben, Matthias Joseph, Joseph Wilhelm, and Thomas Scannell. *A Manual of Catholic Theology: Based on Sheeben's Dogmatik*. London: Kegan Paul, 1908.

Tantra and Yoga

Avalon, Arthur (Sir John Woodroffe). *Introduction to Tantra Sastra*. Madras: Ganesh & Co. Private, Ltd, 1973.

— intro. and trans. *Kulārnava Tantra*. Madras: Ganesh & Co. Private, Ltd, 1965.

— *Principles of Tantra*. Madras: Ganesh & Co. Private, Ltd, 1960.

— commentary and trans. *The Great Liberation, Mahānirvāna Tantra*. Madras: Ganesh & Co. Private, Ltd, 1963.

— *The Serpent Power*. New York: Dover Publications, 1974.

Bharati, Agehananda. *The Tantric Tradition*. Westport, CT: Greenwood Press, 1977.

Cairns, Grace E. *Man as Microcosm in Tantric Hinduism*. New Delhi: Manohar Publications, 1992.

Feuerstein, Georg. *Tantra: The Path of Ecstasy*. Boston: Shambhala, 1998.

— *The Encyclopedic Dictionary of Yoga*. New York: Paragon, 1990.

— *The Yoga-sutra of Patanjali: A New Translation and Commentary*. Rochester, VT: Inner Traditions, 1989.

Kumar, Pushpendra. *Introduction to Tantras and their Philosophy*. New Delhi: Rashtriya Sanskrit Sansthan, 1998.

Sinh, Pancham, trans. *The Hatha Yoga Pradipika*. Allababad: Sudhindra Nath Vasu, 1915.

Studies on the Tantras. Calcutta: Ramakrishna Mission, Institute of Culture, 1989.

Taylor, Kathleen. *Sir John Woodroffe, Tantra and Bengal: An Indian Soul in a European Body?*. Richmond: Curzon Press, 2001.

White, David Gordon. *Kiss of the Yoginī: "Tantric Sex" in its South Asian Contexts*. Chicago: University of Chicago Press, 2003.

— ed. *Tantra in Practice*. Princeton, NJ: Princeton University Press, 2000.

— *The Alchemical Body: Siddha Traditions in Medieval India*. Chicago: University of Chicago Press, 1996.

Taoism

Chang, Chung-Yuan. *Creativity and Taoism: a study of Chinese philosophy, art, & poetry.* New York: Julian Press, 1963.
Chao, Pi-ch'en. *Taoist Yoga: alchemy and immortality.* London: Rider, 1970.
Legeza, Laszio and Philip Rawson. *Tao: The Chinese Philosophy of Time and Change.* London: Thames and Hudson, 1973.

Writings on Spirituality

Brunton, Paul. *A Search in Secret India.* London: Rider, 1969.
Bucke, Richard Maurice. *Cosmic Consciousness.* New York: E.P. Dutton and Company, Inc., 1969.
Fox, Emmet. *The Sermon on the Mount.* New York and Evanston, IL: Harper & Row, Publishers, 1938.
Greeley, Andrew M. *Ecstasy: A Way of Knowing.* Englewood Cliffs, NJ: Prentice-Hall, 1974.
King, Ursula. *Spirit of Fire: the life and vision of Teilhard de Chardin.* Maryknoll, NY: Orbis Books, 1996. Prometheus Trust, 1997.
Teilhard de Chardin, Pierre, *The Heart of Matter.* London: Collins, 1978.
— *Writings in the Time of War.* New York: Harper & Row, 1968.

Index

Feuerstein, Georg, 241, 242–243, 246
Fiery Muse, The (Degler), 78, 117,
126, 207, 252
"Fire of the Spirit" (Hildegard),
111–112
Flanagan, Sabina, 79
Flowing Light of the Godhead, The
(Mechthild), 167, 172–173
Four Horsemen of the Apocalypse,
282–283, 303n2ch15
Fox, Emmet, 66, 67, 179, 225,
292n3
framework for spiritual experience
(exercise), 200–201

Gelpi, Donald, 149, 150, 152, 155
Gnosticism, 84
God, 84, 89
    immanent or transcendent,
    126–127
    reaching out, 234, 238–239
God-with-us, 122, 125, 155, 159,
283, 288
    Christian theology, 126–127
    exercise, 142–143
    Hinduism, 128–132
    Holy Spirit, 150, 288
    Kabbalah, 132–141
    Mechthild's writings, 165–166,
    234
    Sophia, 144–147

Haggadah, 134
Harrigan, Joan, 255–256, 302n4
hatha yoga, 242, 243, 301n1ch13
Hermaphroditus, 263–264
higher consciousness, characteristics,
289–290n5

Hildegard of Bingen, 29, 67,
301n1ch12
    creativity, 81, 82, 104, 203–204, 287
    on divine feminine, 78, 83, 86–87
    fight for justice, 82–83
    kundalini, 101–102
    on "living Light," 93, 102, 103
    self-doubt, 180, 203–204,
    222–223, 224–225
    theology, 83, 86
    transformation, 80–81, 108, 110,
    111–112, 204
    visions, 79, 81, 82, 86–87, 90,
    299n1ch11
Hildegard of Bingen (Flanagan), 79
Holy Spirit, 30, 297n1
    comes to Britta, 96–97, 98–99,
    104, 155
    creativity and, 153–155
    as divine feminine, 148–149, 151
    divine light, 150–151, 152
    God-with-us, 150, 288
    Paul's transformation, 151–154
    Sophia and, 147–150
Humperdinck, Engelbert, 76, 273

immanence, 126, 127
    (*see also* God-with-us)
inspiration, 26–27, 207, 273, 276
    exercise, 33–34
intuition, 195–196
invocation (exercise), 279–280
Irenaeus, St, 147–148

Jesus, 29
Joseph (Old Testament), 29
Judah ben Barzillai, 135
Judaism

creativity, 47–48, 51, 108, 109,
120–121, 152
exercise, 123–124
light imagery, 47, 108, 109–112,
113, 119, 121
mental, 108–109, 110–113
physical experience, 112, 120,
121, 122, 246, 247, 283–284
Tantras on, 109, 110–111, 112
Tree of Life, 137–138
Trinity, Christian, 148

union of self with Divine, 21–22,
231-232, 288

Victorinus, 148
Virashaivism, 43–46, 47, 291n6

Wagner, Richard, 76, 89, 273, 277,
279
Wallace, Edith, 220, 221
Wendi, 114–122
creative yearning, 116–117, 120,
206

divine feminine in, 156–159,
210, 287
reawakening, 118–122, 196–197
writing, 114, 116, 118–119,
120–122
Whitman, Walt, 27, 76, 89
Wisdom, 19, 83–84, 86, 87–88,
111
Wisdom books of Bible, 83–84,
111, 293n5
women's rights in 1200s, 168–169
Woodman, Marion, 19, 31, 114
on masculine-feminine balance,
267–268, 270–271, 275–276
Woodroffe, Sir John, 110,
295n2ch6
Word or Logos, 85

yang and yin, 244
yoga
breathing exercises, 33–34
union of self with Divine, 21
yogic texts, 19, 26, 109
on kundalini, 101, 102, 112–113

About the Author

Originally from Idaho, Teri Degler is an award-winning writer who currently lives in Toronto with her husband and teenage daughter. She is author/co-author of ten books, including one for young adults, the Canadian bestseller *The Canadian Junior Green Guide*, and *The Fiery Muse: Creativity and the Spiritual Quest*, published by Random House of Canada.

For more than twenty years Teri has been researching and writing about yoga, Tantra, the divine feminine, and the lives of highly creative women mystics from different spiritual traditions. Her own interest in the mind/body/spirit field was sparked early in her life when she began studying hatha yoga in Paris with Monsieur ben Simone, a yoga teacher who had lived in Mahatma Gandhi's ashram in India for many years. She soon began writing on yoga, kundalini, and other spiritual topics. Later she traveled to India to meet with Gopi Krishna, the Indian philosopher, writer, and yogi who was widely recognized during his lifetime as the world authority on kundalini.

A widely experienced public speaker, Teri has taught many workshops on creative inspiration and creative writing. She has also appeared on numerous national television and radio programs. Her freelance writing has appeared in many periodicals including such widely divergent publications as *Family Circle* and *New Age Journal* in the U.S. and *More Magazine*, *Today's Parent*, *The Toronto Star*, and *The United Church Observer* in Canada.

Teri has a Master of Arts degree from the University of New Mexico. An active member of PEN and the Writers' Union of Canada, she represents the union on the Board of Directors of Canada's Book and Periodical Council. A long-time member of the Institute for Consciousness Research, she was also one of the founders of the Kundalini Research Network in the United States.

For more information please visit her website, www.teridegler.com.